D1615709

The BLISS *of* SOLITUDE
A Conservationist's Tour of the Lakes

The BLISS *of* SOLITUDE
·*A Conservationist's Tour of the Lakes*·

JOHN WYATT

Ellenbank
Press

Published by Ellenbank Press
The Lathes, Selby Terrace, Maryport, Cumbria CA15 6LX

First published 1991
Text copyright © John Wyatt 1991

Illustrations copyright © Fiona Porteous 1991

Designed by Linda Blakemore

Author photograph on jacket courtesy of Eric Whitehead

Typeset in 11/12½ Bembo by Butler & Tanner Ltd, Frome
Printed and bound in Great Britain by Biddles Ltd,
Guildford and King's Lynn
Jacket printed by Belmont Press, Northampton

British Library Cataloguing in Publication Data
Wyatt, John, *1925–*
    The bliss of solitude: a conservationist's
    tour of the Lakes.
    1. Cumbria (England)
    I. Title
    942.78
    ISBN 1–873551–01–0

Contents

•

Illustrations

•

Overture

•

You may have picked up this book and thought, 'Not another book about the Lake District!' (And by the way if you are a person who likes crowds and noise put this down at once. It is not for you.) This book's purpose is to try to bring a hint of that fresh Lakeland air, and some of the district's special magic, to its explorer, whether on foot, on wheels, or both. It is about one area which happens to contain examples of all that is best in the British landscape; with some subjective, sometimes critical, thoughts of someone who has lived and worked in it for most of his life.

I have served a very long apprenticeship in the Lake District, so a sentimentalist about it I am not. I have been harnessed to work here since my teens. I have mucked out on farms and felled in forests. I have ditched and dyked. In rain, shine, frost and snow I have pick-axed, mattocked, crow-barred, sickled and scythed and mowed my way through acres of this land. At the last I worked for twenty-six years in the service of the Lake District National Park; and have endured some backache, heartache, blisters and strains; also pain and pleasure; bitterness and consolation, frustration and release. I have spent many ecstatic hours on the hills and sometimes less pleasing ones as a mountain rescuer. I have ascended its crags and descended its holes. I have enjoyed working with like-minded conservationists; and endured the misdeeds of a miscreant minority; I have spent hours in committees discussing the area's problems, real, and sometimes imaginary. I have built walls and demolished eyesores, and praise be, planted countless trees. I have lifted litter and put out fires, I have been social worker and policeman, and done all manner of unpleasant and pleasant, curious and interesting things in the cause of conservation. I have occasionally done what I should not have done and left undone so very many things that I ought to have done; and the more I know, the less I know I know.

I have been a willing slave to the Lake District, and there is nothing romantic or superficial about my feeling for it. Or for that matter, any other area of countryside.

Having said that, of course the Lake District to me is not just the taskmaster. It has all been a labour of love: every job of work, from the digging of a drain to the writing of this book. I suppose one could call my feelings for the countryside of the Lakes a deeply respectful reverence.

This then is a guided tour led, not by one who walks about in a perpetual pink haze of poetic joy and wonderment; not with the eyes of a theoretician, not of one who sees the countryside only as a recreational resource; but as an enthusiastic long-time countryside worker who has got his hands dirty in the cause of conservation, and is anxious to get others to feel, at least, involved. I believe that we begin to get involved when we enjoy any spiritual contact with the countryside which fuels our enthusiasm and concern. It is my hope that, though you, the reader, will not necessarily always agree with me, you might share some of my thoughts and feelings.

We sleep in everyday routine. We awaken in adventure. In that sleep we live in ourselves. In that awakening we become involved in all around us. Let us then leave the diurnal round, close that door to the darkened room behind us, take a deep breath of clear bright air, and step out into an exploration of the Lakes!

· A Contained Conflict ·

To its devotees, not least to me, the Lake District is a feeling. It cannot be simply explained any more than one can explain why music can stir the innermost sensibilities. Music is a harmonious pattern of notes and rhythms. Lakeland landscape is a harmony of forms and light and colour and movement. Its appeal is immediate. It has a tranquillity; perhaps suggested by a conciliation of contrasting shapes: mountains and lakes, the active and the passive elements, male and female, yang and yin. It is a contained conflict.

Perhaps the immediate appeal of sublime landscape is the meaning that, subconsciously, we can see in it. The life which we share with all the creatures on the earth is essentially, in the cosmic sense, an ever-moving balance, a harmony. The pattern of great landscape gives this reassurance: that in spite of all the abuse of humankind the earth's essential forms remain. But it goes deeper than that. It is a reminder, a recognition of what we have known always in spirit. That no matter how we pretend to distance ourselves from the cycles, the tides, the phases, the waxing and the waning of life on earth, we belong to it. We are part of all that we see. We are looking at life, not as we might think that it is *meant* to be, but how in reality it is.

But surely one can feel this in the viewing of all great landscapes. Any area of the world where nature shows its perfection; or where the man-made scene reveals a natural sensitivity; or where its vastness cuts humankind down to size. Any prospect which shakes the senses into wakefulness and demands a reaction. What is so special about the English Lake District? To all 'Lakers', and to me, it has a peculiar sort of magic that compels an addiction. There is an instant feeling of affinity. It is not a large area; and as locals are prone to say, maybe pretending to be puzzled by the region's popularity, 'There's nowt here but hills and watter.' But it has very much to do with the fact that it is *not* a large area; that there is so much in so little. Its gems are all tight-packed, they unwrap themselves and surprise at every turn.

Father West, author of the first best-selling guidebook to the Lake District in the eighteenth century described the attraction in the decorative language of his day. The connoisseurs of scenery, he says, are induced to

visit the Lakes of Cumberland, Westmorland, and Lancashire; there to contemplate, in Alpine scenery, finished in
nature's highest tints, the pastoral and rural landscapes, exhi-
bited in all their stiles, the soft, the rude, the romantic, and
the sublime; and of which perhaps like instances can no
where be found assembled in so small a tract of country.

Later, Wordsworth, who admired West's book, agrees:

I do not indeed know any tract of country in which, within
so narrow a compass, may be found an equal variety in the
influences of light and shadow upon the sublime or beautiful
features of landscape.

The 'compass' covers about 1,000 square miles, or much wider
if one includes the less visited delights and interests in the Lake
County's eastern hills and valleys, the Solway coast, and the Furness
peninsula; and one can be assured that the terrain is so complex, fold
within fold, that an explorer cannot hope to get to know it all very
well in the limited human lifespan. An exploration can never be
boring. But what the explorer observes he can enjoy. Much earlier
than West and Wordsworth, Camden, the Elizabethan historian,
wrote of it: 'for the variety thereof it smileth upon the beholder and
giveth contentment to all that travaille it'.

That is it then. Like me, the keen observer of Lakeland should
expect to find enjoyment and contentment in the contemplation of
'the soft, the rude, the romantic, and the sublime'. Which is which
depends upon the explorer. The author's opinions are offered for
what they are worth and should not be taken as gospel!

· *'Hills and Watter'* ·

The central Lake District's dominating feature is of course the mountain landscape. The Lakeland fells within the National Park are
not the rounded hills of the neighbouring Pennines or the heather
moorlands of the Borders. This is a heaving, thrusting land. A lean
and ravaged land showing bare splintered bones of sharp crag and
rock. The fell wears its lower sheep pastures like a thin old jacket,
out at the elbows. The scene appears timeless. The man-made does
not intrude. The high net of dry-stone walls spreading down towards
the curving valley floor or the levels of the lakes seem to have grown

out of the land. Like the two-centuries old farmstead too, crouching on its hillside shelf, the stone of its building quarried and sledded from the fellside only a whistle call away, and the roof slate horse-carted from the next dale.

Above all rise the crags and peaks. No matter that they are not all that high compared with other Alpine regions. A fit, competent map-reading walker can accomplish any ascent, even to the highest points (just over 3,000 feet), and a return to his starting point very comfortably in a day. In less favoured areas at home and abroad that might not be as easy, for there could be weary miles of rough approach. The mountain scene here is as impressive as any, and more impressive than most.

Proportion in landscape is more important than mere height. In other regions of comparable size to the central Lake District one might expect to find just one mountain with its attendant foothills. But here there is a magnificent tight cluster of fells and peaks all soaring from tortuous, almost at sea level, valley floors. They crowd the scene. It is a geological rugby scrum. There is no great distant skyline of peaks seen across a plateau or a great expanse of lake, no monster of a mountain towering above the hamlets to shut out the light. The fells are in a happy balance with the sixteen lakes. There are a thousand classic scenes; those happy partnerships between contrasts.

Typically, we can hardly choose better than a viewpoint easily reached, even by wheelchair. Friar's Crag, on the shore of Derwent Water, is an easy stroll from the centre of Keswick. Yet it commands a view which is uniquely Lake District: up the lake into Borrowdale; superbly beautiful in early morning before its crowds of admirers arrive; or at sunset in winter. Here, according to tradition, the friars would wait to be blessed by St Herbert who had his hermitage on St Herbert's island. The wait would be a good preparation in the contemplation of 'the soft, the rude, the romantic, and the sublime'. The level spread of lake reflecting a soft light in the foreground; the distant island where the hermit had his hut, perhaps seen through a faint haze of mist; the thickly wooded heights around, narrowing in the jaws of Borrowdale; the peak beyond the lake head crowned with its ancient fort. John Ruskin, the supreme Victorian connoisseur of landscape, records that a visit to Friar's Crag was his earliest recollection of childhood.

Did I say typical? There are multiple variations on the theme. It has all to do with the complicated geology which, at the risk of bringing down the wrath of knowledgeable geologists, I will try to explain in a few words, and in ridiculously simple terms, for it helps an appreciation.

· *Lakeland Rock* ·

Rocks were formed in layers, oldest at the bottom, newest at the top. Without earth movement they would remain so, but of course the earth is buckled by contraction and collision, and torn by climatic erosion. The scenery of the true Lake District, within the boundaries of the National Park, is dominated by three main layers of rock types, which might be termed the soft, the rude, and the romantic.

In this case the oldest lower massive layer was formed from underwater muddy sediments 500 million years or so ago and they are the series known as the Skiddaw Slates. These rocks are shale-like, relatively soft and break down into small fragments, so that after the fells of this rock were lifted by earth movements and later eroded, their shapes tended to be angular and not too craggy. Blencathra and Skiddaw, hunched magnificently over Keswick, are of this rock, and the fells west of Derwent Water.

Next came the volcanic activity, and the various kinds of volcanic rocks built from lava, ashes and dust, known as the Borrowdale Volcanics, make the next layer. They are very hard, and when they were lifted, tilted and eroded they made up the greater mass of the rude, aggressive central fells which challenge the fell-walkers and climbers, in a glorious wide area west to east, from Wasdale through the Scafells and Coniston Old Man, Bowfell and the Langdale Pikes, through Helvellyn to High Street. They are stupendously rough-and-tumble all the way; generally whale-backed on their southern and western slopes; with crags and cliffs on their northern and eastern where the Ice Age snows stayed longest.

Ignoring a hardly visible, relatively thin layer of Coniston Lime-stone, the next huge mass of rocks was again formed from vast mud and grit sediments laid underwater when the seas rose to cover most of the land. These are known as the Silurian Slates. They are a more friable rock type and they break down more easily into an acidic soil which supports tree cover. Standing on the volcanic Loughrigg fell, above Ambleside, one can look down Windermere where, off into the distance on the hills and slopes of Silurian soil, woodlands delight the scene. This to me, and to the early artists who flocked to the Lake District, is romantic landscape. A steamer trip from Lakeside to Waterhead tells it all. A trip on the National Trust's *Gondola* on Coniston Water, with its wooded shores on its Silurian east side, is a similar delight.

The story continues. After the three main layers were formed the area was again inundated several times and sandstones and limestones were laid down. Many of these rocks were swept away by the Ice Age glaciers, but the Lake District is left with a rim of carboniferous limestone, and new red sandstone. There is a magnificent limestone scar west of Kendal, offering an excellent wide view over the district. And the red sandstone is in the outer areas, mainly outside the National Park, seen at its best in the dressed stone of the castle ruins, and the superb Furness Abbey.

Following the formation of the rocks and the upheaval of the land came the latest episode, in geological time only minutes ago. The rocks were broken up, plucked away, or scoured by the vast seas of moving ice of the Ice Ages. In the process some of the volcanic rocks which much earlier had cooled and formed underground became exposed. These are the granite types one finds in Eskdale, Wasdale and Ennerdale in the west, and Shap in the east.

The sixteen lakes and the numerous tarns were scooped out by the weighty glaciers with basal fangs of rock debris, grinding down from the heights, moving the softer material, being checked by the harder. In the process the geological complexity was translated into the fascinating profusion of land forms.

· *And Then Came Man* ·

After all came the flows of nature's colonisation, fen and forest. The forest grew almost to the summits of the greater heights. Then, from more than 4,000 years ago, came the gradual human incursions and the growth of the Lake District's first major industry: the making of stone axes. The axe 'factory' sites have been discovered in several places on the fells wherever a particularly hard rock, a 'tuff', outcrops in the Borrowdale Volcanic. The axes were roughed out on site, then sharpened and polished in the coastal sandstone. They were traded all over Britain and there are 'Langdale' axes in many museums. Axes of stone, through bronze, then iron and steel, with the help of the torch, and grazing animals, reduced the forests over the centuries. The demand for charcoal in the smelting of the area's metal ores, from the sixteenth to the early nineteenth centuries, saw their complete devastation. Much of the broadleaf woodland, which now enhances so many scenes, was planted after that.

Rock and climate created the structure. Man created the texture. The green cloak which covers this delicious land; its fibre, the pattern, the warp and weft, is of human making – with a good deal of help from nature.

When I feast my eyes on the hill pastures with their miles of walled enclosures and their cleared and drained green intake and 'in-by' land, I sometimes feel for the stubborn hill-farming generations who have come and gone, who sweated and strained through all manner of weary hardships in their making. They were often hungry; for this is no fat and prosperous land. It never was and never will be. No saints they; no better or worse than anyone else. But they added that last ingredient to the district's supreme harmony of forms. It is visible evidence of what man can create with cooperation, rather than contention, with nature.

Yet, sadly, the human touch can also be unwelcome, as we know to our cost. Are we not told that the Lake District is now too popular? That it is overcrowded? That it is no longer possible to obtain tranquillity, even on the fells? The evidence is cited: enormous traffic queues in the height of the holiday season; the human chaos in Bowness, Ambleside, Grasmere, Keswick. But this messy congestion is packed into only a tiny part of this most beautiful area of England and for only part of the time. It can be avoided. There is no doubt that at holiday times the Lake District can be overcrowded with cars. Movement then requires patience; but there is plenty of room for people in the 880 square miles of the Lake District National Park. It is even possible to enjoy solitude, if that is needed. This very special region still has everything to offer to those who seek unspoilt countryside with open eyes and mind.

CHAPTER ONE
The Skiddaws

•

In the beginning there was the Skiddaw Slate, and the Skiddaw Slate area is where we start our exploration, for one could justifiably say that here, too, was another beginning; the first practical steps in the conservation movement. The first 'greens'.

Our base is Keswick, sitting below the great wall of Skiddaw, which to me has always looked like a great petrified prehistoric monster. In fact, though, an exciting place for a walker to start, given clear weather, is up the hill which peers immediately over the little town. Latrigg ('latter rig' – the 'hill behind') seems impossible of easy ascent from a front view. It is, as a Cumbrian might say, 'gey brant', which means literally 'fairly steep' (but what the local farmer calls fairly steep might mean to most of us fairly perpendicular). Never fear, an easy track curls around the side for a gentler approach. Moreover, the less able walker with a well-sprung car can cheat by risking a drive up the unmetalled 'Gale Road' round the back to reduce the climb even further. Fit persons of course would be ashamed to do that.

· *The First Conservationists* ·

Remember with gratitude as we walk, those who first voiced that need to preserve the beautiful landscape of the Lake District, and to recognise the rights of public access. One tremendously important event took place here in October 1887. A year earlier some Keswick worthies, inspired largely by the incumbent of Crosthwaite Church, the formidable Canon Hardwicke Rawnsley, concerned about the growing loss of public footpaths, formed the Keswick Commons and Footpaths Preservation Society. When the owner of Latrigg blocked off the traditional route up to its top with locked gates, wire fences and notice boards, and challenged the claim of rights of way there, the Society had to take action.

The first move was to raise funds to fight a court case, which would surely come. A mass protest walk was planned to take down the obstructions and a leaflet was produced instructing the protesters on how to proceed without spoiling their case by doing undue damage. After the first foray the obstructions which had been forcefully removed were replaced, and a further demonstration was needed.

This time the support exceeded expectations. Two thousand members of the public arrived representing all walks of life, some carrying crowbars. Among the leaders was Samuel Plimsoll, MP, a Mr Routh Fitzpatrick, and Henry Irwin Jenkinson, Secretary of the Society. Before the foray began Henry Jenkinson addressed his fellows in the following rousing terms:

> Today, you are showing the world a spirit which will kindle such a fire as will light up all the British Isles! If we have no right of access to the summit of Latrigg, then we have no right to ascend other similar mountains in Great Britain.

A pity it was three weeks early for St Crispin's Day!

His feelings were endorsed by the MP, and a blacksmith forced open the chained gate. On the ascent the crowd began to sing 'Rule Britannia' and on reaching the summit gave rousing cheers and sang a verse of the National Anthem. And anyone who was not there would think themselves accursed and hold their manhood cheap ...

Of course the matter was not ended. Seven months later a suit was begun against the Footpaths Society in the Court of Chancery. In the dock were Canon Rawnsley, the Reverend Goddard, W. Routh Fitzpatrick and H. I. Jenkinson. The defendants had a formidable array of witnesses who swore that the routes in question had been in use from time immemorial. Jenkinson again spoke in stirring terms:

> The defendants in this case feel that they are not acting for themselves. Behind them stand the people of England who will be the chief losers should these ancient rights be lost.

There was an out of court settlement which was a virtual victory for access. It is generally acknowledged that the mass trespass on Kinder Scout in the Peak District in 1932 was the decisive battle in the fight to gain access to mountains and to produce our National Parks Act. But there were other days and other battles. Let us not be deceived – there may well have to be more.

The view from the top of Latrigg is a feast. This height of over 1,200 feet (368m) on a foothill of Skiddaw immediately commands a prospect south beyond Keswick over all of glorious Derwent Water and into the shaggy jaws of Borrowdale. Here we can sit, in a little favourite hollow, forgetting all the cares of the world, refreshing the senses. To the west of Derwent Water the nearer array of fells and hills are of Skiddaw Slate; there are something like 200 square miles of them, partly seen here through Causey Pike, Grasmoor to Grisedale Pike, and all around Bassenthwaite Lake, and to the north-western heights of Skiddaw itself. We should see the difference between those shapely fells, and the more dramatic craggy look to those Borrowdale Volcanics: these are to the left, and beyond Derwent Water into Borrowdale, and in the blue distance beyond that. With a map a pleasant time may be had identifying among other distant volcanic ranges from the left, the greater heights of Helvellyn, and Bowfell, and between some 10 and 13 miles away, Scafell and Scafell Pike, and Great Gable.

Looking nearer our viewpoint; beyond the less than beautiful roofs of Keswick, and the unmentionable A66; around the delightful shores of Derwent Water one can see where more battles – for practical conservation – started. Canon Hardwicke Rawnsley, again, that determined man of many parts, was concerned about the damage being done to the property around Derwent Water by thoughtless landowners. He thought that the only certain protection that the land could be given, so that its beauty could be enjoyed by the public for all time, was by acquisition. With two like-minded conservationists and footpath campaigners who frequently visited the Lakes – the social reformer Octavia Hill and the Post Office Solicitor Sir Robert Hunter – the National Trust for Places of Historical Interest or Natural Beauty, that typically British charitable institution, was formed in 1895, with acquisition and protection as the aim.

Appeals were launched to purchase important properties. At the far end, the head of the lake, on the west, 106 acres of Brandelhow Park was the first. That was in 1902 and since then in this area the Trust acquired directly at the lake head, Manesty Park, in 1908. Then in 1910 Grange Fell, the height beyond the lake in the jaws of Borrowdale. To its right, Castle Crag, the small peak crowned by the earthworks of a Romano–British fort, in 1920; with the highest land in England, Scafell Pike, way in the distance in the same year. Since then almost all one sees in that direction, including the lake itself, is in the care of the famous charity, from long before the Lake District became a national park. Heaven knows what would have happened to this delectable area by now but for the Trust. Lakeside chalets? Huge caravan parks? 'Private Land' signs all around the lake? Commercial conifer plantations?

There, below and beyond, utterly unspoilt, near and distant, is our dear, magic land of placid lake, hummocky hills, expansive frondose woodland, crumpled crags, hanging woods, rugged ramparts, shoulders of fell, beyond and behind, knuckles and folds and piles and peaks, and clouds and sky and clear air. Stay here a while. Stay. What's the hurry?

· Skiddaw and Beyond ·

However, if on another clear day an assault up to the 3,000-foot summit of Skiddaw can be made... Actually Skiddaw is a good first-time fell for less experienced hill-walkers. It is one of the Lake District's four highest, rising to 3,054 feet (931m). I think though that the Skiddaw Slate fells always look larger than they are. Maybe it is because they take the majestic mountain shape, a tremendous obesity; while the volcanic fells are often fronted with a chaos of foothills with the summits hidden from sight. Norman Nicholson, the Lakes poet, said that the fells are a gigantic confidence trick. I think that this is particularly true of the Skiddaws. They distort the estimate of distance. If they are topped with snow they look truly Alpine. But there is no difficulty in the ascent. Taking the traditional route from the back of Latrigg, there is no rough ground, no scrambling. Given plenty of time, a family with small children can manage it. Seasoned fell-walkers might scorn Skiddaw. They might feel that the ascent is a dull featureless slog. I have heard the fell called 'a slag heap', which is a scandalous libel! Skiddaw is undervalued. Not least it offers some thrilling views from its various heights and peaks.

Each mountain to me has its own unique personality. Each has a physical part and a mystical part. Each has something to say. Skiddaw is different to the others in the Lake District; it is one of the mysterious fells. What is it that makes me feel uneasy on its ascent when danger is absent? The routes up other Lake District fells waver around crags and cracks and corners; with zigs and zags, side slopes and slabs; strides and pace checking and changing with each hindrance and hazard. Here, on this crumbled rock of unimaginable age, it is simple, direct. Maybe I sense that it is hardly natural. I feel the way through my feet. Most other mountains have cobbled summits that snag and block, and try to turn and trip each tread. Walking on Skiddaw's summit is like walking up the vicarage drive. Why do I tread so warily, I asked myself on one of those visits. Perhaps it is that ridiculous fancy: that massive recumbent scaly prehistoric monster. If I trod its summit gingerly was it because I was making ready to move if the great beast sighed, and turned in its sleep?

It is possible that Skiddaw and its neighbour Blencathra were once by far the highest mountains in the Lake District. During the enormous mountain-building upheavals of the earth in the early Devonian period, which threw up the Cumbrian mountains, the hard rocks of the Borrowdale Volcanics resisted the thrust, and cleaved and fractured and buckled. The softer Skiddaw Slates offered little resistance and were heaved to a far greater height. That their once permanently snow-capped summits have been devastatingly reduced is wholly due to the fact that, over the millions of years since, the soft slate has also been massively eroded.

The traditional ascent shows obvious evidence of other very

recent erosion caused by the thousands of feet pounding out a trough. From a distance the straight up-and-down path shows as a scar on Skiddaw's side. This is a problem nowadays on nearly all of the fells and we must consider it in this book later. The way passes Skiddaw's 'Little Man'. A diversion to it gives a much better view southwards than the summit; more expansive, but I think not superior to Latrigg.

Skiddaw's summit itself has the views between south and west to the high fells, and westwards over the Skiddaw Slates to Snaefell, the Skiddaw Slate mountain on the Isle of Man. But to me it has its drama in a prospect over its northern arc across the Solway Firth to the hills of lowland Scotland in the north-west; and north-eastwards over the vast moorland expanse of the Uldale and Caldbeck Fells, largely common land in the care of the National Park Authority.

There is no true wilderness left anywhere in Britain, though this moorland below us, so unique in the Lakeland landscape, looks as if it fits the description. But what we see here in this land of hills and hummocks and hollows is evidence of long exploitation. More obviously over what was once dense forest there have been many centuries of hill farming. Less visible are the effects of mining.

It is a land open to the north and east. Snowfalls are less common in the Lake District than may be supposed, because the climate is affected by the Gulf Stream. Generally the winters, compared with the rest of Britain, are mild and wet, the summers cool. But if snow falls it is more likely to fall here in this exposed countryside than most other places, and the winds can be very cold.

· The Hill Farmer's Heritage ·

The first Cumbrians were Britons, then the area received Angles and Norsemen. The Norsemen came in great numbers into this north-western corner of Britain around the tenth century. They came as refugees, if the thirteenth-century Icelandic historian Snorri Sturluson is to be believed. He states that the Vikings of western Scotland, the islands and the Isle of Man declared independence. This did not go down well with Harald Finehair, the King of Norway, and he descended upon the rebels with a battle fleet. Sturluson records that when the King reached the Isle of Man the inhabitants had fled, every one, into Scotland. At that time, and long afterwards, Cumbria was part of Scotland. Conclusive evidence of Viking settlement is everywhere in the placenames as we shall see; though Skiddaw and the name of its noble neighbour Blencathra, and Carrock Fell to the north-east, have a less usual, Celtic ring to them.

The Vikings, it is thought, brought in what has become the successful local breed of sheep, the tough winterproof Herdwick: a handsome little beast with a pretty white face and wool like fuse wire. (Buy outer suiting or a jacket made of this wool and it will keep you warm and last forever. But keep it away from your skin!)

The Viking blood in the Cumbrian fellsmen, it has been said, accounts for their tough stubborn, laconic character, their traditions, and their peculiar dialect. This is quite convincing. But it has also been written that the Viking can be seen in the true Cumbrian's appearance: typically tall, fair-haired and blue-eyed. Now I know a lot of farmers with impeccable Cumbrian pedigrees and, to be honest, I cannot recall one fitting this description.

Hill farming was always marginal; more particularly here because of the climate, but also for other reasons. For five centuries Cumbria was subjected to periodic visits from Scottish cattle raiders crossing the low-tide fords of the Solway. Not that the inhabitants here were all that passive: there were also tit-for-tat raids the other way. And there were the troublesome border wars. Farm tenants were obliged, under tenancy agreements, to provide themselves with horse, spear and body armour, and to ride to their sovereign's service when commanded by the Lord Warden of the Western March, by proclamation or by the firing of a beacon. There was a beacon here on Skiddaw.

It is true that today's Cumbrian farmer is a rugged individualist. He has to be, his survival depends upon it. Let us wander down somewhere into this extensive 'Back o' Skiddaw' country and meet a typical (though fictional) farming family. We will call the head of the family 'James B.' James is forty-five, stocky, dark-haired with strong eyes, barrel-chested, with a hearty voice and a laugh to match. He comes of a farming family. His solid-looking farmhouse, 900 feet above sea level, set with its back to the fell and sheltered by elderly sycamores, is eighteenth-century, with later additions and improvements.

His wife, Joan, a slightly built handsome brunette, constantly on the move, is also of farming stock. As well as helping with physical labour, and keeping house, she takes care of the book-keeping, and pays the bills. They have two sons and a daughter. The eldest son, eighteen, works full-time on the farm. The daughter, twenty, works part-time on the farm, and part-time at a guesthouse 5 miles away in the village. The youngest son is at school. The farm has 150 acres of valuable improved 'in-by' land. On this land there are 100 head of cattle, half of them dairy cows. The farmer enjoys fell rights on the open common, where he runs some 500 Swaledale sheep. Some poultry is kept. The farm is eligible for government grant aid as it is in a designated Less Favoured Area. This means that James is paid to plant trees, build walls and generally improve the landscape. He does it with some skill.

The difficulties of running this farm might not be apparent to the layman. Firstly of course it is a seven-day-per-week job, with milking to be done twice each day. The milk is taken away by tanker. If snow blocks the narrow approach road, milk has to be pumped into a relief tank and taken by tractor across the fields to meet the tanker in the village. Lambs are due in April. Work days, and some nights, are long then, with snatched meals, and if the weather turns bad, as it can, it threatens the survival of his lambs and raises problems which would seem insurmountable to anyone but a hill farmer. Another busy time is at haytime, but then there is a programme of mutual help with a brother (with retired father), brother-in-law, and a cousin who farms in the area.

Is the farm viable? 'Nobbut just' (only just) says James. He cannot afford to make mistakes. The fact that he and Joan make so few is due to their long experience. Joan is vital to the decision-making. Only people like James and Joan could possibly run a hill farm of this kind on this land and make a reasonable profit. It is the long experience that is vital.

Both parents enjoy good relationships with the children. Will his eldest son Robert take over the farm on James's retirement? That is the intention. Robert is a good judge of stock and a tireless worker and likes farming. He is also skilled with machinery. (He prizes a veteran 500cc motorcycle and is working on souping up a Ford Escort.) If things go wrong for farming, or – and this may not be all that unlikely – he marries a woman who is not interested in living and working on a farm, he could finish up as a motor mechanic in Carlisle. The daughter will most probably marry a farmer, though the young men she meets at the Young Farmers' Club, are not all farmers. The youngest son is not sure of his future. Although he is handy on the farm he thinks he might like to join the police or the army.

Like all farmers, James will enjoy a good grumble now and then. He has hard things to say about politicians. He is very sad at the worrying number of Cumbrian farms that have gone to the wall in recent years, including those of distant relatives, their houses sold and taken as holiday accommodation, the farm land taken on by other farmers, sometimes miles away. But in more relaxed mood he is optimistic. He enjoys farming and cannot imagine himself doing anything else. He is aware of the dangers of wrong political decisions, outside his control, which could ruin the hill-farming economy; but, going back as he can over his ancestry, he reckons that there have been very bad times before and the family has hung on.

Both James and Joan, while being a little apprehensive, cannot see a totally black future, although they have reason to worry. EEC policy to cut milk production has meant that many lowland dairy farmers have gone into sheep rearing, and a reduction in grain production has put some arable farmers into sheep. Hill sheep farmers cannot compete with farmers who own those better lands. Furthermore EEC policy to cut subsidies on sheep when the country's total production exceeds a fixed level means that hill farmers are penalised at the expense of the growing lowland production. Farmers are urged to diversify to replace losses. High in the bleak hills, what scope is there for that?

It has been fashionable for centuries to romanticise the hill farmers' life. Shakespeare's characters wished to be carefree shepherds. Poets have longed nostalgically for the idyllic simple life in a humble cot (while doubtless enjoying something rather more comfortable). Wordsworth, who pretended to be on more intimate terms with Cumbrian farmers, popularised the myth of the essential purity of character of the simple rustic. Even Robbie Burns, who came of farming stock himself, found it advantageous to pander to the popular view with 'The Cotter's Saturday Night'. There probably still are hill farmers who read their Bibles by the fireside, are completely content to live in 'happy poverty', and are exceptionally kind to their animals and fellow men. If so I know none. The fact is that hill farmers, like anyone else, have their quota of gentlemen and rogues.

Having said that, what is remarkable about Cumbrian farmers

like James and Joan, and probably farmers in other relatively isolated areas, is that they have an unusual perception of time and place. James can trace his farming family back into the eighteenth century. Joan could do so for hers as well. (One farmer by Ullswater reckons he can go back to the fifteenth). They have all farmed in north Cumbria. James's father and grandfather were tenants of the farm before him. He has uncles, aunts, cousins and half-cousins farming all over the area, some as tenants and some as owners. Indeed the pages of his surname in the telephone directory show a wider spread into Carlisle and across the Scottish border.

There is then a sense of belonging to this particular land, bound to it by time; caught up in the seasonal routines which have changed little over the generations: winter feeding; daily milking; lambing in April, putting out to the fell in May; stock buying and selling, striking a bargain; walling, hedging and fencing; haymaking in June and July; clipping; dipping; lamb sales in September, ewes in October. That is how it will continue through this generation and most probably the next. There is an urgent sense of purpose; a responsibility handed down through the generations. This is the reason why so many hill farmers, come economic hell or high water, will cling to their hard seven-day-a-week all-weather way of life with all its ups and downs and burdens, when common sense would persuade anyone else to get out of it and invest their talents in a more profitable and congenial vocation.

The Cumbrian sheep are 'heafed' to their particular fell. In other words they have descended from generations of sheep that belong to that farm and have always fed on that land. Although the land is unfenced, from genetic instinct they will not normally leave it. In a similar way I reckon perhaps the farmer too is 'heafed' to his land. By contrast who are we who live in towns? Where are our family roots? Only aristocrats can pretend to trace their long-past ancestry. Most of us have no great knowledge of our forbears, who were most likely much less attached to one place.

It is obviously unwise to try to generalise too much about people, particularly those who, because of their way of life, have to be stubborn individualists. However I have good reason to believe, from experience, that the hill farmers are traditionally and correctly hospitable to a fault – even if you have to pay a visit to their farm to air a disagreement with them they will likely argue the point over an offered pot of tea and a slab of pie. What is refreshing to me is their tendency to think first and say what they think, and in matters of importance, to choose their words carefully. They are not always right, and can overstate their case, but it is refreshing. Do them a favour and they may not thank you for it; but the likelihood is that they will pay you back in kind, given the chance. And I enjoy their very dry straight-faced sense of humour.

As one might expect, the hill farmer's tough individuality is reflected in the character of his home. The traditional Cumbrian cottage is solidly built with small windows, usually facing away from the view, for they are built as a Cumbrian might say 'arse-to t'wind'. The walls are stone and rubble and if you try to make alterations, such as putting in an extra window or door, or even knocking a hole through, there are enormous problems.

Although the Lake District supplies millions of urbanites with a water supply, the Cumbrian cottage must make do with water piped from a hillside beck or a well. In the many years I have lived in the area I have never enjoyed a mains water supply. In times of drought a private supply often means carrying water from elsewhere; a terrible job for a farmer if he has stock to water. Sewage treatment is by private septic tank which needs occasional emptying, and a prolonged wrong choice of detergents can cause a malodorous malfunction.

Mains electricity has now reached most of the farms, but failures are rife in some areas and it is foolhardy to have no emergency plans. A telephone is a necessity, and can be subject to faults. Television reception may be poor or even impossible. The cottager relies greatly on personal transport, especially since public transport, being uneconomic, is extinct. A vehicle is not, as it is in the towns, a convenience, it is a necessity. The nearest hospital can be many miles away and emergency treatment can only be achieved after a long and uncomfortable ambulance ride. The cost of basic food and fuel is higher than it is in the towns. Life in 'the cot beside the hill' is great if you accept all that goes with it.

· Castlerigg ·

The farmers of Neolithic and Bronze Age days had it easier. The soil, fresh wrested by axe and fire from the forest, was good, and the climate was more temperate than today. It can be assumed that they were relatively prosperous. The labour demands of mere subsistence farming could hardly allow opportunity for such time-consuming production of structures that had nothing directly to do with agriculture. We should not visit this area without seeing one of the number of Neolithic/Bronze Age stone circles in Cumbria: the remarkable Castlerigg Stone Circle. At holiday times it is best to go there early in the morning or just before sunset. It is hard to enjoy the experience with too many people there trying to do the same.

The first thing to strike us is the setting, which is superb. The most impressive backdrop to the north-east is Blencathra (Saddleback), the noble neighbour to Skiddaw, which is only here seen end-on across the Greta Valley. Somehow Blencathra always seems to be very much higher than its 2,848 feet (868m), especially with some snow on its tops. From this point one cannot see its savage south-east facing cliffs and screes. As a fell walk it is much more of a challenge than Skiddaw. Southwards we look into the Naddle Valley with the lava-rock ridge of High Rigg to the left, and beyond the next valley of St John's to the south-east, the Helvellyn range. The question often asked is, did the builders deliberately choose this amphitheatre site for these views? It is impossible to answer. When this circle was built, perhaps over 3,000 years ago, the area could have been surrounded by trees. The circle might have been in a sacred grove.

Many similar structures of this period have been built to accord to astronomical alignments. There has been no absolutely convincing theory about Castlerigg's, though the entrance is on the due north end. Outlying stones might have been lost: one possible entrance is by the gate into the field. The rectangle on the east side is a puzzle.

We will never know for sure why the circles were built. But they would certainly have been meeting places for all the clans in the area: the lake fishermen, the farmers and huntsmen. Castlerigg used to be called 'the druids' circle'. In fact it was built long before the coming of the Iron Age culture and the druids. Because we cannot understand the significance of these stones we might regard their builders as obscure aliens, foreign Indo-Europeans who spread themselves over most of Europe, bringing their strange religions with them. But these were our ancestors. They may have occupied the country for around 2,000 years before a new wave of immigrants came among them. We carry their genes. These, our mysterious forefathers, 400 generations back, were not wild men dressed in skins. They wore woollen clothing and enjoyed some form of settled social life. If they understood the movement of the stars they must have understood a great deal about this precious land in which they lived.

They placed these stones as a response to this environment. More than we, they understood its significance. Being wholly dependent on what nature could provide for them in the valleys and the hills about this place, they had to be in close communication with it. They had to be not only familiar with all that shared life with them, but with the source of life-sustaining energy itself. Like all farmers they had to have a keen perception of time and place. They measured time by the natural cycles of sun and moon through the seasons, marking the movement with stones and stakes. It was vital to their understanding.

We think of environment as a locality. In environmental studies with students we survey the land in sample kilometre squares. The method is convenient. But nature does not live in isolated portions. Nature is a common sharing of the whole biosphere. Every single living thing is dependent upon a whole. If the definition of environment is 'everything external to an organism which affects the fulfilment of that organism' where does the environment end? Ninety-three million miles away? For the sun has a major effect on the fulfilment of any organism. These, our early ancestors, had an understanding that reached into the nature of things as near as the earth and as high as the stars. They marked the movement of those stars. If they did it with a religious fervour that is understandable.

People have always reached for a religion. I believe that there have been throughout human existence, even in primitive races – perhaps especially in primitive races – those who live so close to nature, who come to know, by intuition, that there is an authority higher than chiefs or kings. For there is a voice in the wind and storm, a message in the cast of the hills or the brooding silence of the forest, and the movement of the stars. We have largely lost such sensitivity. We do not feel the earth through unshod feet. We do not taste the air. We do not continually observe the changing pattern of nature. Our senses have atrophied, losing the fine-tuning that was once needed for a full life in the wilderness. But the people who placed these stones were surely responding to the deep-down mystery of life. The struggle for an identity; a response to a universal feeling that there must be a meaning; a feeling that lifts perception above the daily level of existence; and a hope that there is an inner part of humanity that can have no end but is embraced by the earth's and the firmament's eternal round.

Life may be seen as a strange predicament. The thinking man is plagued with ideas and half-felt beliefs. Afraid of lone confrontation with them, he seeks refuge in some sort of ordered society. But there is a need for an answer to a question that cannot be shaped. There is an unexpressed hope that some mentor will put words to feelings and interpret the mysteries. On to this ancient stage comes the shaman. Perhaps he has sincerity and integrity. Perhaps he is a ruthless power-seeker. But whatever, he calls the people to this wondrous place, thrusts his stave in the ground, and orders the positioning of the circle of stones. This is the sacred centre. Here the laws and habits and customs will be devised. Here will be the magic rituals that might be thought to ensure survival; here is where the gathering might try to reach a communion with the higher authority. Here perhaps is where our forefathers tried to make that spiritual journey, deep down into the essentials of human existence.

The builders speak to us through these stones. But somewhere between the time of their wisdom and ours there has opened an abyss. We can only place our hands upon these stones and wonder about our ancestors' strength which carried, moved, and erected them.

The stones belong so well in this place, fitting perfectly and solidly into everything you see around them, it seems that the circle *had* to be just here. The landscape spoke to our forefathers and their response has become their monument. Our response to this environment might take different forms. It can inspire rapture and reverence; an urge to protect; a compulsion to fight for the right to enjoy it. What will be our monument?

CHAPTER TWO

Keswick and Beyond

•

Keswick's River Greta has its source in the Borrowdale Volcanics on the eastern arm of the Helvellyn range. It begins as northward-flowing Thornsgill Beck (Norse *gill*, meaning 'ravine'; 'beck', from the Norse *bekkr*, meaning 'stream'). This becomes Trout Beck as it enters the Skiddaw Slates and turns due west. It is joined by many waters, first one flowing from Blencathra that rejoices in the Celtic name of the River Glenderamackin; then notably Mosedale Beck, which flows from Helvellyn. By the time it reaches Threlkeld, Trout Beck has become a formidable flow. It cuts its way deep through the Skiddaw Slates and is joined by a beck draining the facing sides of Skiddaw and Blencathra, the Glenderaterra Beck – here again, pure Celtic. (Coincidentally, in local dialect 'to glender' means 'to wander around aimlessly'.) It then becomes the Greta and cuts through a beautiful wooded gorge.

The railway line which once ran from the main line at Penrith, through this Greta Gorge to Keswick, and from thence to Cockermouth and the west, was axed by Beeching in 1972, in spite of protest. It was a popular tourist route, so how could it be said that it was losing money? At the time the poor receipts at Keswick station were quoted but of course only a relative few actually booked a ticket there; the tourists came to Keswick on a return ticket from wherever. I remember the excitement I felt journeying on this line longer ago than it pains me to remember. Greystoke, Penruddock, Troutbeck, Threlkeld – the very station names were so suggestive of adventure. But the spectacular single-track line, a Victorian masterpiece opened in 1864, is no more. It was not built to carry tourists, but iron ore from Cumberland's west coast to the blast furnaces of the north-east, and transversely with coke for Cumberland's furnaces. Tourist traffic came later, attracting nearly half a million passengers annually before the First World War. In that great Victorian age of railway mania the line was constructed in two and a half years. It meant building 135 bridges in 31 miles. It was reckoned that the navvies, with pick, shovel and wheelbarrow, could each move 20 tons of rock and soil per day on a diet of 2 pounds of beef and a gallon of beer. Just to think about it, makes my back, and stomach, ache.

Picture then these sweating, cussing, blaspheming, earth-moving labourers, smelling of soil and sweat and tobacco, sitting in a room at Penruddock, hearing Bible tracts and taking part in Sunday hymn-singing; or better, listening to lectures 'on suitable topics for their station in life' and politely drinking tea served by ladies of the parish; all provided free by the Cockermouth and Penrith Railway Company!

'Will ye be after passing me the sugar, Murphy me old friend, if ye please?'

'Sure an' it's a pleasure, Paddy. Allow me. Will ye be takin' one lump or two?'

What, we might wonder, would have been a suitable lecture topic for their station in life? Gardening? Embroidery?

This was the company's solution to the difficulties encountered in the building of the line from Lancaster to Carlisle when navvies rioted. (Did someone there try to water the beer?)

To me the surprising thing about the line is its beauty. I am sure that at least some of those hard-working navvies would have looked back with satisfaction at what they accomplished. The rails of course are gone, but the route of it, cut and fill, tunnel and bridges, between Threlkeld and Keswick is almost intact, and – great news! – in the ownership of the National Park Authority. Sad to me that the Authority did not have the courage to go the whole hog and accept the line all the way eastwards to the park boundary. But through the wooded gorge it makes a delightful, sinuous and secluded level walk, away from noisy traffic, crossing the river seven times. The tracery of the beautifully curved iron bridges actually adds something to the sylvan scene. In May and June the length is a botanist's and entomologist's paradise. Why do wild strawberries always seem to flourish by railway lines? We can never make a meal of the tiny things, but they titillate the tastebuds most pleasantly. The general quietness is refreshing, and I have my favoured picnic spots. My only grumble is that a walk from the best end by Threlkeld is hardly possible as there is no car park, although the National Park Authority could have made a modest secluded one at Threlkeld Station.

A serious question: if I admire the line now, would I, if I had been around in the middle of last century, have felt opposed to its making? Almost certainly I would have agreed with John Ruskin's bitter and eloquent diatribe:

> ... the stupid herds of modern tourists let themselves be emptied, like coals from a sack, at Windermere and Keswick. Having got there, what the new railway has to do is to shovel those who have come to Keswick, to Windermere – and to shovel those who have come to Windermere – to Keswick. And what then?
>
> 'What else can be said? I protest I can find nothing; unless that engineers and contractors must live. Let them live, but in a more useful and honourable way than by keeping Old Bartholomew Fair under Helvellyn, and making a steam merry-go-round of the lake county.

If I would have opposed the line then, and admire it now, could it be that if I live long enough I could grow to love the substitute: the improved A66 trunk road that now links Penrith to Keswick and Cockermouth? I protest that I never shall! It is a hateful intrusion. Why should heavy industrial traffic trundle noisily and malodorously through the centre of a national park? Luckily the road does not closely follow the railway route all the way and it makes only one leap across Greta Gorge at the Keswick end, but what a leap and what a sight! A horrible obscenity of a bridge in ice-cream-coloured concrete. Not everyone will agree. Some will say that it shows the Victorians what the twentieth century can do. Some will say that it has beauty. It might be an engineering masterpiece. But it should not be here, not here!

It was agreed in the 1960s that this new road was needed to provide better access from a proposed M6 junction to serve the industries of West Cumberland. The argument was about the route. There were loud protests when the highway plans were published: very extensive roadworks from Penrith to Keswick, the leap over Greta Gorge, and a road section actually built out into the water on the side of Bassenthwaite Lake. The great body of protesters were accused of being indifferent to the plight of the declining industries of West Cumberland – a lie! The National Park Authority, the Countryside Commission, the Friends of the Lake District, the National Trust and the other supporting organisations detailed an alternative route, to the north of the National Park, 4 miles longer but with easier gradients, with the advantage of giving access to the towns of northern Cumberland. The enquiry lasted six weeks and the protesters were confident that they had made a cast-iron case. The decision then to take the original proposed route was greeted with incredulity. A call in the Upper House by Lord Henley to look at the road policy in a national park was supported by the peers. But the Secretary of State refused to review the decision. The bulldozers were waiting in the wings.

Now that politicians appear to have gone so 'green', you might have thought there was a presumption against such highway policies in national parks. Do not believe it! I have been sickened at the sight of the new Oakhampton bypass (completed in 1989) which, against strong opposition and with good obvious alternative proposals, destroyed a deer park in Dartmoor National Park. Not enough of us care. What is a national park worth against the powerful and wealthy highway lobby?

Still, the A66 with its heavy transports, bypasses Keswick and nothing much has changed in the centre of the old place with its pleasant Victorian eccentricities. The only really ancient building is the church of St Kentigern, at nearby Crosthwaite, thought to be on the site of an ancient cross which marked where the Celtic saint preached (*thwaite* is Norse/Irish for 'clearing'). Keswick was once a mining village; the tourist trade, which markedly increased with the coming of that railway, made the present town. It is still the best of the Lake District's tourist centres, though it gets horribly busy in the height of the tourist season. Somehow the district council struggles to cope with this, and the town centre is normally kept quite clean. Alas though for the litter outside the centre, all of which cannot be blamed on visitors.

How pleasant it must have been, however, in those earlier days to arrive at the little railway station and to have a porter wheel your luggage as you strolled from the platform through the potted palms and ferns of the conservatory of the Keswick Hotel to be greeted by the proprietor himself and introduced to the hotel's modern luxuries, which included 'A spacious Drawing-room for ladies' attached to a 'coffee room'.

Even before the railway, accessible by reason of the new turnpike roads, Keswick must have been an exciting place for visitors, who began coming in greater numbers in the latter part of the eighteenth century. We might arrive by post coach which left Kendal at 5.30 in the morning. Having arrived in Keswick, there was keen and entertaining rivalry between coach houses for our touring requirements, and some of the surrounding journeys were done at terrifying speed. Some of the coaching facts and stories were collected by William Wilson, proprietor of the Keswick Hotel, in 1885.

It is recorded for example, that Jack Sheldon of Keswick, a noted speed merchant who would take corners on two wheels, was driving his coach from Patterdale with one passenger, and met another regular coach on the approach to Keswick. A race began. Jack took the road down Chestnut Hill at full gallop, while the other coachman turned left to go west by Brow Top. The coaches arrived almost simultaneously at The Royal Oak, narrowly avoiding collision. Jack's terrified passenger made a rapid exit. 'Remember the coachman,' said Jack, holding out his hat. 'Oh I'll remember you,' was the reply, 'for the rest of my life!' Concern for road safety was in its infancy then. Poor old Wordsworth himself, driving his pony and trap, was in collision with a coach 3 miles from Keswick and was thrown into a roadside field, demolishing a wall on the way. There was no sonnet forthcoming to record the incident, but then high drama was not his style.

The coming of the railway eventually diminished the coach trade. I like the warning said to have been given by one of the coachmen: 'Don't yer travel by those new-fangled steam engines. Suppose yer travel by my coach, and yer meets with an accident? There yer are! But suppose yer travel by rail and yer meets with an accident? Where are yer?'

· Bassenthwaite Lake ·

Bassenthwaite is the only lake actually owned by the National Park Authority. The A66 trunk road slices through and desecrates its west shore, and we can hear its rumble on the happier east side. The lake is an important habitat for wintering and breeding birds, for aquatic plants, and a rare fish, the vendace, a relic of the Ice Age. Because of this, Bassenthwaite is listed as a Site of Special Scientific Interest, and at the time of writing the Park hopes to have it soon officially designated as a National Nature Reserve. No powerboats are allowed on the lake and human activity is centred on the local yacht club at the lake foot.

The Mirehouse Estate, below Dodd Wood, is one of my favourite places. There is a car park in the wood with a pleasant café in the 1890 water-powered sawmill. From near here, there is a right of way to the ancient chapel close to the lake shore, but we must buy a ticket at the café as we want access to the private land alongside it. St Bega's Chapel and the shore by it is one of the most evocative places I know. Perhaps that is because there is no road to it. Every place of worship should be like this; a sanctuary far from worldly cares and petrol fumes, offering time for peaceful reflection.

Why is the chapel near the lake, far from a settlement? One theory is that it is deliberately built on an ancient pagan site. But the chapel served a large area. Some of the congregation would have arrived by boat.

The link with King Arthur, one of my boyhood heroes, is another reason why I regard this as a special place. On this shore Alfred Lord Tennyson wandered, and surely the moving image of the ruined chapel with its broken cross (before the restoration of 1874) was his inspiration as he wrote about the death of King Arthur in one of his 'Idylls of the King', though he places it near the fatal winter battlefield by the sea. In the poem Arthur lay deep wounded:

> And the bold Sir Bedivere uplifted him, . . .
> And bore him to a chapel nigh the field,
> A broken chancel with a broken cross,
> That stood on a dark strait of barren land.
> On one side lay the Ocean, and on one
> Lay a great water, and the moon was full.

Arthur commanded Bedivere to take his sword, Excalibur, and cast it in the lake. Bedivere agreed and:

> So saying, from the ruin'd shrine he stept,
> And in the moon athwart the place of tombs,
> Where lay the mighty bones of ancient men,
> Old knights, and over them the sea-wind sang,
> Shrill, chill, with flakes of foam. He, stepping down
> By zig-zag paths, and juts of pointed rock,
> Came on the shining levels of the lake.

The images are all there: he first treacherously concealed the sword in 'many-knotted waterflags, that whistled stiff and dry about the marge', as they still do in winter. He told Arthur that he only heard 'the water lapping on the crag, and the long ripple washing in the reeds'. So they do now. Eventually he did as he was ordered and threw the sword into the lake. An arm 'clothed in white samite, mystic, wonderful' caught it by the hilt, brandished it three times and drew it 'under in the mere'. Then, at last, Arthur was carried off into the lake in a dark barge rowed by ghostly figures clothed in black, with three queens with golden crowns; after he made that moving final speech: 'The old order changeth, yielding place to new . . . Pray for my soul. More things are wrought by prayer than this world dreams of . . .'

Oh surely it could happen here in this magic place! Walk off the public right of way, to the shoreline owned by Mirehouse, to see a stone carved with the brandished sword, commemorating Tennyson's vision.

Tennyson was a great friend of James Spedding who owned Mirehouse and he stayed here on many occasions. In 1835, so keen was the impecunious poet to get to Mirehouse that he sold his

Chancellor's Gold Medal for English Verse for £15 to pay for his journey.

Other welcome guests here were Tennyson's good friend and fellow poet 'Fitz' (Edward Fitzgerald) and another great literary figure, Thomas Carlyle. Spedding himself was a man of letters. He edited *The Works of Francis Bacon* in seven volumes ('Literary navvywork,' wrote Carlyle appreciatively) and wrote *The Letters and Life of Francis Bacon* – another seven! The handsome Georgian residence Mirehouse is open to the public on some days of the week in season. It still has a calm studious atmosphere and is one of the best 'open' houses I know; certainly the friendliest. I can imagine Carlyle, with his face in a book, in the library. 'Mirehouse was beautiful and so were the ways of it,' he wrote in a letter, '– not to speak of Skiddaw and the finest mountains of the earth.' Praise indeed from a canny Scotsman.

The present Speddings have done two commendable things. The Mirehouse shore is available to the Calvert Trust, a nearby training and holiday centre for disabled people. It is a tremendous pleasure to see the disabled enjoying handling sails, and canoeing, often with a great deal of hilarity. In the words of the Hobhouse Committee, national parks were intended as places 'where country sports could be available to all who would find in them a source of health and refreshment, a new sense of adventure ...' 'All' should mean all people who seek, again in the words of Hobhouse, 'the refreshment which is obtainable from the beauty and quietness of unspoilt country'. There should be no recreational apartheid. The less physically able are gradually being better provided for, but much more is still required. As an instance the Greta Gorge railway track is available to wheelchairs for a good distance; but there is plenty of scope for improvement in many desirable places. Furthermore, the less able should be making a contribution to conservation. Work parties of disabled people have been organised. The fact that they are rather less productive than those staffed by the more physically able is irrelevant. Conservation work is enjoyable and important, and is itself recreational in more than one sense.

The second thing introduced at Mirehouse itself is the adventure playground for visiting children. You may ask whether there should be adventure playgrounds in a national park. With 880 square miles of park is there not enough? But this one has been built in woodland, using natural materials and a great deal of imagination. Superb treehouses and forts remind me of days when I was Robin Hood or King Arthur and the world was young and I could live forever.

Dodd Wood, on a foothill of Skiddaw, is part of the Mirehouse Estate and is managed by the Forestry Commission as part of Thornthwaite Forest. I have mixed feelings about alien conifer forests, as you will see, due not least I suppose to spending my early working days in native broadleaf woodland. But Dodd Wood at least has a mixture. There are still native oaks, Scots pines, birch and juniper here and there, and a smattering of woodland flowers, including the miraculous foxglove, which is always there, waiting for a clearance, a break in the canopy, to let the sun open its rosy cups; and the dark green of Sitka spruce is broken by the light greens of larch, which turn gold in autumn. The Dodd, however, given clear weather, has a breathtaking summit view. To make it we must be booted for something of a messy scramble at the end. There is a stupendous panoramic aspect over the central fells, all the length of Bsssenthwaite Lake and across the Solway into Scotland.

· *Thornthwaite and Other Forests* ·

Thornthwaite Forest proper is on the far side of Bassenthwaite Lake and the River Derwent. There is another section, west of the Lake round Wythop to Sale Fell. Thornthwaite was the first forest to be planted in the Lake District, in 1919, shortly after the Forestry Commission was established to grow timber after the depredations of the First World War. The forest climbs up to around 1,700 feet (518.5m) on either side of Whinlatter Pass, on Grisedale Pike and around Hobcarton End. The forest now supplies pulp wood, some of which goes to a pulp mill in Cumbria's industrial area at Workington.

There was originally a fair mix of trees. Later plantings have largely been of larch, and Sitka spruce. By far the most popular tree in modern British forestry is the Sitka spruce (*Picea sitchensis*) because it is tolerant of all soil conditions, thrives in a wet climate, can be planted to a fair height on the hills, and grows fast. In some poor soil conditions Sitka is the only tree which can grow successfully. It is a native of the temperate rainforests of British Columbia, and North-West America where it enjoys a wet winter season, and in the summer, the claggy wet mists which drift in from the North Pacific.

I love trees and I have even been called a 'tree freak'. Having made a TV item which was mainly about trees, two girls from the production team were overheard to say that I '*looked* like a tree'! (An old crab or a strong oak?) After a period enjoying bare Alpine scenery I have recently been beset by a gathering unease which I have lately diagnosed as tree-deprivation. But prickly Sitka in the mass, I must admit, I like the least; firstly because it is so favoured by the forestry interests that it blankets vast acres in England, Wales, and particularly Scotland, with little or no consideration of its effect on landscape and wildlife. It is planted thickly to encourage rapid growth in the fight for light in a sort of silvicultural equivalent of intensive farm stock rearing. (Battery trees?) The Forestry Commission, aware of public feeling about blanket monoculture, would like us to love the Sitka and would prefer us to call it, more romantically, 'silver spruce'. Call it what you like, the general effect is the same.

Now I must qualify my prejudice. In its native land Sitka is superb. In British Columbia I have walked among giants over 200 feet high. The highest, regrettably just outside Pacific Rim National Park (in an area under threat from loggers in 1990), is over 310 feet high! In the wonderfully tangled moss-draped unspoilt temperate jungles in the coastal rainforests, protected in the national parks of Canada, and in America's North-West Pacific national parks, it is supreme, living happily in close communities with Western red cedar and Western hemlock over a mass of mixed undergrowth largely made up of the wiry shrub, salal. This undergrowth is so dense in places that it can support one's body weight and progress through it is only possible by 'swimming' over its surface! The whole is rich in wildlife. Massive fallen Sitka trunks, which have dropped to the forest floor after a life of several hundreds of years, become nurseries for young trees which seed on the rotting bark and sapwood. As the survivors of these grow and the dead trunk rots away, we are left with a ruler-straight colonnade of great trees. Some of these tree lines are massive, and over 500 years old. The self-generating process has been going on since long before human history; left alone it will continue into the forseeable future.

We have no very large Sitkas in Britain; after all the tree was only introduced here in 1831. Even so, some park specimens are over

100 feet high. There is an impressive one on National Trust land below Aira Force by Ullswater.

In our forests Sitka is not generally grown for timber. Our forests are cellulose factories. Sitka is good for producing pulp, which is in demand for making paper, but here it is mainly used for cardboard cartons (which are commonly used once and then thrown away). This means close planting, and harvesting at between fifteen and twenty years; no chance for undergrowth to develop under the dense canopy; no big trees, no wildness; no rainforest (though in some seasons visitors might dispute the latter!).

Due to the tax relief involved, quick-growing forestry has for many years offered attractive investment opportunities for anyone who suffered dreadfully from a surfeit of cash. Successful pop stars and showbiz personalities, most of whom have not the remotest idea where the forests are, and could not care less about the ruination of a landscape they will never see, have put their spare cash into the spreading blankets of Sitkas. Sitkas spell greed. The only argument in the Sitka's favour is that it produces a needed crop quickly. It used to be argued that the new plantations provided jobs. Very few. Afforestation is capital-intensive, and modern labour-saving machinery has taken over many forest operations.

Here we are then in the great Sitka controversy. 'Now, John,' a forestry friend told me, 'you will just have to learn to love the Sitka because it is going to be with us for ever. You're biased. Everyone will accept it in time. It will be appreciated as an attractive feature of the British countryside.' Will it? I wonder. What, to me, is wicked is that with the approval of the Forestry Commission – and often in the past by their own direct action – native broadleaf woodlands have been clear-felled to make way for spruce. I have watched it happen with horror and incredulity. Of course the hardwoods were judged to be unprofitable, and the landowners have to make a living. But this policy has resulted in the destruction of some beautiful landscape, and rich natural habitats, here in this National Park. Now 60 per cent of the Lake District's tree cover is conifer. Nationwide, somewhere between 40 and 50 per cent of ancient broadleaf woodland has been lost, all within the last forty years. My forester friend was right – I am biased. (Apart from anything else, Sitka needles are sharp. If you work among them they get down your collar and eventually insinuate themselves painfully into your underwear.)

The Commission will agree that aesthetically the past plantings in the National Park have been insensitive. The problem is the fenced boundaries on the hillside which have always been made ruler-straight. The fells have looked as if they have had poodle trims. Now all that is to end. The boundaries will be nicely broken to give the forest a 'natural' look. The work has already been started here in Thornthwaite and elsewhere. More broadleaf trees will be planted, though nationally Sitka will remain the most economical short-term crop. But in the slightly longer term, is it more economical to go on planting Sitka than it is to maintain and crop the existing broadleaf woodlands that too often suffer from neglect? And would it not be possible, just now and then, to plant whole mixed forests of the slower-growing native broadleaf trees that *we* might not enjoy, but our children and children's children will?

The National Park Special Planning Board is the planning authority but it has no powers over forestry activity – a ridiculous anomaly. However, by a long-standing agreement, the Forestry Commission will not agree grant aid for any new afforestation in the central Lake District. It has sometimes been argued that this is an unnecessary restriction. Since the natural forest which covered the Lake District has gone, it is said – and much of the regenerated and planted woodland since – centuries of sheep grazing on the exposed fellsides has impoverished the acidic soil in great areas. Vast acres are covered in useless *Nardus*, a grass so tough that even Herdwick sheep, which will eat almost anything, cannot stomach it. Other areas have been badly eroded. Sitka here would be a profitable crop, and would in time, it is said, stabilise and enrich the soil. Scientists argue about the latter point. Other vast areas are covered in bracken, which is useless to animals and man. But bracken is an indicator of reasonable soil depth. Where there is bracken, trees will flourish.

In conservation terms the arguments are reasonable. According to many naturalists (though not necessarily botanists), fencing an area off from sheep, and planting with spruce provides a richer succession of habitats. In the early stages it provides a home for bush-haunting birds. In the later, higher stage it provides a home for finches and thrushes. As the trees grow more, tree-nesting birds such as jays and carrion crows favour the area; and it is a delight first to hear, then to see, flocks of goldcrests, our smallest bird. Chattering teams of crossbills feed on the cones. Other naturalists might argue that the water run-off from spruce forest is acidic and can have a detrimental effect on life in becks and rivers; and while new forest provides new habitats for birds there could be a displacement of moorland birds.

Forestry propaganda also mentions the increase in animal populations, particularly deer, but the suggestion is mischievous without qualification. While it is true that mature conifer forest can provide a sanctuary for deer, in the planting process deer, which would browse out the young trees, have to be fenced out. In areas where existing deer are then excluded, the fences can severely restrict deer movement. Traditional deer pathways, some of them probably very ancient, are blocked off. This is very serious. From my own observations I am sure that this causes stress to the animals, and loss of feeding areas. And, incidentally, restrictive fencing offers great advantages to poachers, whose activities are rife, indiscriminate and cruel.

However, if one agrees on the opportunities that conifer plantations can offer for nature, there is absolutely no comparison with the habitats available in the extremely rich environment of an oak or ash wood, many of which are crying out for investment in proper management and expansion.

In landscape terms, and in terms of recreation in a national park, the suggestion that spruce afforestation should be more acceptable, and that we should rethink the prohibition in the restricted area of the central fells, is extremely controversial. The great majority of those who love the Lake District would threaten a revolution if it was proposed to fence off, bulldoze service roads, and cover parts of the mountain walkers' landscape in upper Borrowdale, or Langdale, or even the less familiar areas such as Kentmere or Longsleddale, with spruce trees. And if the soil is eventually enriched, what is to be grown on it? More spruce trees? Or sheep? A naturalist or an economist might well shudder to see the bleached landscape of *Nardus*; or pity the ignorant photographer who enthuses about the autumn gold of the useless bracken. For my part I would be very happy indeed to see the lower fell areas of bracken planted with oaks and other hardwoods; with Scots pine on the knolls and alders in the bogs, and the hill farmers paid to care for them; and existing woodlands better looked after. With careful planning such woodlands would enhance the landscape. Of course, contrary to our modern impatient grasping philosophy, the plantations would not produce any profit for some considerable time. Sitkas for a quick return! But Sitkas on the fells? Never!

Now, having said all that, having got the forests whether we approve of them or not, I hasten to praise the policy of the Forestry Commission in encouraging their recreational use. The forest tracks are great for walking, cycling and riding in any season. They have provided me with many hours of great pleasure and refreshment. They are attractive, particularly in rough weather, when the exposed open country is less pleasant. The dense spruce forest then is a good option; not giving complete protection, but at least allowing a muted perpendicular rainfall, rather than a more forceful diagonal!

Few forests are exclusively Sitka. Some, like Thornthwaite, offer a greater variety of species. To the layman they may be just fir trees but, armed with the Commission's tree identification leaflet or book, one can gain a better appreciation. Literature is available at a commendable little visitor centre and shop in Thornthwaite Forest by Whinlatter Pass, where one can learn more about the Commission's point of view.

We must salute our own native conifer, the noble Scots pine. And you must surely recognise the larch, the second most popular forest tree. Its needles are lighter and more delicate, attractive in spring flush, and it sheds them all in winter after turning an eye-pleasing gold. The absence of continual cover allows some light to reach the forest floor and there is some ground flora, as against its complete absence under the dark canopy of the evergreen conifers. Wordsworth disliked their alien presence. To me, they are a more acceptable immigrant.

· Walking Through Thornthwaite ·

When walking in Thornthwaite, or any forest, we must take care and keep to the paths and tracks! Irritatingly, the Forestry Commission still does not wholeheartedly encourage public access and recreation. One may find in some forests that rights of way are blocked, and if maps and walk leaflets are on offer they encourage one to walk only where the authority wants you to walk. Even then the odds are that sign posts and waymarkers mentioned in the literature will be missing. In these cases you may have to resort to using a compass. Or sometimes you are confronted with a sign saying 'Path closed owing to Forestry Operations', when the operations finished weeks, or even months ago. A warning: if you wander off the path and find yourself fighting your way through, or crawling under, the scratchy branches of Sitkas, you are in for a very painful experience. And if you were not convinced by arguments about the unfriendliness of British plantations of 'silver spruce' before, your mind will now be changed irrevocably.

I remember standing on a forest path above Windermere's western flank some years ago and hearing cries for help somewhere in the dense prickly green canopy of young spruces down the slopes below me.

'What's the matter?' I called.

'We've lost the path. How do we get to you?'

'Keep coming up towards my voice.'

At intervals they cried out and I answered. Their calls were getting nearer each time, and at one stage I could hear the party quite clearly crashing about, arguing with each other and swearing so horribly I could hardly bear to listen. Then, strangely, there was a longish silence, followed at last by another cry for help, but this time so far away as to be quite faint. I decided that to try further assistance was useless and I continued on my way. For all I know the party is still in there!

Even forest workers get lost. On one forest track I met a young man resembling a spaceman in his modern forestry safety gear. We exchanged words about the weather but I noticed that he seemed somewhat embarrassed. Eventually he said, 'Have you seen some felling going on as you came up the track? I can hear the chainsaws going occasionally but I'll be damned if I can find them!'

And that reminds me of a search for a lost person in Thornthwaite Forest years ago. A local and occasionally confused old lady went into the forest to collect firewood and had not returned home by dusk. It was a dangerously cold winter's night so the Keswick Mountain Rescue Team took no chances and called out a full-scale search. With powerful lights we scoured the pitch-black forest all night without result. The old lady was found at dawn. The fact that she had absent-mindedly put on several coats saved her from the bitter cold. She told us she had no idea that rescue teams had been searching for her. She said she had seen lights and heard shouting during the night. It all frightened her – so she went and hid!

The advantage of walking in the forest is that, even on a busy day, it is usually quite possible to get away from other people. The forest is a thousand curtains that open and close about the visitor. It can swallow a crowd and still give the walker an impression of isolation. There are, of course, exceptional days when the forest is the venue for a large event. It is as well if we know beforehand that there is an orienteering meet of a thousand runners, for example. Noise will also warn us when there are timber operations in progress.

Given the absence of disturbing noise, one thing I will allow forest conifers: the sound of the wind in their spires is restful, like sea surf. It is a chorus, whereas wind in the hardwoods is conversational: a humming in the birches, a sighing in the oaks. But on a still day the silence is superb. Wrap yourself in trees – a cloak of comfort for frayed nerves.

We should find a good spot to enjoy refreshment: a sheltered hollow maybe with a stump, a mossy stone, or a log to sit on. Here, more than anywhere else, we will surely find a sanctuary of stillness – the bliss of solitude. Some noiseless nook, tucked in a corner of the forest. But if we sometimes like music with our snack, ideally we should be beside a small beck, and maybe move around until we tune in to the right performance. I like a steady background note, with a purling-over-pebble cycle: pure delight! – a watery pibroch. Or we can maybe choose something less simple: an anthem, or a concerto for ripple and flood. We can hear a stream. But we should sit back and *listen*.

The spot should be open to some light. It often is where there is some running water. It may not be completely open to the sky – we can settle for subdued light filtering through the canopy. That almost compels a feeling of calm; long recognised, and imitated in the stained glass of church and cathedral. Where there is light there are plants. A visit to one of my refreshment stops offers a seat on a carpet of small flowers: deep blue milkwort, the ubiquitous yellow tormentil, and yellow vetch, white of bedstraw, and nearby, a luxury of ferns, male fern, hardshield fern, and oak fern.

Forest light is worth observing. There is the obvious photographer's favourite of sunlight shafts illuminating the morning mist. But there are various subtleties. We might come across, in the dimness, a sudden torrent of light. Here there is a suffused dewy dribbling of light; there a dance of light as the canopy moves in the wind; or again there may be flickering swarms of light. Then there are the sudden revelations: when probing light kindles a spider web into iridescence; or gleams through translucent leaves, or sets a bank of foxgloves ablaze. There is a sparkle and a shimmer on wet branch and frond; lambent light on pools. There is the mystery too of the seemingly inner light in the dimmest places: the luminescence of lichens; the radiance of tree-stump moss. There is a feast of such simple pleasures for those with eyes to see and time to relax and enjoy.

We should not be tempted to step out with speed in a forest; no need here for a purposeful mountaineering pace. Why hurry? Hurry is for slaves. Who would gulp good wine? Savour it.

But give me Lakeland's broadleaf woodlands – oak and ash with hazel and holly and yew growing around and upon rocky knots and steep hillsides, the whole thick with ferns and rich-scented mosses that, not content with covering the ground, climb up the topmost trunks. In winter, with the branches black against the sky or grasping at the sunset as if trying to hold back the life of the day. Or on a high-summer evening when the silence seems to be deepened by the mysterious churl – the 'roding' of passing woodcocks – that most pleasurable and evocative of twilight sounds. And the purpling sky aswoop with bats' wings. Or in the joyful bird-loud spring morning when leaf buds kindle into a green blaze. An exhilaration! Here we are, away from reminders of the new and the man-made, maybe with a warm wistful feeling, as if trying to remember something which has been long forgotten.

All that was best way back, in our wild ancestry in wilderness, seeps into the deep, thirsty hollows of our minds. It banishes all that is trivial. Like all wild things, we carry with us the spirit of the past as well as the prospect of the future. We are part of all that we see; brothers and sisters all, in the eternal round.

· Whinlatter to Cockermouth ·

Thornthwaite Forest is a good place to climb out of; and to spend an idle hour on a warm day it would be hard to beat lounging on a heather couch on the side of Whinlatter Top with a good helping of its plentiful bilberries, and imaging the once busy scene below. The ancient road from the south – once used by the Romans –

through Keswick to Cockermouth, to the Cumberland coast, and to Scotland by the Solway fords, came, not by Bassenthwaite Lake, but below here, by Braithwaite, through Thornthwaite and over Whinlatter Pass. Before the nineteenth century it would have been passable only for horse traffic. Travellers – male and female, masters and servants, with their luggage and chattels – would be on horseback. Trains of pack ponies made regular journeys to and from the Cumberland coast, connecting the area with southern markets. Records show that in the eighteenth century, apart from the contracted trips, there was a regular weekly service of twenty packhorses to and from the port of Whitehaven, and fifteen from Cockermouth. One can imagine them passing and re-passing, each train's lead pony announcing progress with a bell; the south-bound train laden with, amongst other things, tobacco from Jamaica. It would take at least three weeks to reach the London market.

This was also a drove road. Scottish cattle, following the old raiders' routes across the low-tide Solway fords and by Caldbeck and Uldale fells, would be driven this way, the traffic increasing after the fairs at Rosley, and swelling in spring after some of them had wintered on the coastal plains and been sold at Cockermouth market. There were also horses from the horse fairs; farmers taking sheep and wool to Cockermouth market; pedlars and gipsies; beggars, and maybe a few thieves. Was there some ill-tempered chaos at times when pony trains got mixed up with cattle herds? Or did the train captain and the drover stop to exchange news – and maybe something from a flask to keep out the cold? What has been the social cost of tarmac and speed?

The speed came with the turnpike acts, and the improved roads, particularly in the first half of the nineteenth century. There was a daily post coach rattling over the improved Whinlatter from 1811. And this is still the best way to Cockermouth, though by no means the quickest.

Cockermouth is worth visiting. It has been an important town since Roman times; the Roman fort and settlement was at Papcastle, west of the town. The twelfth-century Norman lord, the Earl of Dunbar, stole its stone to build his keep near the present town centre. This was at a time when Cumberland was shuttlecocking nationality between Scotland and England. Forceful arguments over this political point meant that the castle changed hands, and changed shape, a fair number of times. The present structure is mainly fourteenth century with some nineteenth-century restoration.

Cockermouth (population around 7,500) is a very pleasant place as country towns go. The horse trading which went on when the national park boundaries were fixed, just kept the town out. Nonetheless it is a good exploration base for the northern lakes. Shopping is unpressurised, and shopkeepers are friendly even on busy Monday market day when the town fairly hums. But there is more to offer than shops; not least the pleasant riverside walks and friendly hospitality.

Of course we have to make the pilgrimage along the main street to its most impressive house, now in the loving care of the National Trust, where William and Dorothy Wordsworth were born, in 1770 and 1771 respectively. The house was the property of the Lowthers, large Cumbrian landowners. John Wordsworth, head of the Words-worth family of five children, was agent to Sir James Lowther (known at the time as a despotic and mean landlord, 'the bad Lord Lonsdale'), and the house went with the job. To me the house seems to have offered a somewhat stern beginning to the gipsy spirits, William and Dorothy. But William enjoyed a good deal of freedom and was able to experience his early encounters with nature in the surrounding countryside. He wrote in 'The Prelude':

> Fair seed-time had my soul, and I grew up
> Foster'd alike by beauty and by fear;
> Much favor'd in my birthplace . . .

And he writes of his happy times running about the fields by the Derwent, 'fairest of all rivers' that 'sent a voice that flow'd along my dreams', 'a Playmate whom we dearly lov'd', and bathing – 'one long bathing of a summer's day' – in a nearby mill stream.

Dorothy records that their father had no friends in the town, no doubt because of his professional connection with an unpopular public figure. It would seem from William's small reference to him in his works that father and son were not too close. But John taught William early to appreciate good literature, and William had the use of a stimulating library. The poet and his sister did not spend long here. They attended infant school at Penrith, 30 miles away; and from the age of nine to seventeen William attended Hawkshead Grammar School. Until John Wordsworth's death in 1783 (their mother had died in 1778), the brother and sister came to Cockermouth, over Whinlatter Pass, to spend their holidays.

The walled garden is a lovely retreat. The National Trust has planted and maintained it with herbs and flowers that would most likely have been there in the late eighteenth century. Full marks for the Trust's coffee shop and exhibition – a pleasant place to spend a happy hour or more.

· *To Buttermere* ·

From Braithwaite, back at Whinlatter's eastern foot, what was a track and footpath, and is now an unclassified road soon blocked by winter snow, heads south and south-west to cross Newlands Pass to Buttermere; but for the fit and energetic, and given good weather, there are more delectable ways to Buttermere. We can choose the Coledale route. From the foot of Whinlatter, Coledale lies southwest and for 2 miles there is a mine track to Force Crag mines ('force' from the Norse *fosse,* meaning 'waterfall'). The crag is a great perpendicular wall of buckled rock over which two waterfalls spill, though only spectacularly after prolonged rain. The mine was opened early last century to produce lead and barytes, and it continued production on and off to recent times. The mine borings look like impertinent pinpricks in the rockface.

A much-eroded mine track climbs south around the crag and this leads to a deep cove backed by another high crag, the abode of ravens, with additional mine workings and over which falls another force. The track becomes a rough path as we climb higher and at one point it has eaten through peat. This peat has fibres of tree root in it, showing that forest once occupied these heights. When we reach the hummocky grasslands at Coledale Hause there is some more, quite massive footpath erosion in several places. Footpath erosion is often raised as a matter of concern and there are still wild optimists who think that it can all be repaired. Coledale is only one example of the hundreds of miles of fell path severe wear and tear and there is no way that any very serious headway can be made in restoration. This is really an aesthetic issue rather than one of conservation, as footpaths take up only a small fraction of the vast area of fell land. Given the great number of walkers taking to the fells nowadays, my own view is that there is no solution to this problem.

At the Hause we follow the path for Buttermere southwards, then south-west to the top end of Whiteless Edge, and an astonishing view bursts open. How to describe the impression? It is like the ecstatic climax to a great symphony. I am not saying that it is the greatest view in the Lake District. There are others comparable. But, as the Cumbrian farmer says when something is exceptionally wonderful: 'It'll do!'

We are still standing among the fells of Skiddaw Slate but the distant peaks of the Borrowdale Volcanics seize the attention. And what an array! From the distant east we can see the Helvellyn range: Fairfield, then moving south, Glaramara, Bowfell, Great End, Great Gable, Scafell Pike and Scafell. It is a complex gathering of heights.

This expansive view tells a story which tantalises the interpreter. It covers changes over an immensity of time – volcanic eruptions, folding and faulting, and the effects of Ice Age erosion. The change of course continues, for there is nothing in the whole wide world that stands still. Weather erosion is gradually levelling the hills and silting the lakes. There is no beginning and no end; only change, which to us might be imperceptible. The scene is dynamic. If, from our viewpoint, it appears reassuringly and restfully static it is because we are prisoners of human time. And there is no word in any language to describe how infinitesimal that is in the context of geological time.

If we stand in awe at such a scene as this, is it because we are intuitively aware of an existence, an absoluteness, immeasurably greater than we can even dream of? We stand, fragile creatures of a moment, poised in eternity. What are we? What do we pretend to be? What, in the tremendous universal scheme of things, do we possibly imagine is so vitally important in our busy toils and pre-occupations down in our human ant hills?

But we must move on to enjoy the scenic bounty that is offered to us. Below is Buttermere, with the bold Borrowdale Volcanic cliffs of High Crag, High Stile and Ennerdale Granite Red Pike behind; and Crummock Water with Mellbreak behind that; and Loweswater to the north-west. Whiteless Pike is our next destination, hovering at the end of a ridge and saddle before us. From this point it feels as if we might be looking from a masthead towards the prow of a ship. The prow, the Pike, is soon reached and here we are directly above

Buttermere, looking down on the whole of its delectable beauty. We descend southwards to it.

The settlement is a small hamlet of two hotels, a tiny chapel, and one or two farmhouses. Father West, in his eighteenth-century guidebook states that here 'The life of the inhabitants is purely pastoral. A few hands are employed in the slate quarries' and 'the women spin woollen yarn and drink tea'. On this latter point, did some cynical Buttermerian male chauvinist con the cleric? Considering the price of tea in those days, the ladies may have been gaily drinking away the meagre profit on the yarn! Or was it smuggled tea? In 1784 Pitt the Younger calculated that almost half the tea drunk in Britain at that time was smuggled in. The going rate generally seemed to be about half a guinea per pound. Smuggling was rife on the Cumberland and Solway coast, the nearby Isle of Man being a staging post, and there must have been bargain prices for tea here. The women could hardly have been idle. Their way of life must always have bordered on bare subsistence. In the eighteenth century the women commonly not only spun and sold yarn, they also wove and made the family's clothing. Some would specialise, and there was some bartering. For instance probate records show that every dale had its supply of malt for brewing, and if there was no inn as such the early tourist could invariably buy a drink at some cottage door.

But in Buttermere there is The Fish Inn. In the eighteenth century there appeared here one of the early tourists, a jaunty one-armed veteran soldier, Captain Budworth, who was to do the innkeeper a good turn by increasing custom, and his daughter a bad turn by bringing her a good deal of attention. This was the Romantic age when the writings of Jean-Jacques Rousseau, among others, suggested a belief in the essential innocence of those who lead a more natural, rural way of life. To the commercially minded urbanite, the life of the shepherd and shepherdess was further idealised. Thomas Gray, for example, writing of his journeys in the Lake District, referred to a 'happy poverty'.

Budworth, in his *A Fortnight's Ramble to the Lakes,* wrote of Mary Robinson, the landlord's teen-aged daughter, with enthusiasm for her 'fine oval' face, 'full eyes' and 'lips as red as vermilion', 'an angel', 'the reigning Lily of the Valley'. Budworth was widely read, and Mary Robinson at The Fish Inn was soon high on the tourists' itinerary. Poor Mary was gaped at by all and sundry. (I find it hard to understand why that should have included Wordsworth, Southey, and De Quincey!) Eventually a story unfolded which was to be repeated in magazine articles, broadsheets, journals, and a novel, and was even dramatised for the fashionable London stage. The story concerns essential innocence corrupted by evil, the latter in the shape of an apparently wealthy titled tourist.

He called himself the Honourable Alexander Augustus Hope, and was easily accepted by Lakeland society on his arrival in 1802. No doubt familiar with Budworth's book, he appeared at Buttermere, wooed and 'married' Mary Robinson at nearby Lorton. The attention the occasion attracted was his undoing. The authorities knew that the real Colonel Alexander Augustus Hope was abroad, and newspaper reports of the wedding alerted them to the impostor's whereabouts. He was arrested, escaped, recaptured in Wales, and tried at Carlisle. His real name was John Hatfield, already married with a family. He was condemned to death for forgery, and, remarkably again, visited in jail by Wordsworth and Coleridge. He was hanged in September 1803. And Mary? Surely in that romantic period she would be expected to die of a broken heart? There was no such satisfying end. There is nowt so daft about a true Cumbrian. She married a farmer Caldbeck way, raised a family and lived a long and happy life.

Nowadays there is relative prosperity in Buttermere, but there is not a lot of what some people like to call 'progress'. An elderly motorist once got out of his car in the hamlet and asked us 'Where are the shops?' When I told him there were none, he did not believe me. When I convinced him that I was telling the truth his mouth dropped open with astonishment, and he immediately got back in his car and drove off.

It may seem incredible but more than once I have also been asked for directions to the nearest amusement arcade. Thanks to strict planning there are none in any of the towns and villages of the National Park, but that is not from want of trying by entrepreneurs. Why on earth do these people come to the Lakes? These are the type of shally-wallies who would be happier somewhere else. They crowd noisily into the bars, disturb the night in villages, and leave drink cans everywhere. The Lake District National Park should be exclusively for those who appreciate quiet recreation in unspoilt country.

The rest should be turned away at the park boundary. If only that were possible!

Buttermere itself is sublime and I must walk round its lake shore footpaths at least once each year. It is a delight all the way and mercifully cared for by the National Trust. On the north side, the path goes by one of my favourite lunch stops, under pine trees, the property of the National Park, and passes through a tunnel in the Lakeside rock at Hassness. (Rumour has it that the one-time owner of Hassness did not like to see his gardeners idle in wet weather and had them work on the tunnel whenever it rained.) I am particularly fond of this place. Trees I planted here with my colleagues of old have reached a splendid height, but they can get a fearful battering from the spiralling gales that sometimes tear down this valley, lifting the lake surface into racing water spouts, an amazing sight: spires of water that spin upwards and rush across the lakes like demented water-wraiths.

If nearby Crummock Water was in some less favoured part of Britain it would be a very major attraction. It is a lovely sheet of water, like Buttermere in a completely unspoilt landscape, thanks largely to the National Trust. But Crummock lacks the background drama that is Buttermere's, for Crummock with Mellbreak behind, is in the Skiddaw Slates. Mellbreak is impressive enough, and lake and fell make a great picture; but it lacks great spectacle.

Each mood has its time. There is a time to thrill to the classic sights of hills and lake; enormity wedded to tranquil secrecy; but there is also a time for a more restful mood. To stretch in the heather on Mellbreak away from the excitement, and to watch the changing clouds, and let the world roll by. Here, for me, is the place.

CHAPTER THREE

Borrowdale and Round About
·

East and south of Derwent Water the Skiddaw Slate gives way to the more dramatic landscape of the Borrowdale Volcanics. There is speculation about the location of the eruptions which produced these fells. It is usually assumed that there were several volcanic centres, and that there were several periods of eruptions, possibly later ones partially overlapping the earlier. This makes a study of the complex structure difficult, and it is further complicated by the effects of the enormous folding and faulting of rocks during the Caledonian earth movements which followed the volcanic activity and lasted for several millions of years. Furthermore there was the erosion in the comparatively recent Ice Ages.

On a boat trip on Derwent Water today, Walla Crag, Falcon Crag, and Brown Knotts form an impressive eastern wall, and at the lake foot we are at the threshold of the Volcanics at their best. The scene astonished early tourists. In the 1750s Dr John Brown, a renowned essayist and author, wrote a letter to Lord Lyttleton which, when later published, did much to stimulate tourism to the area. He described the Derwent Valley graphically, and of this eastern side and foot he wrote:

> ... you will find rocks and cliffs of stupendous height, hanging broken over the lake in horrible grandeur, some of them a thousand feet high, the woods climbing up their steep and shaggy sides, where mortal foot never yet approached. On these dreadful heights the eagles build their nests; a variety of water-falls are seen pouring from their summits, and tumbling in vast sheets from rock to rock in rude and terrible magnificence; while on all sides of this immense amphitheatre the lofty mountains rise around, piercing the clouds...

Enthusiasm encourages more than a little exaggeration – horrible, dreadful, terrible – flesh-creeping stuff to encourage the early adventurers!

The Volcanics are at their 'terrible' best suddenly and spectacularly as we enter 'the jaws of Borrowdale'. Here we are in a curving steep-sided glaciated valley containing the River Derwent, with a wealth of 'hanging' woodland, opening to pastures, before the valley divides at the point where two glaciers met. Borrowdale continues to the mountain foothills to the south-west; Stonethwaite is the branch to the south-east.

Father West, a Jesuit priest and author of the best-selling eighteenth-century guidebook to the Lake District, wrote of Borrowdale in a style to match Dr Brown's of Derwent Valley:

> The rocky scenes in Borrowdale are most fantastic, and the entrance rugged. – Here rock riots over rock, and mountain intersecting mountain, forms one grand semicircular sweep. Extensive woods deck their steep sides; trees grow from pointed rocks, and rocks appear like trees. Here the Derwent, rapid as the Rhone, rolls his crystal streams through all this labyrinth of embattled obstacles. Indeed, the scenes here are so sublimely terrible, the assemblage of magnificent objects so stupendously great, and the arrangement so extraordinarily curious, that they must excite the most sensible

feelings of wonder and surprise, and at once impress the mind with reverential awe and admiration.

At a time when roads were sketchy, he wrote of the road up Borrowdale: 'It serpentizes through the pass above Grange; and, though upon the edge of a precipice that hangs over the river, it is nevertheless safe.'

For some time after the advent of tourism, Borrowdale was considered to be remote and savage enough to attract only intrepid travellers. The aboriginals of this 'sublimely terrible' region were considered to be backward wild men. Stories were invented about them and laughed over in the Keswick hostelries. One such was that the Borrowdale inhabitants, equating spring with the cuckoo, built a wall across the valley to trap the bird and so have eternal spring. But it did not work – the cuckoo got away. The story goes that the inhabitants thought this was because the wall was one course short of sufficient height!

The road was not safe enough for carriages until fairly late in the nineteenth century. Indeed, it is recorded that in 1824 the road was so bad even as far as the lake foot that the first hired chaise, driven by local coachman Jack Cawx, was almost overturned, to the terror of the occupants, at Grange Bridge.

Presumably the road then was subject to the scouring action of periodical flooding. Schoolchildren were once told (are they still?) that Seathwaite in Borrowdale is the wettest place in England. In fact the 'Seathwaite' rain gauge is not in Seathwaite village but 2 miles away, at 1,500 feet, in the upper part of Borrowdale in the lap of the highest mountains in England. Its records show an annual average of around 131 inches. But the Scafells might well receive some 180 inches of annual rain. Grange in Lower Borrowdale receives only half that, as the guesthouse proprietors will explain. (But in the 1980s when Borrowdale's exaggerated reputation for record wetness prompted a tyre manufacturer to give away free tyres to the residents to publicise their wet-road safety qualities, no one argued. Cumbrians are not daft!) When it rains in the mountains above Borrowdale it rains hard. But the number of rainy days is not exceptional, and droughts in spring and autumn are by no means uncommon.

Every so often, however, exceptionally heavy rain in the mountains brings the floods down into Borrowdale. Then ancient history repeats itself. Derwent Water and Bassenthwaite Lake are joined to become one large lake, as they used to be before the gap between them was filled with silt and debris. Such a flood happened after a heavy mountain storm in 1962, but more notably in August 1966 when Styhead Gill and Grains Gill became raging torrents. It was a fearsome sight. The water, loaded like brown syrup with soil and gravel, had picked up large boulders as if they were mere footballs and bounced them down into the valley. The noise as they collided sounded like a cannonade above the menacing roar of the water. Then the upper fields of Borrowdale were devastated and the main valley was one great flood, with houses and settlements isolated. As the water receded we looked with amazement at the altered landscape above Seathwaite farm. The ancient way to Styhead Pass had been swept away and would have to be re-routed. The lovely curving arch of the old Stockley Bridge over Grains Gill was so battered that it would almost have to be rebuilt.

But normally here in Borrowdale, away from the road, we can hope to find peace and tranquillity. Rocks indeed 'riot over rocks' and are clothed in delightful woodland, some of the best in Cumbria and most interesting for plants and wildlife, and most of them in the care of the National Trust. Borrowdale is sublime. Borrowdale of the green spring and the burning autumn. Borrowdale of the rippling river and lapping lake. Borrowdale of the sunsets. Borrowdale of the thousand happy memories. Borrowdale of the hundred walks.

An American tourist expressed surprise that there were so many 'trails' in the National Park, and so many walkers. We should rejoice that so many choose to leave their stuffy steel boxes at the car park or the station, and head for the fresh air of the open country-side. When the National Parks Bill was to be considered the Hob-house Committee stated that people 'need the refreshment which is obtainable from the beauty and quietness of unspoilt country-side'. Well, not all the visitors to the National Park appear to need it.

Research has shown that 45 per cent of visitors to the Lake District do not walk even a few miles. If we rule out those who are excluded from much physical activity by infirmity; and those who are unaccustomed to walking and are not inclined to walk, yet get some enjoyment at seeing the countryside through a glass darkly; we are left with what I fear are still a high number of people who had much better be somewhere else. It is these latter folk who give the Lake District its reputation for being overcrowded, causing congestion on the roads and in the holiday villages at certain times of year.

Maybe they are motorists with only a very vague notion that a change of scene is a good thing, or they are paying for an expensive car and to justify its existence have to collect mileage. They can make a roadside walk up Borrowdale a very unpleasant experience, with air and noise pollution and threats to safety. There are also, I fear, a proportion of shally-wallies who evidently despise the countryside, for they foul their route with drink cans and take-away food containers and cigarette packets. Why do these people come? They are no small minority. Anyone who doubts this should ask the National Park's mobile litter crew, or join the voluntary wardens on their end-of-season roadside litter sweeps, when hundreds of sacks of motorists' litter are removed.

Is it for the care-less people that we build our car parks and public conveniences in the countryside? Is it for these people that the entrepreneurs move into the area, for these that the planners buckle under pressure to allow planning applications in the holiday villages for new shopping facilities, luxury weekend flats, and take-away food franchises?

There are an unlimited number of reasons why people visit the countryside, and most of those who do so would no doubt have difficulty in explaining why. The Hobhouse Committee suggested that people needed unspoilt country as an 'escape from the routine of working lives'. The value of the experience is surely in getting away from it all; not bringing it all, or a good part of it, with you. In theory, people who live in luxury would get most out of a camping holiday in a remote area. Yet very few would opt for it. But who really needs in our unspoilt countryside, with all its open-air opportunities for adventure, super-luxury time-share cabins and holiday flats, indoor gymnasiums and Caribbean-style swimming pools complete with palm trees? We know who *wants* them but who *needs* them? Perhaps the only people who need them are the underprivileged of inner cities who need a complete change from the routine of *their* working lives?

I have really tried hard to understand some motives. For instance, how does one comprehend the person who admires a scene so much that he must take a photograph, then throws down his empty film packet? This is not at all uncommon, and we may well find evidence of such people's visits at Borrowdale's Surprise View, or by Ashness Bridge. Or how to explain the camper who has made great efforts to find that unspoilt idyllic campsite on the fell, then leaves his food cans and other trash there under a pile of stones?

How much we enjoy the countryside depends on the attitude of mind we take with us. We know that to appreciate it we must have some understanding. The keener the awareness, the greater the experience. It is possible to walk into the countryside and see nothing, for we carry with us the cares, the worries, the problems, which we ought to have left behind. To be truly aware we must dispense with all that, and open up our senses to all around us: the sights and sounds of the immediate environment; the distant view; the pure air. But it is not always easy to do this. We carry with us a mischievous imp which tells us that if we are not worrying about something, we ought to be! That same demon whispers to us that menace lurks behind solitude and silence, and peril in the opening of awareness.

The greater the awareness, the greater the enjoyment. A little knowledge of botany, ornithology and geology – only a modest knowledge – enhances an appreciation of the whole. But there is a natural inclination to specialise, and there is a danger in specialising too much. An ornithologist might see nothing except birds, a mineralogist only rocks, a botanist only plants. Specialisation can put us into blinkers. It is a crippling habit of modern age. As Wordsworth put it, in 'The Tables Turned':

Sweet is the lore which Nature brings;
Our meddling intellect
Mis-shapes the beauteous form of things;
We murder to dissect.

An awareness of the whole interlocking interdependent community of nature – if only a hint of its music, just sitting quietly and enjoying it, more especially in the bliss of solitude – is a spiritual experience.

Some of us, I believe many more of us, could reach a step

higher. To have this awareness, and to get physically involved in conservation tasks to a point where muscles begin to protest – that is, I swear, blissful fulfilment. And this experience is not exclusively for healthful youth. Anyone can do their bit. Some of my happiest volunteer work parties have been beyond middle age, even some physically handicapped. The National Park's volunteer wardens are of all ages and from all walks of life. And probably some of the most enthusiastic are mid-weekly work party all-weather regulars, the majority of which are 'senior citizens' (one group call themselves jokingly 'last of the summer wine') who have trained themselves to do most tasks, including rebuilding dry-stone walls.

I can understand the surprise of the American visitor who remarked about the number of 'trails' in the National Park. In American parks, walkers' routes through the wilderness areas are understandably kept relatively few. I had to explain that most of these trails of ours were ancient footpaths and bridleways over which the public had legal rights. Some have had to be fought for, as in that nineteenth-century demonstration to retain the footpath to Latrigg. The 1949 National Parks and Access to the Countryside Act did much to rationalise the public rights of way system in England and Wales. (It remains Scotland's and Northern Ireland's great loss that there is nothing comparable there.) Under the Act, the parish councils were required to claim all the rights of way in their parishes. A provisional map was then to be produced, appeals heard, and finally a definitive map drawn which had legal standing. The county councils then, as highway authorities, were responsible for ensuring that the routes were kept open and maintained, and signposted at the points where they left the public road. The disgraceful lack of action in some counties shows the weakness of their local government, and the docility of those inhabitants who like to walk.

In the Lake District National Park we do rather well. Cumbria County Council delegated responsibility for rights of way within the park to the National Park Authority. Here we can be reasonably certain that rights of way shown on large-scale walkers' maps (paths and tracks copied from the definitive map) are unobstructed and stiles and gates in place. If not, a report receives an active response, rather than a non-committal bureaucratic acknowledgement.

Borrowdale has a generous share of these rights of way, as

well as the opportunity to wander at will through National Trust properties. One of my favourites is to take the service boat from Keswick landings to the Lodore landing at the foot of the lake. After paying the token fee at the gate by the Lodore Swiss Hotel we walk through hotel land to the Lodore Falls, one of the essential sights in Victorian times – very impressive and noisy after prolonged rain but tame after a dry spell. Robert Southey gives me the impression that he was a rather stuffy academic but he wrote for children (surprisingly, the original 'Three Bears' story). And I have enjoyed getting my tongue round his long description of the 'Cataract of Lodore', from top to bottom:

> ... Pouring and roaring,
> And waving and raving
> And tossing and crossing ...

The ravine is richly clothed in woodland, and a footpath wanders up alongside the lower falls to the upper which we can view from a little platform. This is a pretty walk that I have done time and time again. Up above on the left are the broken crags of the Volcanics, but here this moist place is covered in mosses, ferns, honeysuckle and ivy, foxgloves, and heather and bilberry. Eventually we reach the top and walk through National Trust woodland to the side of the narrow Watendlath road, which is at times ridiculously jammed by cars, some of which have left pretty patterns of body paint on the roadside dry-stone walls.

We will resist the temptation to walk to Watendlath's tiny settlement, and go in the opposite direction to a point where the road comes close to a cliff edge. This is the famous 'Surprise View' framed in trees. As an American visitor was once heard to say, 'That's real awesome!' And it is. Below us is the whole of Derwent Water, with Bassenthwaite Lake in the distance. We are obviously standing on a volcanic rim, while all behind the lake, to the north-west and the north, are the fells of Skiddaw Slate.

Further on, as we descend the road, we come to another famous viewpoint which can be recognised even by those who have never been this way before, for it must have appeared on more chocolate boxes, biscuit tins, and greetings cards than most other scenes in Britain! But here is a case where familiarity does not necessarily breed contempt. This is Ashness Bridge, a small hump-back which, with its bouldery beck, gives foreground interest to a lovely scene – trees again, lovely in autumn, the lake and Skiddaw behind. Film-makers have made fortunes out of this, and I know of at least one photographer who fell in the beck with excitement.

The route leads down to the Borrowdale road, which we can cross and catch the boat back to Keswick at the Ashness Gate landing. We must sit on the starboard side to enjoy the woodlands on the east side of the lake, climbing the 'horrible grandeur' of the tumbled crags, 'up their steep and shaggy sides where mortal foot never yet approached'. Well, this is the stuff of dreams...

· Upper Borrowdale and the Scafells ·

The poet Thomas Gray, best known for his elegy about a country churchyard, visited the Lake District in 1769. In his description of Borrowdale he wrote of Seathwaite, the uppermost settlement:

> ... all further access is here barred to prying mortals, only there is a little path winding over the fells, and for some weeks in the year passable to the dalesmen; but the mountains know well that these innocent people will not reveal the mysteries of their ancient kingdom, – only I learned that this dreadful road, divided again, leads one branch to Ravenglass, and the other to Hawkshead.

Well, the mysteries are out. The ancient kingdom of the mountains now endures the assaults of multitudes. The 'dreadful road' is passable to all able-bodied walkers throughout the year. The roads to Raven-glass and Hawkshead lead upwards to England's highest land: the Scafells in general, the Pike in particular, via the passes of Sty Head or Esk Hause. From Sty Head one can also climb Great Gable; and rock-climbers have access to some of the classic climbs, including the famous Napes Needle.

The roads are of course mere tracks. In those old days they were shown as roads on some of the available maps. But roads were not necessarily carriageways then. They were pack-pony routes. Travellers came on horseback.

So, given a fine day with a good forecast, we will put on boots, shoulder our rucksacks, and ascend what were once called 'The Pikes of Scawfell', particularly the topmost one, now called Scafell Pike, England's highest mountain, 3,210 feet (978m). The very best way is the three-and-a-half-hour journey via Sty Head and the Corridor or Guide's Route. Start early to avoid the crowds of other adventurers, for after Helvellyn, Scafell Pike is the most popular mountain in England; though a fair number never complete the climb, either finding it to be further than they anticipated, or getting lost.

Seathwaite, at the end of a road from Seatoller, is little more than a farm and a mountain hut. The well-known and much-respected farmer must put up with the many thousands of walkers who plod through his yard every year. He deserves a medal for extreme tolerance. There are two routes to Sty Head starting from the farmyard: the popular one, and the route via Taylorgill Force. The rougher, latter one, turning right through the farm buildings, is to be preferred after prolonged rain, as the waterfall is one of the most spectacular in the Lake District. The regular route, though, makes its stony way to Stockley Bridge, an attractive packhorse bridge, at the point where the other track leaves the Sty Head route to go by Grains Gill to Esk Hause (the 'dreadful' old Hawkshead road).

The Sty Head route then ascends a paved path. Little remains of the ancient paving. The pitched paving here, of undressed stone modelled on the ancient system, was laid in the 1980s by work gangs led by skilled officers of the National Trust. It cost something below £50,000, and it won the prestigious Medal of Honour from Europa Nostra, a federation of associations dedicated to the protection of Europe's cultural and natural heritage, in 1990. If it looks primitive compared with urban paving, that is how ancient paving was; and I must tell you that this commendable work replaces a very loose and eroded eyesore that formerly made ascent and descent a trial. The secret of successful restoration is to use large stones and to make sure that any water from surrounding ground is channelled away. The path will then need very little maintenance. My only worry is that, even so, the National Trust, depending on charitable contributions from the public; or the National Park, as footpath authority, depending upon the even more uncertain support of government grants; may not have the staff or resources to do any maintenance. Without maintenance much good work can come to nought. It remains to be seen.

In little more than an hour we should have reached Styhead Tarn at around 1,400 feet (430m), a tarn blinking in a hollow below the windy west-facing Sty Head Pass. On our right towers Great Gable, but we are too near to see its summit, 1,500 feet (457m) above. On our left is Seathwaite Fell, but forward and left is the splendid enormity of Great End, the northern bulk of the Scafell range. Around the tarn is the mountaineers' campsite. But campers have to be prepared for savage storms and severe gales funnelling through the pass. It has been known for the site to be abandoned at the dead of night as campers make a retreat to find shelter. After a spate of such disasters I once took up a gang of students to clear the mess. They found enough unopened tinned food, much of it army issue, to keep them in luxury for several days. It is a great place for finding maps, hats, scarves, and lost walkers.

At Sty Head summit is the strategically placed Mountain Rescue first aid box which contains dressings, splints, and the all-important stretcher. I have mixed feelings about these boxes. The object is to enable climbers and fell-walkers to organise immediate first aid and rescue. However, an ad hoc team of passers by, untrained in first aid, could perhaps aggravate, rather than alleviate a serious injury. I have no knowledge of it happening but a badly handled spine injury could paralyse a casualty for life. Nowadays self-rescue is not as urgently needed; the Mountain Rescue teams are very professional and, with modern communication technology, can reach the casualty very rapidly. In my opinion the box should contain only survival equipment.

Some years ago a walker was foolish enough to climb into the box to rest on the stretcher and escape bad weather. At that time the lid was secured with a hasp. This dropped when he lowered the lid and made him a prisoner. It used to be said that if one stayed on Sty Head long enough, every mountaineer in the world would walk by. (But then this was at a time when mountaineering was more the pastime of an elite.) Luckily for the prisoner, one of these mountaineers heard his knocking and cries for help, and effected the only known rescue from inside a rescue box!

We have our map and can see that the Corridor Route runs southwards along this west side of Great End. It leaves the easterly track from Sty Head and after a short descent the climb begins and is interesting all the way. Here again – praise be – the formerly loose sections have been pitched, many of them very well indeed, and some of the paving is amazingly megalithic. The rugged surrounding terrain, of hard though shattered rock, is very obviously volcanic. The material is Pyroclastic, formed from ash ejected from a volcano and consolidated. Here it varies in texture. Obviously the heavier, large-grained ash falls nearest the volcano's vent; the finer dust falls further away. Some of this 'tuff' is extremely fine-grained and very hard; like flint, it fractures conchoidally (in shell-like patterns). This is one of the materials which was used to make those early stone axes.

It is astonishing to me that Neolithic settlers in the Lake District discovered the flint-like properties of these types of rock more than 4,000 years ago. Where the rocks outcropped high on these fells, our Neolithic ancestors broke sections away, and rough-shaped the axeheads by striking the tuff with granite hammers, before taking them down to the coast for final polishing in the sands. Axeheads from these Lakeland rocks have been found all over the British Isles, showing that there was a flourishing export trade. Museums label them 'Langdale axes', because the first of a number of 'factory' sites in the Lake District was discovered in Langdale in 1947. I actually stumbled upon half an axehead hereabouts. The fragments one occasionally comes across are obvious rejects, and I find it extraordinary to hold something that a Neolithic craftsman threw away (probably with a Neolithic oath!) after it broke, maybe 4,000 years ago. I once felled a tree with a Neolithic axe, but I must tell you of that in another chapter.

It is hard to imagine that this lofty, precipitous, broken, warped and folded landscape was once tree-covered. But so it was when those Neolithic craftsmen plied their trade. Human exploitation and climatic change saw it disappear. Remains of woodland flora, and trees, can still be seen in ravines inaccessible to sheep. Even where sheep graze, I have found dog violets blooming at over 2,000 feet on this route, though typically there is much bilberry, Alpine lady's mantle, some mosses, and *Nardus* grass. In the rock crevices one finds the attractive crinkly bright green mountain parsley fern (*Cryptogramma crispa*), an Alpine which occurs in Alpine country all over the world as well as the highlands of Britain; but in Britain it is nowhere more prolific than in the Lake District.

The route passes by the heads of two ravines: firstly Greta Gill; then at 2,300 feet (700m) we can peer down into the awesome depths of Piers Gill. A descent into the gill might seem too dangerous an adventure. Three climbers did this in July 1921 and to their astonishment came upon a Mr Crump, sitting weak and injured on the gill side. He had fallen there twenty days before on a walk from Coniston to Wasdale Head and had sustained himself on the gill's water after finishing the little food he had. Luckily the temperatures had been exceptionally high and the weather fine throughout the period. Earlier search parties had long since given up hope of finding him. A rescue was organised and Mr Crump made a good recovery. Time and again, when out with rescue teams, searching for long periods for some unfortunate who has not left word where he was going, and becoming inclined to give up hope of finding him alive, we have reminded ourselves of the survival of Mr Crump.

Shortly after Piers Gill, before reaching the subsidiary summit of Lingmell, the Corridor Route turns southwards and up slabs of block scree, to Scafell Pike's summit. Many of the blocks are sand-coloured, which seems very untypical and reminds me strangely of the tombstones in a churchyard I knew in early childhood. The peak of the roof of England is a wilderness of these broken rock slabs, surmounted by a solid round cairn which one can triumphantly ascend by steps. This is it, 3,210 feet (979m) up and visited by many thousands every year. Even if we are here early we will not be alone for long. Holiday groups, family parties, tourists from the world over, will follow and pose for photographs. Frozen time on pieces of card, to be got out and relived, maybe long after. 'Ah those happy days!' – forgetting about the aching thighs and the sore feet.

Given a fine day, as one might expect the view is excellent and one can walk about to get the best prospects. Nearest to us, to the south, is Scafell Pike's neighbour, Scafell, 58 feet shorter than the Pike but once thought to be higher. It is quite a separate mountain. To go from the Pike to Scafell direct is no problem to a rock-climber but it is not a route for walkers. There is a distinct path, but this approach to Scafell is guarded by Broad Stand, a slightly overhanging wall which is a notorious accident black spot.

I once saw a student sitting above this spot, making some holiday money by offering the use of his rope to those who wanted to reach Scafell or return to the Pike. On another occasion I saw a walker being pulled up by his trouser braces! Part of the problem here is that the scramble looks simpler than it is, and if one was to drop off, the landing is on a slanting rock which can pitch the fallen farther down the rockside. There have been more than a few fatalities here, but broken limbs are more common. One man fell off and broke his leg. A year or two later he came back to take a photograph of the place where he had broken his leg. He decided to have another try at negotiating the scramble – and fell off, breaking his leg again! If one really needs to collect summits there is an alternative route to Scafell, descending south-east, then south-west to Foxes Tarn.

Scafell is famous for its spectacular north-facing crag, offering some of the longest and most testing rock-climbers' routes in Britain, and this is indeed where the sport of rock-climbing was born in the 1880s. Some who tried ascents and failed lie buried in the little churchyard at Wasdale Head, 3,000 feet below to the west.

To me the most exciting way to Scafell's summit is not from Scafell Pike, but up the slabby eastern side from remote Upper Eskdale, by the waterfalls of Cam Spout. Coleridge records using it as a *descent* in 1802. The route he chose was fierce and hair-raising or, rather, lump-raising! He described his feelings after completing a dangerous drop achieved by hanging from handholds:

> So I began to descend when I felt an odd sensation across my whole breast – not pain or itching – and putting my hand on it I found it all bumpy – and on looking saw the whole of my Breast and Neck – to my navel – filled with great red heat lumps, so thick that no hair could lie between them.

But back to the Pike. Westwards the nearest fell is Yewbarrow. North of Yewbarrow, Wasdale Head is out of sight below, and through the gap of Mosedale, the western fells with Steeple and Pillar can be seen. Then, northwards, the nearest is Kirk Fell, dropping with knee-wobbling steepness down to Wasdale Head, then nearer still, the spectacular craggy south-east side of Great Gable. Turning east of north beyond Styhead Tarn we can make out part of Derwent Water with Skiddaw behind and Blencathra to the right. Turning north-east, the Helvellyn range can be seen some 10 miles away over the folds of the nearer fells. Eastwards, the more prominent peak is Bowfell, some 2 miles away, Windermere may be seen behind, and south-eastwards, at between 4 and 7 miles, is the bulky mass of the Coniston Old Man range.

There, we have enjoyed the view, but we need to get away from the summit crowd. No problem. A short walk, and away from the paths, we can enjoy the summit experience undisturbed.

Some authors have referred to Wordsworth's account of his ascent of 'Scawfell Pikes' recorded in his *Guide to the Lakes*. He may well have made an ascent of the mountain, but the account in his guide was written by his accomplished sister Dorothy. The intention, with a shepherd guide, was to climb Scafell, which at that time was thought to be higher than the Pikes. But it was accepted that Broad Stand was a barrier and Scafell could not be reached without a descent by Foxes Tarn, so the highest Pike was the ultimate destination. It was a perfectly still October day and they enjoyed 'the majesty of the mountains' in 'the lofty solitude'. They were impressed with 'Great Gavel', 'the Den of Wastdale at our feet – a gulf immeasurable'. As they lingered, a storm brewed, 'a spectacle of the grandeur of earth and heaven commingled' and it passed over while they sheltered amongst the rocks. Dorothy describes the summit with typical attention to detail:

> . . . not a blade of grass is to be seen. Cushions or tufts of moss, parched and brown, appear between the huge blocks of stones that lie in heaps on all sides to a great distance, like skeletons or bones of the earth not needed at the creation, and there left to be covered with never-dying lichens, which the clouds and dews nourish; and adorn with colours of vivid and exquisite beauty.

It was moonlight when Dorothy reached Rosthwaite in Borrowdale. It is easy to misjudge the time needed to accomplish a longish fell walk. If we descend now by what is considered to be the most direct route north-westwards for Borrowdale, under the range's no less impressive peaks of Broad Crag and Great End, we will find ourselves scrambling over block scree and faced with descents and ascents. It will take almost an hour to reach Esk Hause and the cross-tracks below it, and we will only have dropped about 700 feet (213m).

Esk Hause is an enigmatic place. It is the highest point of Upper Eskdale and the point where the path we have taken from the Pike is crossed by the Eskdale to Borrowdale path, and a fell-walkers' path between Esk Pike and Great End. Just below it, to the north, is another 'crossroads' where the well-used Langdale to Wasdale bridleway is met by the Eskdale route which passes a wall shelter. This pass is often called Esk Hause but, strictly speaking, it is some distance away. In fog this area of cross-paths is a notorious place for getting lost. Invariably the wayward walkers, confidently hoping to get to Langdale, finish in Upper Eskdale. If someone is reported missing in this area the search and rescue teams send a party to Upper Eskdale as a matter of course. Who knows why Eskdale is such a magnet? Some years ago a rescue team leader and I deliberately went up to Esk Hause in fog and walked round and round for a considerable time until we felt thoroughly disorientated. We then descended for some distance in what we thought was the Langdale direction before consulting our compasses. The experiment failed to take us into Eskdale; we were correctly on the Langdale track. Eskdale's 'pull' remains a mystery.

From Esk Hause we join the Langdale to Wasdale bridleway, turn towards Wasdale and after walking over red iron-rich ground for about 15 minutes we reach the upper end of Grains Gill. The beck plunges down a deep ravine, and its rock walls are rich in botanical specimens. Although the Borrowdale Volcanic rocks contain many minerals, it is only when water seeps through the rock, particularly through fractures containing softer veins, that these minerals are released. So the botanist must seek out the wet 'flushes' on the mountainsides, where a spring has brought nutrients to the surface. But ideally these areas must be where sheep cannot graze. This makes the sides of wet ravines so attractive, and so dangerous to students of botany. These are *not* places for the solitary adventurer!

An exploration of a sheep-proof gill from its foot to its top might typically have woodland plants at its lower and middle levels, thinning out to Alpines as height is gained. The woodland plants are remnants of those that flourished when most of the fells were covered in forest, before man came with axe and torch, before climatic change, and last, but by no means least, before grazing animals prevented further growth.

In effect a Lakeland gill is a botanical ancient monument. The increasing use of such gills, particularly by outdoor pursuits groups, for adventurous (and wet) fell ascents is a matter of concern; for it appears that ordinary paths and tracks are nowadays considered too tame. There would be less of a problem if the groups kept to the water, or places where water has scoured the gill bottom rocks clean. Unfortunately, 'escape routes' up the gill sides can destroy the fragile plant communities. Concerned conservationists and National Park staff have mounted a campaign to make outdoor centres who regularly use the area aware of the damage they must avoid causing.

Here, at the top of Grains Gill, the rock wall shows a rich growth of a sedum, the Alpine Roseroot; and there are other, less prominent Alpines. As we descend the path alongside the gill, we will see that even trees can regenerate naturally in places where sheep cannot reach the saplings. Naturalists often debate the likely sequence of botanical events if sheep were kept off a fell and there were no human interference. The silver birch is the great first coloniser, as one can see in the abandoned quarries of Borrowdale and other areas. Birch would begin the process; and after perhaps a few centuries, it is usually said, there would be a return to the old oak woodlands with their typical ground flora, which was once the Lake District's main cover. I would like to see a substantial fell area fenced off from grazing as an experiment.

In about 2 miles the Grains Gill path drops 1,500 feet and we arrive in the valley at last with aching muscles that we forgot we had; and other parts of our inner anatomy suggesting that tea and scones at Seathwaite Farm might give the expedition a fitting conclusion.

· *Great Gable* ·

One of the often-heard grumbles is that the Lakeland fells are less appealing than they once were because of their popularity. Too many other people spoil the sense of remoteness.

The feeling of achievement is devalued too: it is disconcerting to make a triumphant ascent of a summit to find someone sitting there whom you might feel is obviously less fit and less well-equipped than you are: perhaps an obese person wearing sandals; a lost-looking man in a city suit, carrying some belongings in a Sainsbury's plastic bag; or a scrawny spindle-legged person in gym shorts and tennis shoes. A consolation to a less sympathetic man like myself is the knowledge that though they might have made the ascent without trouble, they may well find the descent a horrible trial. A few of those with inappropriate footwear do indeed become accident statistics on the way down (95 per cent of accidents happen on the descent). The Stickle Tarn path from Langdale has the record for people stretchered off by the Langdale Mountain Rescue team with broken ankles and legs, sprains, damaged kneecaps, bruises and abrasions. I remember standing at Stickle Tarn and seeing a very, very large lady appearing wearing slip-on slippers, and thinking to myself, if this person is going to fall I don't want to be around. (The impact could reach point six on the Richter Scale.)

But the crowds are not unavoidable. Even on the popular fells I have very seldom found human presence too abundant to be tolerable. Great Gable is one of those popular fells and one for which I have great affection. It is, every inch of it, a mountain, though it is 51 feet (15.5m) short of the magic 3,000 feet (915m). Its colossal dome rises sheer from all its craggy sides, majestic, monstrous, magnificent.

I still remember my first ascent of it in second-hand ex-army boots and paratrooper anorak, feeling as if I were 10 feet tall. I remember it too because the mountain swallowed a precious possession, at a time when I had few. I dropped my much-prized penknife – an old friend – among the great blocks of summit stones and it disappeared for ever down a cavity. But Gable has since repaid my sad loss with interest.

There are many walkers' routes up Great Gable. The direct route from Wasdale I regard as a painful slog and it is best either to go around by Beck Head on the west side of the mountain, or up the bridleway to Sty Head to climb from the east. The easiest way is to cheat, and start the walk from the car park on Honister Pass which knocks over 1,000 feet off the ascent (but because of ups and downs there is still a good 2,000 to go). I did this latter walk recently on a hot day, when, according to a Cumbrian friend in the car park, footpaths were 'gey thrang' (very busy). There were, surprisingly, two unconnected parties of naturalists with cameras and nets on the route looking for the mountain ringlet, an Alpine butterfly in its known location.

It is always a surprise to me that, in searching for something uncommon or rare at a known place, I expect to discover only one or two specimens even though experience says otherwise. That rare Alpine flower, when found, can be very profuse; similarly with the ringlet butterfly. I was suddenly among dozens of them (with none of the naturalists in sight!); though the other thing about rarities is that they are not necessarily exotic in appearance. The mountain ringlet is a rather dull little creature, which is little wonder when you find that its caterpillars feed on the wiry *Nardus* grass, which even the Herdwick sheep cannot stomach. But it seems strange that the ringlet is so uncommon when vast areas of the fells are covered in *Nardus*.

Our route, like most people's, might take in Green Gable, which is a place to rest and enjoy superb views over Buttermere and Ennerdale. Then we must face a descent at well-named Windy Gap, before struggling up rocky slabs and steps to Great Gable summit's stony chaos. Here there is a memorial erected by the Fell and Rock Club for those of their members who fell in the First World War. Usually I cannot approve of man-made artefacts on our mountains. They detract a great deal from the feeling of remoteness. If the National Park, and the National Trust, did not insist on their exclusion some of the fells would be cluttered with monuments. But here we must make an exception. For those who erected this memorial acquired the fell and handed its custody to the National Trust, as the legend says, 'for the use and enjoyment of the people of our land for all time'. And it reminds us of those early fell-walkers who discovered for us the joys of hill-walking. Annually on Remembrance Sunday here, whatever the weather, scores, sometimes hundreds, of walkers congregate for a simple ceremonial eleventh-hour moment of silence for those who loved these fells and died in both wars.

The views are great, as one might expect, though to the southeast the Scafells are a spectacular barrier, with the columns and ravines, grooves and folds, of the great precipice of Scafell Crag seen in its magnificence.

The memorable view is a short walk south-west to Westmorland Cairn, where Wasdale is revealed from head to foot: green Wasdale Head of a thousand walls; the Wast Water Screes sloping into the sheet of England's deepest lake; and across the Cumberland plain to the sea.

We must descend on the north-west. It is very tricky, down slabs and steps for around 600 feet (180m), and we need to take our time. This puts us on Moses Trod, a delectable path back to Honister, away from the madding crowd's ignoble prattle, which tempts a dawdle. Who was Moses? There are several stories. He was, it has been suggested, a Honister quarryman who might have been a smuggler, using the 'trod' (path) as a route from the smugglers' port of Ravenglass, the contraband coming from the Isle of Man, or even the West Indies. Or he may have been a thief, with a hidden hoard of the valuable 'wad' (black lead), taken from the mine above Seathwaite and hidden among the crags. Or, then again, he could have been the owner of an illicit whisky-still hidden among the crags. There is indeed a well-hidden ruin of a stone hut on the north side. I have yet to see it, but I know some who have, including the Lakeland author Harry Griffin. If Moses existed at all I prefer the whisky-still story, as it is wholly compatible with the Cumbrian character, and stills were certainly not unknown at a time when the area was inaccessible.

Great Gable is famous for its crags. The pioneer rock-climbers made them so. The great W.P. Haskett Smith was the first man to climb Napes Needle back in 1886. Nowadays it is sometimes necessary to queue to make the ascent. Most of the rock-climbers' routes can be seen on the girdle traverse which starts at Sty Head and goes westwards around the mountain by Kern Knotts, across a scree, and under the Great Napes which has many famous routes. A detour can be made to view the Needle and the much-photographed Sphinx Rock. There is no recommended way to the summit from the traverse. There are the two nasty scree spills which may tempt, but they are well named as the Hell Gates. I have only once scrambled up one of these downward-moving staircases. Hell, it is said, is paved with good intentions. The 'Gates' are paved with apprehensions!

· *Ennerdale* ·

West of Great Gable is the Lake District's westernmost valley and lake. As of 1991, it is the only one remaining without a public road along its length. This means that it is delightfully free of cars which must be left at a car park provided by the Forestry Commission by Bowness Knott. We can then walk along the reasonably level forestry road by Ennerdale Water as far as we like, with wheelchairs and pushchairs if need be. The fit and energetic can make a walking circuit of the lake. Now, some may ask, why should this valley be traffic-free? Why should motorists be denied access to this road along the delightful valley and lake shore? Why should fell-walkers have to do a 6-mile valley walk before reaching the high central fells? Why are rock-climbers compelled to walk 5 miles to reach the famous rock climbs on Pillar Rock?

It is because it is the one, last valley, the only one free of traffic. For pity's sake let us keep it so! The forestry road is private, and remains prohibited to public traffic by agreement with the National Park Authority and the Forestry Commission. They must not yield to the motoring lobby. Motorists have access to every other Lakeland valley and they do have access to Ennerdale Water's foot. A limited number of licences are issued to climbers who want to save themselves the time involved in walking the 5 miles. Other climbers, and walkers of all people, should accept the restraints on this one and only valley.

From the car park at Bowness Knott, a short climb up to the top of the knoll opposite, Bowness Point, gives a great view of the lake. It is one of the best picnic spots in the whole of Lakeland. I am probably biased – a colleague and I spent hours of sweat and toil to clear it of scrub and bracken. The lake was dammed to provide a water supply for West Cumberland. It is hardly noticeable.

The north shore of Ennerdale Water, and the top 4 miles of Ennerdale, are forest, planted in the early 1930s with larch and spruce. Since then the Commission has been criticised from time to time for the ugly straight-lined boundaries of the fellsides, and for fencing off footpaths, but now they are much more sensitive to aesthetics, and they actually encourage the public to walk in the forest. I hate the ugly view of the alien blanket of trees from the surrounding fells, but I must admit that I have enjoyed some happy hours within the forest. A forest in winter is as good as a topcoat and a walk there in snow is magic. Ennerdale is great. It has a homely feel about it.

The head of Ennerdale is in the Borrowdale Volcanics. We have the southern slopes of High Crag and High Stile and Haystacks above Lakeland's remotest youth hostel at Black Sail. But the southern side of the head is dominated by the lofty sides of craggy Pillar and Steeple, and there is that famous rugged pile of Pillar Rock in all its delightful enormity.

Down valley, the fanning out of the lake foot betrays a geological change. There the Ice Age glacier which carved out the dale met less resistance in yielding rock. In fact there are two changes. From Red Pike, west of High Stile, and a line across the valley to the west of Steeple and then westwards across the head of Ennerdale Water, Ennerdale Granophyre is exposed. This is mainly a fine-grained granite, but in places coarse-grained, formed when volcanic molten magma cooled just under the earth's surface. It breaks down into blocks which are colonised by mosses, and makes a walk around the lake lumpy and sometimes slippery underfoot. Where the lake opens out, betraying the presence of a softer rock, we are back in the Skiddaw Slates. The change from Granophyre to Skiddaw Slate can be seen very clearly in the pebbles on the west shore of the lake.

I made my first exploration of Ennerdale a long time ago, and a recent visit brought back the memory of an early one. I had heard and read a bit about Ennerdale. There was the magnificent Pillar Rock; and the afforestation of the valley much hated by walkers and climbers. It was a fine day in spring and, for the whole long walk from The Anglers Inn (alas now demolished) by the lakeside to the higher forestry plantations, I remember seeing no one. I ascended through the scrubby plantings and over the fence to the approach to Pillar Rock. The rock was magnificent! The mass stood out from the side of Pillar mountain like a great earthquake-shattered tower from the biggest cathedral in the world. I scrambled around the base of Low Man in great elation, staring up at the knuckles and grooves and recesses of the soaring 500-foot-high north face, working out the possible ascent routes and hoping for a return visit with climbing companions. One day!

There followed an incident, which in itself I could have forgotten as a minor one, but I was in a heightened state of enjoyable excitement, a very much alive moment which remains with me indelibly. I was scrambling around the base of the south face looking for Alpines, and had contorted myself up some distance on to a likely ledge when the single foothold gave way and for a second or two I was hanging on shaky handholds, praying that they would stay, heaving upwards, one foot stretching to reach another crack. Below me was another safe ledge, but if I dropped on to it I would almost certainly have rolled off and heaven knows where I would have finished.

Ordinarily, with climbing companions, it would have been a ridiculously minor, very brief inconvenience, and might only have raised some banter and a good-humoured oath. But I was suddenly seized by the horror of being completely alone. Nothing concentrates the mind more than the prospect of an utterly helpless rush to possible demise. This, I thought, was it. Considering the brief moment in cold retrospect I am certain that I was not in great extremity. In earlier times I had been in serious life-threatening situations, and I was in later times to be in much more potentially dangerous straits; but all sorts of emotions raced at a tremendous pace through my mind in the brief time between the sudden danger and the stretch to relative safety. I was in the grip of hostile forces, confronting an immediate menace from what had seemed a friendly rockface. A moment before I had been feeling completely safe and confident, master of my situation. Now this great tower of rock had shaken off my foothold. It was no longer passively inanimate. I was suddenly an unwelcome guest in that place, an unwanted alien. Even the grass and plants and moss and detached rocks seemed to be unmoved witnesses – like the vacuous crowd that gathers round to stare at a street accident. It was only a brief moment in actual time. But in the conscious period of extremely rapid, shunted impressions, it was an age.

I at last got a good purchase with my foot in a crack and was able to move upwards to safety, then climb off. Having gratefully reached terra firma, and capable of rationality, I became aware of my stupidity. If I had fallen there it would have taken hours for an alarm to be raised and then many more for a rescue team to find me.

We are given opportunities to learn from experience. Fools forget them. After that I was to take fewer chances when alone. When I had to be in potentially dangerous situations, particularly in night-time search and rescue, I admit to reciting to myself, sometimes earnestly, sometimes elatedly, from Psalm 121: 'I will lift up my eyes to the hills, from whence cometh my help . . . He will not suffer thy foot to be moved . . .' But I learned something else on Pillar too. In the mountain rescues in which I was to be later involved I could understand the shock of the casualty: hit by an instantaneous catastrophe, helpless, desperately alone, in pain, very afraid, a captive of suddenly uncaring hostile natural forces.

The adventurer courts a certain amount of danger. It is to be expected, otherwise it is not adventure at all. Adventure is an over-reaching. The adventurer has climbed out of common personal experience and ventures into the unknown. But somewhere a line has to be drawn. The risk must, to some extent, be calculated. One encounters the unfortunate adventurer who has not done his homework: not listened to a weather forecast; not learned to read a map; assumed that trainers are all right on wet rock; over-estimated physical fitness. They are on our fells every day. Fortunately the guardian spirits of the hills take care of most of them. What else can account for the fact that only a tiny proportion of fell-walkers have to be rescued? Even so, the Lake District Search and Rescue deal with a greater number of incidents than anywhere else in Britain – 200 per annum in the late 1980s.

Pillar is a fell, a great hump of a fell, which is well worth an ascent. However, being closer to the coast, it catches more mist than most other fells, and we must choose our day well. I am not completely against walking in mist, but it does make navigation difficult and one misses the great airy prospects. My favourite route to Pillar has some exciting ones. I think the obvious, more direct route from Gillerthwaite in Upper Ennerdale is something of a slog and one well deserves the reward of the summit views. It is a descent route. We should really make a day of it and take the longer way: walking to and up Black Sail Pass on the way to Wasdale, then turning west to Looking Stead, pausing to enjoy the offered prospects, then joining the superb High Level Route to Robinson's Cairn; one of Lakeland's classic walks, with views all the way. It is like walking on the clouds. From the imposing cairn there is the stupendous sight of the rock tower which gives the fell its name: an enormous soaring mass, unbelievably buttressed, grooved, turreted, striated, creased and folded by aeons of erosion. The rock-climbers' paradise. The rock of ages!

We then have several choices of route to the top of the fell; generally it is southwards and struggling upwards, but a popular way is to make for the upper portion of Pillar Rock, turning left under it and going upwards; a path can then be picked up going above the rock along a safe ledge, before going up a scree slope to the summit. The summit is not broken into blocks like Great Gable, not all that far away and only a little higher. It is a restful plateau, just the place to get out the flask, and to break open the 'bait box' for an oatcake or two. The views are superb – best to walk about to enjoy them. The route down is a longish one by Scoat Fell, with a view of Steeple on the way. This brings us to the bridge across the River Liza by Gillerthwaite. The day ends with a level walk along the scenic treat of the vehicle-free lake shore track. One long and happy day.

CHAPTER FOUR

The Helvellyn Range

•

So far as locals are concerned, though not now as concerned as they were, there are two Lake Districts: north, and south 'o't'Raise'. The 'Raise' in question is Dunmail Raise, the top of the pass from Grasmere to Thirlmere, the A591, which is the old boundary between Westmorland and Cumberland before the counties were amalgamated in 1974 into one Cumbria. But the division goes further back than that, for this was probably at times the boundary between England and Scotland. Until the second half of the twelfth century the boundary line between the two kingdoms wavered somewhat, Cumberland being generally considered to be historically part of Strathclyde. Indeed the name 'Dunmail' celebrates one noted dispute. In 945 AD King Dunmail of Cumbria took exception to the claims of Edmund, King of Northumbria, and their two armies met to settle the dispute on Dunmail Raise. Dunmail was defeated and Edmund gifted Cumbria to Malcolm, King of the Scots.

There are two other legends concerning Dunmail. One is that he was killed and buried under the large cairn which crowns the Raise. This cannot be true for there is some historical evidence to show that he was in Rome some time later. The second story is that he fled with his followers by Raise Beck and Grisedale Tarn to Patterdale, casting his crown jewels in the tarn as he passed. This escape route under Helvellyn seems logical, but if jewels there are, they have yet to be found!

There is another strange but, to me, attractive suggested explanation for the large cairn on the battle site. At that time it was a Celtic custom before a battle for each man to pick up a stone and place it upon a pile in the field where they were to fight. At the end of the battle each survivor would take a stone back off the heap and cast it aside. The remaining stones were a record and a memorial to those who fell. If this is so, the battle must have been devastating, for the cairn contains many thousands of stones. However it may have grown a bit when the highway authorities carried out improvements. The cairn could not be moved, and the highway passes it on both sides; you cannot mess about with the marker on this historical border!

Now all this business was centuries ago but the boundary line between north and south still divides two types of Cumbrian. Before local government reorganisation it was the boundary between Westmorland and Cumberland, and even the dialects were quite different. There is an old saying: 'Nowt good comes o'er t' Raise.' I first heard it said in Windermere, as a lad: 'Watch out. They're a canny lot o' folk i' Cummerland.' It was only years later that I heard the same said in Keswick of Westmorland folk. A middle-aged Windermere farmer asked me once what was it like 'o'er t'Raise'. He confessed that in all his years he had only been as far north as Grasmere, on sports day. Nowadays easy mobility has changed everything; a farmer selling stock can choose a far distant market if necessary. And it would no longer cause wonder and surprise if an Ulverston lass (once Lancastrian) were to marry someone from Threlkeld (once a Cumberland man).

Actually the A591 road over Dunmail goes along an old geological fault line which divides the central fells of Borrowdale Volcanic into west and east. To the east of that line on the old Cumberland side is the Helvellyn Range, 7 miles along from Grisedale Tarn in the south to Threlkeld Common in the north, with a 5-mile sprawl west to east between Thirlmere and Ullswater. There are several peaks: notably Dollywaggon Pike, Nethermost Pike, Raise, Catstye Cam, the three 'Dodds', and the highest, Helvellyn itself, 3,116 feet (950 m).

Like the great majority of Lakeland's fells, there is a soft side to Helvellyn, on the west, and a craggy side to the east. This is all to do with Ice Age glaciation. The ice lingered longer on the east side where there was less sun and less effect from thawing westerlies. On this east side there are the classic coves, deep-gouged hollows which were the snow- and ice-gathering grounds at the head of glaciers. Red Tarn, below Helvellyn itself, is a remnant of what would have been meltwater. Glaciation has cut deep into Nethermost Cove, to the south of Red Tarn Cove, and Brown Cove, to the north, leaving two notable arêtes or sharp edges: Striding Edge and Swirral Edge, curving round to Helvellyn's summit.

Helvellyn is the most popular mountain in England. This is no doubt because of its accessibility, the fact that it is again over that magical 3,000 feet (915 m), and I think it may have something to do with its romantic Celtic name. Whatever it is, thousands of walkers head for the summit every year. Some of them, maybe a lot of them, will be content with having done the ascent and will never ever climb another mountain. To them Helvellyn is the first and last – something to boast about for the rest of their lives. An observation of the crowds making the top on a fine day, or even on wet days (maybe a thousand or more at holiday times), will confirm this, for most of them are certainly not equipped for fell-walking. Trainers are the favoured footwear on Helvellyn nowadays. They slip on wet rock, and they are no protection against sharp rock edges. But we are just as likely to see wellies, or slippers, or even fashion shoes! Clothing can be in delightful and colourful variety, but it can be very cool and windy on the top and this takes many by surprise.

I can quote one example of the strange visitations to this summit. A girls' school arrived in the school uniform which included an ankle-length blue cape. It was windy and the girls were buffeted about the place, cloaks flapping, like a flock of great dark birds – griffon vultures? The mistress asked of a colleague, David, the best way down to Glenridding. He strongly recommended a route via

Raise to avoid Swirral Edge which would be tricky in the wind. Later a walker told us that there was a party having problems on Swirral Edge. We walked to the summit's edge and we could see the girls struggling along the Edge in their long cloaks. They looked as if they were running on casters. 'It's a posh finishing school,' David remarked. 'I think their leader intends to make a quick finish.'

Many make the ascent from the car park by the little church at Wythburn at the foot of Thirlmere. To me, this is a long drag up an upturned pudding basin of a side. If one must approach from the west, a better route is from the Station Coppice car park at the far end of the Water Authority's Thirlmere Forest. After a promising start this makes a rather painful ascent to Lower Man and on to the summit plateau.

By far the most popular route is the exciting one from the east side along Striding Edge. Ideally, public transport being unavailable, we should take the car and park at Patterdale, and start the walk up Grisedale. But the National Park Authority, after closing the car park in Grisedale, up the road above Patterdale, have not been able to replace it with another car park anywhere nearby. We are therefore forced to park a mile further on at the Authority's car park in Glenridding and pay for the privilege. The charge discriminates against the walker for whom in the first place the car park was made. If you are a motorist driving casually about the Lakes you need only stop for an hour and pay only the minimum charge, so the Park Authority seems to want to encourage motorists to move off and contribute to road congestion. It is a scandal that the Park Authority is so starved of funding that it has to make money by holding the walking public to ransom. Many of us might find the charge (£1.35 in 1990) a trifle. But it is the principle! National Parks are all about *free* access, or they ought to be.

Having started at Glenridding, we are then forced to make an unsatisfactory start by climbing over a hump of fell into Grisedale, gaining then losing height in the process. This route may be no hardship, but psychologically it is all wrong. A look at a map will show that one can walk from Glenridding direct by Birkhouse Moor, but this means missing the attractive prospects over Grisedale Valley.

Either route leads to the 'Hole in the Wall' and the start of the Striding Edge path. In half a mile we are on it. It is soon apparent that the Edge is not as fierce as photographs may have led one to believe, certainly not as sharp as the crenated knife-blade arêtes one can encounter in some Alpine places. In fact the Edge top can be avoided by paths just below and alongside. The sure-footed with a head for heights will choose the airy top; the views down into Red Tarn Cove with Catstye Cam behind are thrilling. Those who are a little nervous will be impressed by a memorial to a huntsman who fell to his death at that very spot. At the end of the Edge we are confronted with the 'bad step'. But even this scramble descent can be avoided by retracing one's steps and taking a path to the south side of the Edge. The 'step' is tricky to non-scramblers. The easiest and safest way is to face into the crag so that footholds and handholds can be seen, and to keep handholds low, although they are only necessary to maintain balance; there are footsteps aplenty.

It is something of an education to watch the gay pageant of humanity, crawling, sliding, and stumbling down this obstacle; listening to the exclamations, the execrations, and the shouted advice. There are very few accidents, however; the only serious ones seem to occur when walkers attempt to avoid the problem by going off to the right side, only to find themselves in a worse situation. Sometimes on busy days there is a traffic jam here. On very busy days at peak times walkers spill over continually, several abreast. A voluntary warden on duty on the Edge once radioed down to me in the valley: 'My God, John, they're pouring over here like lemmings!'

Even then all is not over, for we are faced with a steep ascent on an unstable fellside. There are pathways in every upwards directions as walkers have tried to choose the easiest way. Regrettably, this means that the area seems to get more and more worn and loose every year. The erosion is very bad and it spreads. To add to the difficulty, if there is only a little snow on the top there will certainly be snow here too.

One of the first things to be seen as the summit plateau is gratefully reached is the Gough Memorial, a monument to Victorian sentimentality which may bring a lump to the throats of dog-lovers when they read the inscribed poetry. It celebrates the faithfulness of a dog which stayed by its master's side for three months after he died. The man was Charles Gough who fell to his death when walking from Patterdale to Wythburn. (We are not told the name

of the dog, which seems wrong.) Wordsworth and Sir Walter Scott
wrote poems about the episode after they climbed the mountain
together in 1805, and there are excerpts on the memorial which
was erected in 1890 by Canon Rawnsley. I remember being very
impressed by Scott's first words on my first Helvellyn ascent as a
young boy scout. (The other memorable thing about the ascent was
that we ate *kipper* sandwiches!) The summit was shrouded in fog,
which made the sudden sight of the monument the more dramatic.
I remembered the lines and have recited them in my mind for many
years since:

> I climbed the dark brow of the mighty Helvellyn,
>> Lakes and mountains beneath me gleamed misty and wide;
> All was still, save, by fits, when the eagle was yelling,
>> And starting around me the echoes replied.

Great stuff! But the poem goes on in a tear-wrenching address to
the dog, a 'little guardian', 'faithful in death':

> How long didst thou think that his silence was slumber?
>> When the wind waved his garment how oft didst thou
>> start?
> How many long days and long nights did thou number?
>> Ere he faded before thee, the friend of thy heart?

And there is more!

Wordsworth was not to be outdone; he has a shepherd following
the strange dog to Gough's remains, but he puzzles over its survival:

> This dog, had been through three months' space
> A dweller in that savage place.
>
> —How nourished here through such long time
> He knows, Who gave that love sublime;
> And gave that strength of feeling, great
> Above all human estimate!

When, in later years, I was on a Helvellyn patrol I always had my
dog sit in a moment's respectful silence at the memorial.

Scott writes 'when the eagle was yelling'. There are several
references to an eagle around Helvellyn and Patterdale. A pair
probably nested then on the east face, in one of the coves. In fact,

in earlier books on the Lake District, eagles are mentioned not infrequently. There must have been a few pairs nesting into the early nineteenth century, though ornithologists have commonly assumed that they ceased to breed in Cumbria after the late eighteenth century. The White Tailed Eagle (local name 'Erne') was certainly nesting on Eagle Crag in Borrowdale, in Eskdale, Martindale, and Mardale, into the late eighteenth century. Eagles, like other species of birds, return to old nest sites which may have been abandoned many years before. Thus when eagles ceased to nest on Helvellyn, an odd one, or even a couple, would return and assess their chances of nesting. So there were occasional Helvellyn sightings into this century, even if we rule out the odd false identification. (Buzzards are common and often mistaken for eagles.) One golden eagle certainly frequented Helvellyn in 1921, 1922 and 1937. They have been seen around in recent years, but it has been assumed that they are one or other of the pair which has nested in recent years in Mardale.

What happened to the eagles? Since time immemorial they lived in the Lakeland hills. On the whole the inhabitants accepted that they were there. They might take a weak lamb occasionally but this made little impact on the farmer's living, as the bird's main food was small mammals and carrion. Better communications killed the eagles. The new waves of tourists included trophy hunters with better guns, later the egg collectors; with greedy farmers, and those meddlers who regarded natural predators as an evil intrusion in a civilised country. The eagles had to go the same way as the bears and the wolves. Are we now more enlightened? Not a bit of it! It was not enough that the populations were diminished by the use of farm pesticides. In the eagles' last strongholds in the Scottish Highlands they are frequently poisoned by gamekeepers, or shot or trapped, or their nests robbed by collectors. No eagle dare show its beak in a landowner's estate in Wales. We have a nesting pair in the Lake District. But what must one do? There is a day and night guard on the nest. And if it is not under threat from nest robbers there is the danger of disturbance from troops of over-keen bird-watchers, photographers, and researchers, and the plain bloody-minded. One might think that the farmer has the most to lose from the return of the eagle. But one farmer in the Lakeland pair's range has been quoted as saying that he did not mind if an odd weak lamb was taken; he liked to see the birds. There is hope.

You can very seldom find Helvellyn's summit unoccupied by other walkers, whatever the weather, or time of day or night. Just below the summit there is a cruciform wall shelter. That is always occupied, and someone is always eating there. The early guidebook writers, back to Victorian times and into the 1960s, complained about the picnic trash left in the shelter. Originally the shelter was built of dry-stone. It was a source of great annoyance to us that walkers thought the way to get rid of their litter was to push it into the gaps in the wall. At times the tottering shelter seemed to be built of 25 per cent squashed tin cans. In 1968 I suggested to the Park Authority that we should cement the structure and it might end the nuisance.

There began the big lift. Sand and cement had to be carried up to the summit. How to do it? We made it up into 30-pound plastic sacks and organised our voluntary wardens. We also appealed to the public for help and, to our surprise, assistance was very readily forthcoming. On one special public work day an unknown, and not so young, volunteer made three trips to the summit. On one wardens' day I found my journey a struggle. Maybe old age was creeping up on me? On the summit I discovered that some trickster had pushed an extra bag into my rucksack when I was not looking! A pony-trekking establishment offered their help. Well, the Victorians could hire ponies to ride up to 'within twenty minutes of easy walking to the summit'. In fact there is a bridleway from Glenridding via Glenridding Common. The voluntary wardens working on the shelter did not believe us when we said that a consignment of sand and cement was arriving by horse. When the train appeared dramatically out of the mist the workers raised a cheer.

It was a success. The shelter looked exactly the same, as the cement mix was the same colour as the stone, and was largely hidden within the walls. Since then the litter problem has not been a tenth of what it once was. It still means though, alas, that volunteers have to make occasional clearances. 'There should be a litter bin here!' a seemingly intelligent school teacher suggested when she saw me picking up drink cans. I told her I would have one there if she volunteered to empty it several times each week. It really had not occurred to her that receptacles have to be emptied. Litter disappears once it has hit a bin? Incredibly it also had not occurred to her that it would be very easy to carry trash down which had been brought up.

Helvellyn's summit is a little beyond the shelter and is marked, not by a cairn, but by the Ordnance Survey's Triangulation column. The view westwards is sensational: from Coniston Old Man Range in the south, through the crinkles of Crinkle Crags about Langdale, the pyramid of Bowfell with the Pikes of Scafell behind, the great dome of Great Gable, Pillar and the Buttermere Fells, Bassenthwaite Lake overlooked by Skiddaw, then Blencathra to the north. To the east is Ullswater, and way behind, weather permitting, one can see the Pennines. To the south-east is the High Street range, then nearer to hand, Fairfield.

We might find it difficult to enjoy solitude on Helvellyn, but it has everything else. Its popularity is understandable. What is less acceptable is that walkers will make the ascent when the weather is completely unsuitable. Even when there is ice on Striding Edge walkers will attempt it in trainers. When there is a covering of snow, and a snow cornice hangs over the eastern rim, walkers still struggle up, then find the way down hair-raising. Those who make the round – up Striding Edge and down Swirral Edge – find the latter dangerous. The first part of Swirral is an accident black spot in snow. It is an ice-axe route. Indeed, walkers who intend walking in snow should not venture on to the fells without an ice axe and knowledge of its use. The Ranger Service runs winter ice-axe courses.

One Easter Sunday not so long ago, a fine but very cold day when Helvellyn's summit was deep in frozen snow, there was a procession still trying Striding Edge. Some turned back, and some made the summit without ice axes by kicking footholds into the steep hard snow that overhung the approach. But, having looked down at the slippery way back, and discussed the problem with me, they decided to go down the easier way to Thirlspot and share taxis back to Glenridding. 'Don't put too many on the right track,' said one man after one of my lectures. 'I have a living to make!' He was a taxi-driver.

The eastern face of Helvellyn overlooking Red Tarn is a Site of Special Scientific Interest because of its interesting flora. Here again the wet flushes offer a huge variety of plants. It is a dangerous place to research, for there is not only wetness and unstable rock, but sometimes missiles rolled from the summit by idiots. This eastern part of Helvellyn, north from Striding Edge to Glenridding Common, was acquired by the Park Authority from the mining company after the mines at Greenside (above Glenridding) closed.

Greenside Mine was producing lead from the eighteenth century until the 1960s. Few signs remain of the buildings; and the leats (water channels), tunnels, and the long flue of the chimney, three-quarters of a mile up the fell, are blocked. The vast 'tailing dams' of waste material give some idea of the great extent of the underground workings. Attempts are being made to establish grass and shrubs on them. Brown Cove and Keppel Cove, 1,000 feet above the mine, were dammed by the mining company to provide a head of water. In 1927 a dam burst during a storm and a wave of water hit the mine workings and roared through Glenridding. Miraculously there were no fatalities, though the villagers had to rescue their belongings from the far side of Ullswater. The story has it that some silver ingots were washed away from a mining company's building and never found. The Glenridding peninsula, from which the lake steamers now sail, was formed by the disaster's flood debris. Maybe the silver is in the earth there somewhere – deposited in the bank?

Those who say tranquillity has been lost from the fells may point to crowded Helvellyn. If, by tranquillity, we mean 'undisturbed quietness', then I can say it is always possible to enjoy tranquillity there, though we might sometimes be sharing it with others. We might be lucky to find solitude on the busiest days, but even that is not impossible, away from the popular routes and the summit shelter.

· *Ullswater* ·

Many rate Ullswater, Lakeland's second-largest lake, as the most beautiful. I reckon Windermere has the edge on it; the fact that the larger lake is often overpopulated does not detract from its scenic quality. Ullswater is schizophrenic. In its upper crescent amongst the Borrowdale Volcanics, with its head in Helvellyn, it is riotous; and probably best viewed from a boat. The landscape around the lower curve has a different, rather passive beauty, for it is in the Skiddaw Slates: hilly, pastoral; then at the very foot, north and westwards, it blends more subtly into limestone levels.

Ullswater supplies water to the North-West Water Authority but you would not know it. The pumps which extract the water pipe it to Haweswater are underground. Manchester Corporation sought to take water from Ullswater and Windermere by a Water Act in 1965. This sparked off a fight, led by the late Lord Birkett, which has passed into National Park history. Manchester got their water, but a masterpiece of compromise (forcing the Corporation to accept limitations on extraction and development), and some exemplary engineering, left the lakes and surroundings virtually unchanged.

Unlike Windermere, Ullswater has a 10-mile-per-hour speed limit, so the lake is not noisy with big powerboats. It was a different story before 1983 when the speed limit by-law was introduced after a public enquiry. The lake was becoming increasingly popular with powerboat owners and water-skiers. Water-skiers need a lot of room and they do not mix easily with sailing boat owners, and anglers. They also exclusively take over the lake shore areas from which they operate, and there were the inevitable complaints about noise. This was obviously a minority activity completely at variance with every-thing that a national park is supposed to offer (informal quiet rec-reation in unspoilt country), and the water-skiers' public image was not enhanced by the activities of a strident minority. For example, their protest against the introduction of the by-law included a much-publicised bid for media attention when a female skier threw off all her clothes! One of the arguments for the retention of large power-boats was that their withdrawal would cause some loss to local traders. This did not happen. Hotels and guesthouses have done rather better on the return of visitors who like quietness, and had previously been put off by the lake's increasingly noisy activity.

One of the best walks in the National Park, an easy one well away from roads, is along Ullswater's eastern shore under Place Fell, with some great views over to the Helvellyn Range. We need to get the service boat (Ullswater Navigation Company, summer only) to Howtown from Glenridding, or have a friendly car driver take us round. The walk then goes up the lakeside back to Glenridding, along terraces, and the shore – about 6½ miles and a treat all the way. It is becoming increasingly popular, especially at weekends.

Howtown is no town; it does not even qualify as a hamlet. From its jetty the walk goes around the shore to the lake's narrowest point where hard volcanic lava resisted the push of the glacier which carved out the lake, before the flow turned north-eastwards into a softer exposure of Skiddaw Slate. Skelly Nab here ('nab' meaning 'promontory') is so named because in old times a net was strung across the narrows to catch the 'Schelly' (*Coregonus lavaretus*), a rare gregarious white-fish resembling a herring (but no relation), which is an Ice Age remnant. It is only found in Ullswater and in Red Tarn on Helvellyn. It was a much-prized delicacy in the nineteenth century, and is now rarely caught. The only ones I have seen were dead ones washed up on the lake shore.

Halfway along, the walk gives a view up into the eastern coves of Helvellyn, excellent examples of glaciated valleys. In fact there is a great fan of these deep valleys which fed their huge weight of ice and meltwater into the lake: from Dovedale by Brothers Water in the south, then Deepdale south of Patterdale, both biting into the Fairfield Range; then Grisedale from Nethermost Cove on Helvellyn, Green Side from Keppel Cove and Red Tarn, then Glencoynedale, the whole joined to gouge out the hard rock of the lake bed to below 200 feet. All these valleys are worthy of exploration.

The west side of Ullswater has the A592 along its length. Lacking a rail link, and with the barrier of Kirkstone Pass, the highest road pass, from the south, the small villages of Patterdale and Glenridding lost out in the Victorian holiday resort building boom. Glenridding is where we board the boat for the lake trip. There is nothing visually attractive about the place. 'Herbie', the prominent roadside fibreglass monster children's slide at the Ullswater Hotel, is an eyesore which would surely repel any discerning clientele. The woodland owned by the National Trust by the lake shore is the best feature but too near the road to be a haven of peace.

The best thing about this side of the lake is a couple of miles further on: Aira Force, a waterfall in a wooded gorge, also owned by the Trust. However it is so accessible that it gets quite crowded. Nevertheless I have enjoyed some restful moments here. So did Wordsworth. His short poem 'Airey-Force Valley' is very evocative. Here we are, sheltered from the breeze:

Not a breath of air
Ruffles the bosom of this leafy glen.

From the brook's margin, wide around, the trees
Are steadfast as the rocks ...

Then a ripple of air:

... to its gentle touch how sensitive
Is the light ash! that, pendent from the brow
Of yon dim cave, in seeming silence makes
A soft eye-music of slow-waving boughs,
Powerful almost as vocal harmony
To stay the wanderer's steps and soothe his thoughts.

'Eye music' it is indeed. By the edge of the falling water it is fascinating to watch the air currents moving the fern fronds and the overhanging boughs; pleasurably hypnotic, a concerto for water and leaves.

After rain the falls are very spectacular and there are two stone bridges offering viewpoints; leaving the paths is dangerous. The Victorians were obsessed with waterfalls and Aira Force was a must on their itineraries. Someone earlier, heaven knows who, invented a romantic story to enhance its attractions: knightly hero and fair lady heroine, resident at nearby Lyulph's Tower, pledge their troth by the side of the waterfall (presumably it was not in spate at the time or they could hardly have heard each other speak!). Hero goes off to Crusades. Heroine languishes. Will he never come back? Time goes on. Begins to doubt his love for her. Worried. Takes to walking in her sleep. Hero returns at night and takes a moonlight walk to the place with romantic associations. Is surprised to see his lady taking a somnambulatory perambulation by the waterfall. Unaware of her nocturnal habits, he rushes to her side and touches her. She wakes with a start and falls into waterfall. Hero effects rescue, heroine realises her doubts of his love were ill-founded, but too late! She is too far gone. Deceased. Knight upset. Builds cell on spot. Mourns for lifetime as hermit.

Do you believe this? Wordsworth gave it credence, and immortalised the tale in his sickening eighteen-verse poem 'The Somnambulist'. How is this for vintage Romantic? After the hero has plucked her from the stream's 'foaming bed':

She heard, ere to the throne of grace
Her faithful spirit flew,

His voice – beheld his speaking face;
And, dying, from his own embrace,
    She felt that he was true.

Having wiped away a tear, we must go on. There are one or two places by the lakeside where the Park Authority has provided car parks and there is some limited lake access. One can hardly get near them on busy weekends but there is another car park at the lake foot at Pooley Bridge, which is a good starting place for some walks. There are the remains of a Romano-British hill fort on Dunmallard Hill above here, but only the ditches remain.

· Dacre and Dalemain ·

Going northwards we should leave the volcanic and Skiddaw rocks for a while and venture into the limestones and sandstones to view three attractions. Branching off the A592, a narrow road leads across the River Dacre to Dacre hamlet and we must visit the churchyard. There are few clues in the church (largely nineteenth century with features dating to the fourteenth) as to the importance of this site, except for parts of carved cross shafts, one with a human-faced animal, another with animals and Adam and Eve. These have been dated back to the tenth and ninth centuries. In the churchyard, however, are four very ancient stone bears. Although they are weather-worn, moving anti-clockwise from the north-west, it appears that the first bear is standing with its paws on a staff; the second is being attacked by what looks like a cat; the third is reaching over its shoulder for the cat; and the fourth is eating the cat. There is a story, or a parable, here, but I cannot find any reference to it, or anyone who can suggest the bears' origins with any certainty. One suggestion is that they merely depict the sport of bear-baiting, the attacking animal being a dog. But why should that particular sport have been celebrated in stone in ancient times? Another suggestion is that they may have come from Penrith Castle which was owned by the Nevilles. Warwick ('The King Maker') occupied the castle for a time in the mid-fifteenth century, and his emblem was a bear and ragged staff. The only certain thing is that these carvings do not belong here. I have a wild theory which I will come to later.

Here at Dacre we are standing on the site of a very ancient monastery. There is no obvious sign of it now, though recent archaeological digs have found the evidence. It was surely here in 926 AD, when Dacre was still in Scotland, that the Peace of Dacre was signed between Athelstan of England and Constantine of Scotland. Athelstan was too involved in the re-conquest of the Danelaw to afford to be at odds with Scotland.

In his *History*, the Venerable Bede mentions the monastery at Dacre ('near the river Dacore, from which it took its name') which had been 'in course of construction' about 698 under Abbot Swidbert. He relates that a young monk there at that time had a tumour growing on his eyelid. The monastery had a holy relic in the form of some hair from the head of St Cuthbert. The young brother touched the affected eyelid with the hair in the course of replacing it in the holy casket. A few days later the tumour miraculously disappeared.

From the churchyard we have a good view of the Norman castle (not generally open to the public). It dates from the fourteenth century on the site of an earlier construction, most probably incorporating stone from the old monastery, but there have been several restorations since. The Dacre family had a chequered Border history. The castle became the property of the Earl of Sussex in 1675 after Leonard 'Crookback' Dacre had led a disastrous rebellion against Elizabeth I.

East of Dacre, and within walking distance, is Dalemain. This delightful house, long owned by the Hasell family, built of a purply-pink limestone (which reminds me much of St David's cathedral), is a masterpiece of seventeenth- and eighteenth-century architecture. When open to the public it is a restful place to spend an afternoon. One can contrast the gracious eighteenth-century portion with the dark-oak look of the earlier. There is a Chinese room, with wallpaper hand-painted in China. And in the tower is a portrait of the formidable Lady Anne Clifford who figures very largely in the history of Northern England. Sir Edward Hasell, who purchased Dalemain in 1679, became her secretary late in her life. There is a tea-room in the old hall serving home-made fare, as well as exhibits in the sixteenth-century barn; and a deer park containing fallow deer.

The third of these north Lakeland attractions is one of my favourite Lakeland churches: St Michael's at Barton. To get to it we must return to Pooley Bridge and take the B5320 to Eamont Bridge, turning west after 2 miles. Most churches to me give a guarded, conditional welcome, as if saying that people of their parish own the rights to worship, and a stranger is accepted on their terms. Other, rarer, churches say: 'Come in, welcome, sinner or saint!' Barton church is one. It persuades me to stay a while – perhaps it is the unusual architecture which is steeped in so many centuries of worship. The immediately obvious feature is the heavy Norman tower structure with a double rounded arch, contained within the thirteenth-century north and south aisles. The church was given into the care of Augustinian canons of York in 1318, and they made a better access to the chancel by widening and lowering the tower's earlier Norman arch. There are many other Norman features.

Sometimes old stone architecture gives a suggestion of distant history, but it is an exhibition. It is impersonal. Here at Barton I feel that there is no present time. The past is here in the now. It seems as if the brothers, good-humoured workmen all, only finished work on the tower an hour ago and have just popped outside for a tankard of ale and a breather. It is almost certain that, being in a fairly isolated situation – there is no Barton village – and being dedicated to St Michael, the church has been built on a former pagan site. A sacred well perhaps?

Returning to the B5320 road and leaving the National Park's boundary, we meet two important pagan sites as we approach Eamont Bridge. Mayburgh Early Bronze Age Henge is reached by a minor road to the left, shortly after crossing the bridge over the M6. The Henge consists of a 10-foot-high circular bank 360 feet across, built of 'beck-bottoms', hundreds of tons of round stones possibly pulled out of the River Eamont. There is one standing stone left within the circle. Originally there were more.

Why it was built must remain a mystery; it represents an enormous amount of work. But across the road is another mystery. Why did the Bronze Age builders later decide to construct another circle 300 feet across, this time using the easier technique of digging a ditch and throwing the spoil up to make the 5-foot-high bank? This is 'King Arthur's Round Table'. Whether King Arthur was ever here is unanswerable; he seems to have been everywhere else. The odd name originated when the land came into the ownership of the Cliffords of nearby Brougham Castle, who claimed descent from the ancient British kings. Both henges most probably had religious significance. Did they belong to different branches of the same religion? The old church and a protestant one? Like the neighbouring Catholic and Anglican cathedrals in Liverpool?

· Brougham Castle ·

Since we have stepped out of the National Park we must go a little further to what is, to me, one of the most evocative medieval castle ruins in the area. Brougham (pronounced 'broom'), like the henges, is close to what has always been an important natural crossroads: north and south (now the A6) linking Kendal to Carlisle; east and west (now the A66 trunk road) linking a cross-Pennine route with West Cumbria. The M6 has placed the new crossroads a little further west.

There were most probably ancient British tracks here when the Romans came and built their roads in the second century. Their north–south road linked the key cities of Chester and Carlisle; the western route, the 'Second Iter' to York. The crossroads, and the river crossings, had to be defended. They built a fort at the nearby confluence of the Rivers Eamont and Lowther and called it Brocavum. Covering $4\frac{1}{2}$ acres, it could house 1,000 troops: infantry to hold the fort and cavalry to patrol the roads. Outside its walls there grew a considerable civilian settlement.

In medieval times the area was finally wrested from Scotland, when Henry II put down an invasion by Scotland's King William the Lion in 1174. The Scottish King was captured near Alnwick. It was then necessary to strengthen the English position in the Borders, and it was in this period that Brougham Castle was built, first as a keep, using stones from the Roman fort, by a grant given to Gospatrick, son of Orm.

Now comes my wild theory about the Dacre bears. Wherever Henry went he was accompanied by a royal bear. Could the story told by the four stone bears be an allegorical record of William the Lion's attack and defeat? Does the bear represent Henry? Is the 'cat' a rather diminutive lion representing William? Did the four bears come from Brougham's original battlements? A ridiculous fancy?

The castle passed into the hands of the Vipont family in the late twelfth century, and to the Cliffords by marriage a century later. The defences were extended and the accommodation improved.

We see now a red sandstone ruin in the good care of English

Heritage. But there is still a great deal to stir the imagination. First we meet the outer gatehouse. It carries the inscription 'Thys made Roger'. This was probably Roger Clifford who was killed at the Battle of Bannockburn. It can be seen that the defences here were two gates and a portcullis. Any invader who got through the first gate would be halted by the portcullis and would find themselves under fire, particularly from the battlements above. Even if the invader got beyond this, there was still a formidable obstacle: an inner gatehouse (which pre-dated the outer). This also had two gates and a portcullis.

In the outer gate-hall, an inscription records that the structure was repaired in 1651 by Lady Anne Clifford. We saw Lady Anne's portrait at Dalemain. Her father was George Clifford, third Earl of Cumberland, and Queen Elizabeth's Champion. As Anne's brothers had died before her, she was the last of the Clifford line but had to engage in a single-minded and determined legal fight to inherit the large family estates. Brougham was only one of the Clifford castles, but here she lived. Having altered the inner structures to give herself more comfortable quarters, living in and receiving guests at the gate tower, she died in her chamber in the upper room of the inner gatehouse in 1675 in her eighty-seventh year. It was after her death, when her properties passed into the hands of the Earls of Thanet, that the castle fell into serious disrepair.

The keep stands to a respectful height; originally it was four storeys. The foundations of the great hall remain. There is sufficient of the ruins of kitchen, chapel, and lodgings to enable imagination to see it as it once was. The fourteenth-century south-west tower, the Tower of League, rises to its original three storeys. The curtain wall is not everywhere intact. Age has at last undermined a stronghold impregnable to man.

· High Street ·

We must now return to the Lake District National Park. How to know when we cross its boundary? The fact is that it is unmarked and this is a major mistake. The future hope for national parks lies in their recognition by everyone. How can this be achieved if the public have no idea where they are? Ask a visitor where the National Park is and you would get some very varied answers. 'Brockhole, Windermere' (the National Park's Visitor Centre) was once a popular answer. There have been years of discussion about boundary signs with little result. 'No signs are needed,' said one of the Authority's planning officers in the National Park's earlier years. 'The public will know immediately when they enter, when they see the change. The exceptional care of the landscape.' What a piece of arrogance – assuming that the rest of Cumbria receives third-rate care.

The problem with entry signs has been partly financial, partly some sensitivity about signing when planners are keen to limit commercial signing, and partly some small-mindedness by the Highway Authority. The Park Authority wanted prestigious entry signs: a plinth supporting a sign mounted on a large piece of local stone. These are expensive and would be a drain on limited resources. Even so, it would be possible to implement a gradual programme. But the Highway Authority (the County Council) pointed out that the verges on which these substantial signs were to be erected were part of the highway and the signs could constitute a safety hazard. There the problem stayed, but surely this should be history. A start has been made in one or two places, but not enough. Our other national parks have managed to arrange a signing system very well. I wonder if we will see them in our lifetime?

We left the park after Barton church. South-east of this is a large and less-frequented area of the National Park. East of the lower part of Ullswater, a large stretch of open, largely uncultivated country lies under the easternmost fell range in the Borrowdale Volcanics. The range is High Street, a line of hills and ridges some 12 miles long, and 2,719 feet (829m) at its highest point.

High Street? 'Street' in this case means Roman road. And here it means a link of the most exciting Roman road in the country! High Street, now of course only a bridleway, is probably the oldest public right of way in the district. In fact we can be fairly certain that it was in existence before the Romans 'improved' it. The people of Westmorland knew this, for into the thirteenth century they called it *Brettestrete*, meaning 'the street or road of the Britons'. The Roman road linked their fort at Brougham with their fort at Ambleside. The first sign of it, though, is at Tirril, south-west of Eamont Bridge, a ruler-straight line to Celleron on the National Park boundary.

From there the course of the road is followed by the public bridleway, crossing two other bridleways as it rises through moorland, then crossing another by a strange Bronze Age stone circle known locally as the Cockpit. Here the circle's stones are small, but the ring very clear. There are a great many Bronze Age burials on the moors hereabouts. Indeed, the atmosphere of the whole largely open area to the east suggests intensive human occupation long ago. Man, as he exploits the environment, toils and spoils, clears and smears. Human beings once made a living from this landscape; they took too much, but that was long, long ago. The land has forgiven, and offers what it has left to sheep.

Long periods of settlement explain the existence of the 'British' road. The High Street bridleway makes a great walk. I remember, on my first visit, being shown some worn grooves in the bedrock at one place, made by chariot wheels, I was told. I have not been able to find the place since. In fact it is hard to believe that there was enough wheeled traffic on this route to wear away hard volcanic rock. Why take this way at all, high up between the farmed lands and the sky? It was the obvious way in those ancient days when large areas of the valleys below were covered in forest, or undrained bog. In Roman times the valley jungles too could have hidden bands of plundering British guerillas. The Street is the best way, the straight way. Walk it and you are bound to agree.

I feel that to absorb the atmosphere of the place properly we must really be on track at sunrise. That could mean a fine-weather walk by moonlight, or better, a night bivouac. One such occasion I remember very well. The night was absolutely still with a healthy nip to the air, and the canvas of my tent was unstirred. The moon rose in a clear sky. I fell asleep to be awakened, startled by a strange noise. The excited chatter of ancient Britons? It was coming nearer! A host of people hurrying along the Street just above me, intent on some frantic chase, calling to each other in some strange language. Some apparently calling commands, some questioning them. Louder and louder! Nearer and nearer! More of them! I imagined that I could hear muffled running footsteps. A panic! Were they running after something, or from something? They were getting very close! Now alarmed, I dragged myself more fully awake.

It was, of course, a flock of geese, flying low over my head, probably using the moonlit ridge as a nagivation line.

I have another memory of High Street. It was a mountain search, on a foggy cold November night, for a West Cumberland youth who had earlier become detached from his walking group. I kept my search party as near as possible to the Street itself, as visibility was almost nil. At intervals we called the boy's name. Then at last – tremendous relief – we got an answer: 'Aazere!' (West Cumbrian for 'I is here!'). And he homed in on our calls none the worse for his ordeal.

In a little less than 3 miles after the Cockpit, High Street rises to over 2,000 feet (610m) by oddly named Loadpot Hill, then climbs in a straight line to High Raise, before curving and straightening again with the ridge as it wraps around the west-facing crags of Rampsgill Head and on again along the Straits of Riggindale (meaning 'the narrows of the dale of the roof'). Then the climb reaches 2,700 feet (823.5m), on to the plateau of High Street's summit.

Every year, from time immemorial, there have been shepherds' meets in Cumbria. Although sheep normally keep to their own 'heaf' (pasture) instinctively, some wander off and find themselves among a neighbour's flock. They can be identified as wanderers quite easily, for every flock has the special mark of its owner. The marks are recorded and illustrated in *The Lakeland Shepherds' Guide*, a book possessed by all sheep farmers (sometimes very old, well-thumbed copies passed down from forefathers, as the marks change little over the years). The book will record and illustrate, for instance, that sheep belonging to a farm below us on the west, have a 'slit near ear, forked far ear, two red pops on far side, G on either horn, tag in near ear'. This means that the left ear has had a long slot cut out of it, making it a fork, while the sheep's right ear has had a V-section removed. Two red spots are made with 'ruddle', a red dye, on its right side; a G is burnt into a horn, and there is also a tag fixed to the left ear.

Actually the shepherd would never use the word 'ear': the identification is a 'lug mark', and there are several ways of marking ears with different cuts, called variously: 'rits'; punch holes; forks; crops; key and fold bits; upper and under halves; shear halves; and 'sneck bits'. My old friend historian Bill Rollinson suggests that the word 'lug' comes from the Norse word *log*, meaning 'law'; the lug mark is the shepherd's mark of ownership according to the law. I remember a sheep farmer telling me that 'in the owd days' when large families were the norm his great grandfather had contemplated giving his children a lug mark to distinguish them from his neighbour's!

Shepherds' meets are organised by long tradition at pre-arranged places so that wandering sheep can be exchanged; formerly they were held twice each year, in July, and 'at the back end' (November). But the meets are far more than just a sort-out. They are also days when hard-working friends, neighbours and distant relatives from many miles around can come together (they were once the only opportunities) and have a good 'crack' at all the news. A meet has to be experienced to be appreciated! It is a good excuse for what Cumbrians call 'a bit of a stir' – a drink or two (or six) and a singsong. But it can be more than that too. It could mean a bit of sport (though nowadays sports days are generally held on other days).

A glance at our large-scale map will show us that this plateau on High Street's summit is named Racecourse Hill – so named for, until the end of the last century, it was the place for the most famous of the July shepherds' gatherings, when they brought up their sturdy fell ponies and had races. No doubt hard-earned cash was laid out in bets. There were also the 'rostlin' (wrestling) matches, foot races and trials of strength. To fuel this meet, said to have gone on for several days, the ponies came up with barrels of ale and vast quantities of food – mainly 10-pound cheeses of various kinds, smoked mutton and hams, and oat bread.

Nowadays shepherds' meets are based on public houses and sheep can be easily exchanged at any time by vehicle and farm-trailer, so there is less need for a more formal event. But even the present-day meets should not be underestimated. They are still spirited social events.

From High Street summit there is a very wide view of all the central fells, and in the east the Pennines. Below is Haweswater, a reservoir, for the old lake was dammed by Manchester Corporation, raising the water level and covering the village of Mardale. The tarn – another of those remnants of the Ice Age – is Blea Water (meaning 'blue water'), at 207 feet (63m) deep, the deepest of the mountain tarns.

After High Street summit we lose some height to gain some and reach Thornthwaite Crag. Haweswater is seen below to the north, and here Windermere comes into view in the south. From this point, the fell-walker wishing to collect more summits can divert due south to take in the southern peaks of the High Street range: Froswick,

2,360 feet (720m); Ill Bell, 2,480 feet (756m); and Yoke, 2,315 feet (706m). But we will continue, straight down the Roman Road, which goes by Hagg Gill ('hag' meaning 'marshy hollow'), past the Tongue, where there was an ancient British settlement, then by Troutbeck Park where we lose the Road. It must go to Ambleside fort by a route I will later suggest.

Long after the Romans left their High Street, it continued in use. The dales folk needed to watch it. One route down to the valley is still known as 'Scots Rake' ('rake' meaning 'fellside path'), for this is the way the Scots cattle thieves came. They seem to have given up the sport nowadays.

CHAPTER FIVE
Thirlmere and Beyond
•

Below the steep but rounded western side of Helvellyn is Thirlmere, and I would certainly have been among the protesters in 1877 when Manchester Corporation promoted an Act of Parliament in order to dam the lake for a water supply. At the time there were immediate and wide protests. Canon Rawnsley founded the Thirlmere Defence Association, and led the battle to keep Thirlmere as it was then – a long lake almost divided in two by a narrow waist near Armboth. The Association aimed to protect the interests of the inhabitants of the lakeside settlements of Armboth, and Wythburn (mysteriously named 'the City') which were to be flooded if the scheme was approved, as well as the interests of tourists who appreciated the unspoilt beauty of the lake ('one of England's chief recreation grounds,' as the Bishop of Carlisle put it). Rawnsley's other prominent supporters included John Ruskin, William Morris and Thomas Carlyle.

The debate was sometimes heated – those in favour of the reservoir were called 'vandals', those against 'sentimentalists' – and it raised some interesting issues. When the Bishop of Carlisle objected to 'the substitution of engineering contrivance and ultilitarianism for nature in her most primitive and untouched beauty', the Chairman of Manchester's Water Committee made a typically Victorian reply:

> Nature has been at work for ages destroying her most primitive and untouched beauty. Perhaps he prefers the swamps and bogs which Nature always tends to make whenever she has a chance (and never removes again except by great convulsions) to – the artificial conversion of them into dry land.

Victorian pragmatic enthusiasm could then improve the 'primitive beauty' of the landscape (which nature was destroying!), just as it was everywhere 'improving' the interiors and exteriors of ancient and primitive churches and cathedrals.

In the event Manchester got its way. The scheme was approved by Parliament in 1879 and the water level was raised by 50 feet, more than doubling the lake's size and flooding farmland and woodland to more than a mile south. Armboth and Wythburn were lost, buildings above the water line abandoned to ruin. All that remained of Wythburn was its church, school and pub, as these were on high ground to the south-east. Public access was denied to a large area of land, including some fellside, but there was still access to the high fells.

I find it intriguing that, having lost the fight, Canon Rawnsley appears to have become very rapidly reconciled to the situation. At the official opening of the reservoir in 1894 it was he who opened the proceedings with a prayer!

> Let this river of God flow through the far-off city to cleanse and purify, to help and heal. Pour it with full refreshment for the bodies of our fellow townsmen. – Send it with cheer and comfort to their homes, with health and life into their dwellings.

To be fair to the good Canon, he was energetically involved in the setting up of the National Trust in the same year.

So, what do we see now? Only the church remains. The Nag's

Head pub and the school – the latter quite a sound building when I last inspected it – were demolished in the 1960s, for no real reason so far as I could see. The old school site is now a car park for Helvellyn-bound walkers.

The old road was flooded and we have another road – the present A591 – built into the side of Helvellyn's foot; there is also a road on the west side of the lake, which was added in 1889. The Corporation pledged, in Section 13 of the Act, to plant 'indigenous forest trees and underwood'. In 1908 they began planting – 2,000 acres of alien conifers! It was not until 1985 – just over 90 years after the official opening – that the North-West Water Authority, as successors to Manchester Corporation, were taken to court for not complying with the Act. The action was taken by a Mrs Susan Johnson, a West Cumbrian, and the magistrates found her case proved. However they chose not to take action on the promise that the Authority had already embarked upon a scheme to increase the planting of broadleaf trees.

There are those who hate the alien look of Thirlmere and its environs. The lake itself can be subject to a rise and fall of 30 feet; when low this shows an unsightly bleached and sterile rim. The surroundings are all conifer, even the lake's islands, and many feel that the effect is completely incongruous; it is a Scandinavian or North American landscape. I wholeheartedly agree, and I am impatient to see the present trees replaced by native ones; but I also have to admit that I have always been attracted to the area. The only things that have made me angry are the 'Trespassers will be prosecuted' notices all around the lake. Now, of course, since the addition of a new purification plant in 1982, we can wander freely where once we were denied. When interested parties and the media assembled for the official announcement by a Water Authority chief that the barriers were down and there was free access for all walkers, there were one or two red faces when I asked, if there was free access, why there were 'Trespassers will be prosecuted' signs still in place around the lake. I suppose, to be kind, after 88 years they were so familiar to the Water Authority staff that their presence had gone unnoticed.

What is to happen next? The water industry has been privatised, and the Water Authority owns over 12,000 acres of land in the Thirlmere area. We are assured that there will be no restriction on access, but will not the new owners seek to make some sort of profit from the purchase? How?

Most of the old road at Thirlmere is under water, but the line of the new section past Wythburn's little barn-like church is not far from the original route. Between here, over Dunmail Raise to Grasmere, the volcanic rocks are a mixture of lavas and tuffs. The sight of Grasmere as I travel south always makes me feel good. There is the jagged top of Helm Crag on the right, with the rock which, from this angle, is called 'the howitzer'. As we descend to Grasmere we can see another formation on Helm called 'the lion and the lamb'; it looks vaguely like a lion *couchant*, with a lamb between its paws. From another angle which we will miss here, there is 'the old lady playing the organ'. Why an old lady and not a young one, or why not a man, I cannot say. A guide who used to take walkers on the nearby fells would often say, 'There's the old lady playing the organ, and if we are all quiet for a few moments we will hear it playing.' For a second or two everyone actually did go quiet – until they realised they were being ridiculously fooled.

· Grasmere ·

Grasmere opens before us and I must repeat the oft-quoted words of the poet Thomas Gray who made this journey in 1770. After remarking on the strange structure of Helm Crag he continued:

> Just beyond it, opens one of the sweetest landscapes that art ever attempted to imitate. The bosom of the mountains spreading here into a broad bason discovers in the midst Grasmere Water ... from the shore, a low promontory pushes itself far into the water, and on it stands a white village with a parish church rising in the midst of it: hanging inclosures, corn fields and meadows green as an emerald, with their trees and hedges, and cattle, fill up the whole space from the edge of the water. . . . old woods which climb half way up the mountains side, ... discover above them a broken line of crags which crown the scene. Not a single red tile, no gentleman's flaring house, or garden walls, break in upon the repose of this little unsuspecting paradise; but all is peace, rusticity, and happy poverty, in its neatest and most becoming attire.

From a distance there do not seem to have been all that many changes since Gray's visit. There are no red tiles: there are gentlemen's houses though they do not 'flare'. But there is no 'happy poverty' where once farmers struggled to make a living from lean fields. The Romantic observer liked to believe that simple rustics, most probably living on bare subsistence level, were enjoying their happy lot; and comfortable gentlemen and ladies, with their easel and palettes and sketch pads, pretended to envy their rural innocence.

In this later part of the eighteenth century the comfortably-off seekers of fine landscape, unable to make the 'Grand Tour' because of political problems in Europe, had discovered the Lake District. The ideal landscapes were Romantic 'Arcadian', painted by famous Continental artists of the previous century – particularly Nicolas Poussin, Salvator Rosa, and Claude Lorrain. Indeed the tourist, familiar with the works of art, could not look at the scenery 'raw'. He or she must see it through a 'Claude-glass', a pocket-book size mirror in a pretty frame. A stance was taken with back to the view and the mirror held above the head, thus capturing and containing the scene like a Claude painting.

Many artists, real or aspiring, came to the Lakes. Gainsborough came to paint in 1783, J. M. W. Turner in 1797, Constable in 1806. 'The finest scenery that ever was,' Constable wrote on one of his pictures; but he made only one trip, confessing to a friend that he found mountains 'oppressive'. Gray's account of his Lake District visit had been widely read and the typical itinerary had to include the 'unsuspecting paradise' of Grasmere.

A lot of people now come to this paradise. Indeed the non-gregarious amongst us, visiting the village at midday in a holiday season, would think that the opposite place to paradise would claim better title. At certain times of the year the village sports field is taken over by caravan rallies. Visually this is absolutely disastrous, but the Park Authority has no power to prevent the intrusion. They can only obtain an agreement that the rallies will be restricted to 150 units for thirty nights. The Caravan Club, which organises rallies, and the Grasmere Sports Committee, which owns the field, seem unrepentant; the latter saying that they need the income generated to support Grasmere Sports Day. The effect on those villagers who do not profit from the invasion is not considered. I am reminded again of the Hobhouse Committee's policy of national park management, to:

> ... ensure [that] the peace and beauty of the countryside, and the rightful interests of the resident population, are not menaced by an excessive concentration of visitors, or disturbed by incongruous pursuits.

What use is a policy without power?

There are only three attractions in the village itself: the church, which is an eccentric little gem; the humble Wordsworth graves in the churchyard; and the gingerbread shop. For the rest – well it is a good place from which to walk; a good base to stay for a walking holiday. At least there is relative peace in the morning and evening.

We must now leave the village proper and go to Town End on the other side of the A591, to Dove Cottage, home of the Wordsworths from December 1799 to 1808, and Thomas De Quincey for twenty years after. There has been criticism of 'the Wordsworth industry' for practically taking over Town End. Considering that Dove Cottage attracts great year-round international interest, criticism hardly seems justified. Apart from the cottage itself, there is a museum/art gallery, and a great bookshop.

It was at Dove Cottage that William wrote some of the best poetry in the English language (there were some mediocre poems too – even he could not win them all). Much of his inspiration – even an odd line or two – came from his talented sister Dorothy. How to compare 'Daffodils' with the soul-stirring philosophy of 'Intimations of Immortality' which, I contend, can stand with the best of Shakespeare?

Of childhood, he wrote some his best-loved lines:

> Our birth is but a sleep and a forgetting:
> The Soul that rises with us, our life's Star,
>   Hath had elsewhere its setting,
>   And cometh from afar:
>   Not in entire forgetfulness,
>   And not in utter nakedness,
> But trailing clouds of glory do we come
>   From God, who is our home:
> Heaven lies about us in our infancy!

I only 'discovered' Wordsworth in later life. Perhaps school days (and those daffodils) had put me off. Wordsworth was rather unappealing as a person but, like many others, I relate very closely to what he saw and felt. I have, for instance, often experienced a strange sense, that Wordsworth also had, of the unreality of all about me. Perhaps something about the Lake District suggests that it is too good to be true – a contrived landscape manipulated by hidden hands. This may be the meaning of those puzzling words in 'Intimations of Immortality':

> . . . those obstinate questionings,
> Of sense and outward things,
> Fallings from us, vanishings;
> Blank misgivings of a Creature
> Moving about in worlds not realised . . .

An Oxford professor asked William what he meant by those words. In answer the bard grabbed the rail of a gate with both hands and said:

> I have again and again in my life been driven to grasp the nearest object, like this, in order to convince myself that the world is not an illusion. It has seemed falling away, vanishing, leaving me, as it were, in a world not realised.

I have, on many occasions, fancied that what I could see was unreal. I remember feeling it once most strongly at the head of Dunnerdale when the surrounding fells looked exactly like slabs of scenery cut out of hardboard, a stage set arranged for my viewing. It was as if unseen scene-shifters had set sections of scenery. And I noticed with amazement that *the pieces had not been put in quite the right place*. I had taken the workers by surprise and they had not had time to make the right adjustments!

At other times and places I have felt as if the stage directions have gone wrong. The distant shepherd has missed his cue, and should be heading to the right towards his flock instead of left. Sometimes the scriptwriter has stretched the plot to incredulity. On an idle day I was wandering at random in a large woodland area, and suddenly found myself jolted wide awake and looking at a tree that I distinctly remembered planting thirty years before – a job long forgotten. Perhaps the Lake District does this to people?

Yet, paradoxically, it sometimes seems like the only reality. London, to me, is a sort of giant human ant hill, with the scurrying crowds pretending, or trying to convince themselves, that they are involved in something important. An elderly man in Buttermere told me he had lived there for twenty years. He had come to this delectable spot on holiday – and had forgotten to go home. His home, and his jewellery business, he said, belonged to another, unreal life. Coming to Buttermere, he said, was like awakening from a dream.

But Dove Cottage is real enough; it was formerly a public house called The Dove and Olive Branch. William and his sister Dorothy rented it in December 1799. Then William brought his new wife Mary here in 1802 but was forced to move out to a larger house in Grasmere, when his family increased in 1808. In the Town End period he walked the footpaths, composing as he went along, repeating the lines aloud, to be written down later by his devoted sister or wife. He composed 'Intimations of Immortality' here (a Dove Cottage guide told me he was once asked when Wordsworth wrote 'Imitations of Immorality'!), the later Lyrical Ballads, the Lucy poems, and 'The Prelude'. His friend and collaborator Coleridge frequently stayed with the Wordsworths until he fell out of favour. He had acquired a home in Keswick, Greta Hall, later to be also occupied by his brother-in-law Robert Southey. At this time Coleridge, William, and Dorothy would think nothing of walking to each other's homes across Dunmail and by Thirlmere. Dove Cottage had other visitors too: Sir Walter Scott, for one, though it was hard that the Wordsworths did not keep a drop of the water of life – he had to go to The Swan for his noggin.

When the Wordsworths left, Thomas De Quincey, another fascinating literary figure, moved into Dove Cottage with his huge collection of books. He had married Peggy Sympson, his former landlord's daughter, who was beneath him, according to the surprisingly snobbish Wordsworths; but it was a happy partnership. There he wrote the great autobiographical work *Confessions of an Opium Eater* and the very readable, almost conversational *Recollections of the Lakes and the Lake Poets*. In *Recollections* there are moving passages which, I feel, place De Quincey very firmly among the greatest writers of his day.

Charles Lloyd, who held open house at his home by the River

Brathay near Ambleside, was a writer himself and very popular with all in the poets' circle. He is now forgotten as a scholar, poet, and writer, and is not even listed in *The Oxford Companion*. But De Quincey, who had tragically lost other great friends, writes movingly of sitting by the River Brathay thinking about Lloyd's passing after mental illness. His words must strike a chord with many who have been devastated by a sense of waste at the tragic passing of a great friend:

> ... very early in the morning, when the dawn was beginning to break, all things locked in sleep, and only some uneasy murmur or cock-crow, at a faint distance, giving a hint of resurrection for earth and her generations, I have heard in the same chanting of the little mountain river a more solemn if a less agitated admonition – a requiem over departed happiness, and a protestation against the thought that so many excellent creatures, but a little lower than the angels, whom I have seen only to love in this life – so many of the good, the brave, the beautiful, and the wise – can have appeared for no higher purpose or prospect than simply to point a moral, to cause a little joy and many tears, a few perishing moons of happiness and years of vain regret! No! that the destiny of man is more in correspondence with the grandeur of his endowments, and that our own mysterious tendencies are written hieroglyphically in the vicissitudes of day and night, of winter and summer, and throughout the great alphabet of nature ...

He could also write with humour about Wordsworth cutting open the pristine pages of a new book with a greasy butterknife; or comment on the bard's 'inelegant' legs, though he states appreciatively that, according to his calculations, those legs had strode over 180,000 English miles.

· *Helm Crag to Easedale* ·

We must now tear ourselves away from Dove Cottage and the bookshop or we will get nowhere. For Helm Crag we must head towards the 'black quarter' the Wordsworths called Easedale, and up the Easedale road, but turn off at the Easedale Beck crossing to go by Lancrigg and straight up the Helm by the new path engineered by the National Trust. The old path was a dreadful straight up-and-down; this new path, paved in some sections, does a sensible zig-zag. It is still steepish and on reaching the summit we will feel that we have achieved something much higher than its 1,300 feet (396m). But the summit is a choppy chaos of broken rock, turrets and towers, pillars and pinnacles, hollows and holes. Lion and lamb, old lady and organ, are lost in the scrum at close quarters. The view takes in Helvellyn northwards, and there is a peep of Blencathra. Fairfield can be seen quite nearby, and there are good views over to the Langdales in the south-west.

Twice I have stood on Helm Crag and seen military jet planes roaring *below* as they make for the Dunmail Gap. This is very common, almost a daily occurrence at times, weekends excepted. (Once an aircraft tragically failed to make it, and there was a fatal crash by Thirlmere. On another occasion two aircraft collided over Borrowdale, killing one of the pilots.) The tremendous noise as a plane explodes past almost bowls one over. I was leading a party on one such occasion; they did not immediately react because they were all deaf – I was helping the social services – and this time it was only I who was handicapped. These military exercises, sometimes multi-national, take place all over the Lake District; fell-walkers can expect to see, and hear, the planes roaring horrendously by at their level, or below. The pilots are practising low-level attacks, to avoid detection by enemy radar.

We are told that this training is essential and, to minimise inconvenience to civilians, areas are chosen which are sparsely populated. But a national park? Where people 'need the refreshment' of the 'quietness of unspoilt country'? No use complaining that you have come to the National Park to get away from the bustle and noise of modern urban life. No use the farmers complaining that at lambing times ewes are made to have miscarriages. These brave young men have to be trained and the Lake District is not the only place to suffer.

At least, one might gratefully acknowledge, the Ministry of Defence does not own a fifth of the area for military training, as it does in Northumberland National Park; nor are there military exclusion zones in the most spectacular area, as in Pembrokeshire Coast National Park; nor are 33,000 acres set aside for firing ranges and exercises, as they are in Dartmoor National Park; nor is there a prominent and unsightly military early warning system on the high ground, as there is at Fylingdales in North York Moors National Park.

Though noisy and intrusive military activity in a national park is deplored by many locals and visitors alike, discussion about it is inhibited by concern that one might be considered unpatriotic. But surely a patriot is one who has a passionate love of his country. Is a person who loves the best of his country so much that he deplores any damage to its special quality – any desecration of it, from whatever source – not then a patriot?

An air force officer suggested to us that there had to be low-flying training here because the terrain was right; it was the ideal place. That is no argument. Westminster Abbey might be the ideal place for a pop concert. 'We should not complain, this is training for the defence of the country!' said a local county councillor. It is training for attack actually – let that pass – but why should we not complain? Unless more and more of us complain, the Ministry of Defence will not be under any pressure to seek alternatives. The national park authorities have no power to prevent any military training activity. But what have we achieved in designating national parks for quiet enjoyment if war training activities can negate so much of what they stand for? We should not be afraid to complain. The Countryside Commission, the national parks and countryside watchdog, should complain. Their book celebrating forty years of the National Parks and Access to the Countryside Act, *A People's Charter?* (HMSO Books), has only one sentence which refers to military activity in national parks.

A report of the Defence Committee on Low Flying, published in May 1990, stated that 5,500 complaints were received by the Ministry of Defence between 1986 and 1988. And this in the United Kingdom, a country where only a tiny minority take the trouble to complain; it is not in the national character. The Ministry states that it takes around six weeks to answer letters. They also state that 'There are no plans to alter the basic structure and use of the current UK Low Flying System'. But of course they say that regulations and procedures 'are kept under continuous review'. There you have it. If tranquillity is lost at times on the fells it is not because there are too many people. It is lost in the interests of defending our freedom to enjoy it.

We can descend from Helm Crag by Bracken Hause to Styth-waite (pronounced 'stithat') Steps in Far Easedale. Bracken Hause is well named; there is a lot of it on this steep descent. I am constantly amazed by the way bracken seems to have spread, even in the last twenty years. Since my teens I have fought the stuff in woodland where it was threatening to drown young trees. The hard way is to dig it out. But the weight of fronds and stems can come to around 6 tons per acre; and there is, below ground, something between 20 and 50 tons weight per acre. The black, tough-stranded roots spread in every direction except up, and you need to dig very deep. If even a little of the root is left behind, it can start off the spread again. Another way is to attack the new shoots with a swishy hazel rod, keeping the work up at close intervals from spring to high summer – for around four or five years or more. Lastly there is a chemical treatment, which seems to have only a short-term effect, and I worry about what happens when it gets into watercourses.

Stythwaite Steps used to be stepping stones. Young volunteers built a bridge and it was a hard slog to manhandle the materials to the site in hot weather. There are hundreds of places in the National Park where I can recall volunteers doing the necessary improvements. Surely the amount of voluntary help available in Britain cannot be matched anywhere else in the world? It ought to be used much more than it is at the moment; some national parks have yet to realise its potential.

From the bridge a path winds up and round, westwards, to Easedale Tarn. The tarn was high on the Victorian tourist's itinerary. There was a refreshment hut here then, but it became a litter-filled ruin and was demolished in the 1960s – by volunteers.

Here is another attractive, typical glacial feature: a tarn in a hollow gouged out by the moving ice. All around this valley are moraine heaps – grass-covered mounds formed from debris left by stationary melting ice. It has been suggested that the moraines found here and elsewhere – for instance around Dunmail Raise – look fairly fresh, and were most probably left when the Lake District endured a late minor Ice Age during the ninth millennium BC. This seems to be confirmed by some fascinating studies of lake sediments. The Freshwater Biological Association (which has its headquarters at Ferry House, by Windermere) devised a method of extracting a core of sediments from a pipe bored into a lake bed. It was possible then to lay the core on a laboratory bench and use radiocarbon techniques to date the sections, from the earlier period at the bottom, to later periods at the top. Pollen grains immured in the sediments revealed the types of vegetation prevalent in each period. And this research showed that around 10,000 BC there was a warmer period after the retreat of the late Ice Age, when scrub and birch trees colonised the land. After this, average temperatures must have dropped again for at least 500 years during the ninth millennium BC. The scrub and trees disappeared and Arctic Alpine plants took their place. On the heights winter snows did not melt in the summer and small glaciers grew in a landscape already shaped by previous glaciation. When the temperatures began to rise again after this, the quickly melting ice produced those late moraines.

From Easedale Tarn a path descends to Grasmere beside the spilling waters of Sour Milk Gill. This is the favourite tourist route to and from Grasmere by Lower Easedale. A person using this path to Easedale Tarn with solitude in mind had better do the walk by moonlight, as I did once, though I did have my dog with me. A trained dog is a great companion. On a walk a dog does not want to start a conversation, or suggest an alternative route, and will not complain about stopping or starting, or of the walking speed, or lack of it; or make critical noises if your map-reading goes wrong. Stop to listen and it will stop panting and hold its breath. Its friendship is unquestionable – especially when you stop and open a snack.

From Lower Easedale, 'a land-locked little park within ring fence of mountains', according to De Quincey, a path ascends by the side of Blindtarn Moss to Great Langdale. Blindtarn is one of those areas with little obvious beauty, but to me it has a kind of mysterious magnetic attraction; I was only a little surprised when I was asked to take a party there one night to look for a flying saucer which someone swore they saw landing in that area. There was a tarn there long ago which gradually filled with silt. By its boggy basin there is an extensive growth of juniper scrub. Juniper here and elsewhere in the Lake District grows to various shapes: some are squat to the earth; some rounded like umbrellas; some grow as spires to around 10 feet high; some are as spiky as a hedgehog. There are almost impenetrable thickets. At night the strange groups, black in the moonlight, might look a bit like alien astronauts from a flying saucer.

When I first felt this strange fascination of Blindtarn Moss it was suggested to me that I was a sensitive person who had somehow got 'tuned in' to the atmosphere of tragedy that hung around the place. I know that some sensitive people can pick up an atmosphere, often in a room of an old house, and become uneasily aware that something unpleasant happened there in the past. But personally I rarely have such feelings about places on the fells, even though, after nearly three decades with Mountain Search and Rescue, I know that there have been tragedies enough.

I was fairly well acquainted with Blindtarn before I became aware of the sad story which was told and retold in the nineteenth century, and which moved Wordsworth to write his 'Elegiac Stanzas Composed in the Churchyard of Grasmere'. If De Quincey is correct there was an isolated cottage called Blindtarn in the Blindtarn area, in which George and Sarah Green lived, at bare subsistence level, with their six children. It happened in 1807.

De Quincey tells the tale fully. It was wintry weather when George and Sarah took the path by Blindtarn Moss over to the head of Langdale to attend a sale of household goods; such sales were social occasions, with food and drink, and there were always opportunities to meet old friends. The children were left in the care of the eldest, nine-year-old Agnes. On the walk back from the auction at dusk a blizzard blew up. And it would seem that on climbing and approaching Swinescar Hause, the pass into the Blindtarn hollow, they missed their way. The story has it that George gave Sarah his cloak, told her to stay put, and went in search of the path. In doing so he fell over a crag. This could have been on either side of the Hause. He was killed and Sarah died of hypothermia. Both were covered in the drifting snow.

Back in the cottage Agnes put the children to bed and waited anxiously for their parents' return. The weather worsened; the children waited all the next day. Agnes, in spite of a growing fear, fed the cow in the barn and managed to get some milk from the ailing beast. She fed the children with porridge, and baked some cakes for them. She continued to feed and care for the children for three days and nights while the foul weather continued. It was too dangerous to go out and, though by this time the child was torn with fear and anxiety, she had somehow to comfort her charges. At last the weather improved enough for Agnes to leave the children and set off through the snow to the nearest cottage.

The alarm was raised. The children were instantly collected and taken into the care of neighbours, and every able-bodied man turned out to search for the Greens. Their bodies were not found for several days.

The story of little Agnes's bravery and care touched everyone in the area, and there were many offers to take the orphans. Everyone in Grasmere turned out for the funeral. The Wordsworths organised an appeal, and we are told that when the Royal Family were acquainted with the story, they responded with generosity.

CHAPTER SIX
The Pikes
•

The indefatigable Captain Joseph Budworth was one of the most adventurous of the eighteenth-century tourists. He would have felt at home among the Lakeland rocks for he was not unaccustomed to a rocky environment; he had fought at the Siege of Gibraltar where the Spaniards had relieved him of an arm. Writing as 'The Rambler', he had a refreshingly rumbustious style: none of your 'arty' nonsense. 'Whatever I have written,' he said, 'comes warm from the imagination – I have no fine houses, no fine paintings, no compliments to great people to swell out my book with.' Grasmere's island was 'rump shaped'; the fells were 'beautifully misshapen'; Helvellyn from one viewpoint was shaped like a pair of breeches; its Red Tarn was 'shaped like a Bury Pear – if I had a draught of it, it would be worth all the fruit in the world, for my tongue cleaves to the roof of my mouth.' He ascended Helm Crag, but by no means on an empty stomach. First, at Robert Newton's in Grasmere, he feasted on: roast pike, stuffed; a boiled fowl; veal cutlets and ham; beans and bacon; cabbage; pease and potatoes; anchovy sauce; parsley and butter; plain butter; butter and cheese; wheatbread and oatcake; three cups of preserved gooseberries, with a bowl of rich cream in the centre. He found the climb a bit of a strain, no less, he said, 'from having a complete bellyful'!

He wrote with warmth about the local people, reminisced about his life in the army, and admitted frankly that he fell into a quarry after having too much to drink. However he also spiced his Lakeland adventures with a bit of drama. He climbed Langdale Pikes (nowadays among the top attractions for fell-walkers), said little about the ascent, but gave a hair-raising account of the descent over a 'large bulging part of the mountain, across a sward nearly perpendicular and of an immoderate height ...' The drop below, to his right, was apparently so fearsome that he could not proceed until he had bandaged his right eye and taken a hold of his guide's staff! The guide was fifteen-year-old Paul Postlethwaite who did not know why the Captain was apprehensive – he had used the path 'hundreds of times'.

Later writers have suggested that the Captain's route was Jack's Rake on Pavey Ark, which, though safe enough for fell-walkers, is on an exposed cliff face. But this is bare rock and does not tally with Budworth's description of a 'sward'. If it was a route used by shepherds 'hundreds of times' this would exclude Jack's Rake, and I would suggest it was the direct descent from Harrison's Combe, between the Pikes, which begins over by a dizzy ravine of Dungeon Ghyll. I confess I once found a descent at this place 'interesting', when I unexpectedly encountered some sheet ice.

The valley of Great Langdale is immensely popular with walkers and climbers; and the most-used walkers' path is up to Stickle Tarn from the Dungeon Ghyll car park. I suppose I have trudged up the path to Stickle Tarn, bound for the Pikes of Langdale, and down again, far more times than any other path, in all seasons and all weathers, day and night. This path has seen more minor accidents than any other path in the Lakes. The route takes an enormous volume of fell-walkers, many of them very ill-shod. If nerves can stand it we can sit within view of the path and watch the slithering procession descend. (The ascent is easier.) Since the National Trust has paved sections of the path, though, it is not nearly as dangerous as it once was. There used to be a great deal of loose stuff – in places it was almost like walking on ball-bearings.

I remember when the media picked up my report on the state of this path and a TV crew arrived by arrangement one weekend to 'take pictures of people falling'. It was a good day and we got some nice shots of people sliding and falling on their bottoms, giving me ample chance to comment on the need for proper footwear. Satisfied, the cameraman was dismantling his equipment, when, on the opposite side of the gill a man slipped, somersaulted and rolled spectacularly down 100 or so feet into the gill bottom. Luckily he was only bruised, but the cameraman was very upset to have missed the shot, and suggested that the man might go back and do it again!

The footpath improvements have certainly made the route a lot safer. In 1989 only one accident, a leg fracture, was recorded there: an unfortunate lady fell off a ladder stile! I must admit that I had reservations about the paving of the path. If it was made easier for poorly shod walkers to use, would it not be a case of pushing accidents on to less safe paths further up the fell? Rescue team leaders share this concern, but so far there is no hard evidence to suggest that this is happening. However the National Trust was quite right to deal with the spreading erosion here; the footpath was becoming a terrible eyesore. The walkers are now concentrated on to a clear path, and there has been some effective tree planting.

· Stickle Tarn and Pavey Ark ·

'The Pikes' deserve their popularity. Originally they included all the protuberances on the north side of the head of Langdale: Pavey Ark, Loft Crag, Thorn Crag, Pike Howe, and the most distinctive bosses of Harrison Stickle and Pike o' Stickle. Now 'Langdale Pikes' are considered to be the two latter.

On reaching Stickle Tarn, however, the overwhelmingly dominant feature is the great straggling dome of Pavey Ark. Its rugged cliff spreads across behind the tarn. There again is the classic view repeated thousands of times in every Alpine area: level smooth lake and towering scarred and wrinkled crag face; beauty and the beast; the harmony of contrasts. At times when I was working on dam repairs, and up at the tarn early, long before the arrival of the first walkers, I found myself listening to a conversation, primordial and awe-inspiring: the happy lapping of the water against the shoreline rocks, beneath the frowning disapproval of the great Ark.

I say it is awe-inspiring, for if I am in such places alone, or at least utterly undisturbed by busy human conversation, I am privileged. Once we were creatures of nature. Rocks and water, animals, birds, and trees were as real and familiar to us as people. Preoccupied with power lust, with the greedy exploitation of nature, seduced by material toys, we chose to drift away from the natural world. Now, at last, many of us feel a pull to the outdoors, to free and unspoiled countryside, or to wilderness. Whether it is only a vague attraction or a great, it is an aching nostalgia, a sickness of the spirit, seeking the only possible medicine. The problem is that many of us feel that we must take it in small doses; or that it needs to be taken with sugar – in a cocoon of comfort, or diluted with distraction by crowds of other people.

Landscape has its own language. It is a conversation between its elements. Our enjoyment of the best of it lies in a crude appreciation of what is being said. When the elements speak in harmonious accord – so much so that they seem to form part of a whole greater than their sum – there is total rest. It is a rest in which we can share.

No matter that Stickle Tarn is partly artificial. Many years ago the tarn was dammed to assure a head of water for a mill below. In the 1950s the dam had been neglected to the extent that water leaked away. Drawn down, the tarn was much reduced to its original size, with its original surrounding bog. Walkers who knew the fuller tarn of old complained. The sheep farmer complained that his animals were getting stuck in the bog. Something had to be done. The National Park Authority acquired the tarn, the dam was repaired and the water restored to the original level. Since then it has needed maintenance and a number of repairs using many volunteers. And this is one reason for my familiarity with this scene: a bond has been sealed with sweat.

Most casual walkers satisfy their spirit of adventure on an hour's climb to the tarn, but our appetite is only just whetted. There are many options. The most obvious is the direct route westwards to the Pikes but it is one of my least-loved ascent paths. 'These high wild hills, and rough uneven ways, Draw out our miles, and make them wearisome,' says the Earl of Northumberland in *Richard II* – and he was only in hilly Gloucestershire!

We could climb Pavey Ark by that exciting route up Jack's Rake. Or we could take another favourite round walk by Sergeant Man. For the latter we walk north along the bank of the tarn and upwards to the Easedale and Grasmere track, but on reaching its easterly dive, we climb north-west. In a little while there is a strange outcrop of stepped rock to the right of the path. This is one of my refreshment stops, for it offers a place to be 'lounded' as Coleridge would say, sheltered from any wind, and there are very accommodating steps on which to sit. We can see that the rock is built up of layers of lava flows of different consistencies, like several layers of fat sandwiches: some of plum jam, complete with plum stones, some showing raspberry pips, some chunky marmalade! It stands out amongst the surrounding rocks for it is harder and has resisted natural erosion. It has the added attraction of a pleasant eastern prospect: Easedale Tarn is below; Grasmere is hidden but we can see a part of Windermere; and there is a good view of the Fairfield range.

· *Sergeant Man and High Raise* ·

The path up to Sergeant Man is now quite clear and we should be challenged on the way by wheatears, flitting from rock to rock, showing their white rumps, for here is a favoured ground, where areas of broken rock offer good nest sites. More often than not we should hear that complaining 'chack, chack', but their song is a delicious warble, interrupted with amusing creaks and grumbles, as if saying 'Life is wonderful! Life is great!', then, *sotto voce*, 'Not another fell-walker!'

Sergeant Man is little more than a prominent rocky knoll and its top is an easy scramble from the path. Here, though, we are higher than the Pikes of Langdale. Looking westwards we can see Bow Fell, Scafell and Scafell Pike, Great Gable, and Pillar. Skiddaw and Blencathra are to the north, and eastwards we have the Helvellyn and Fairfield Range. Southwards lie Pavey Ark and Harrison Stickle with the Coniston Old Man Range way behind.

We must now head north-west, avoiding boggy ground, to High Raise. This, the centre of the central fells, is a fairly featureless plateau, and it can be confusing in mist. On a winter's day I was once guilty of stupidity here. I had been instructing a companion in the use of an ice-axe. We were approaching High Raise when we were hit by a very heavy blizzard that rendered visibility almost nil. Not to worry, I'd just get out the map and take a compass bearing from it. I put my hand in my rucksack. No map! I had left it at base. I asked John, my fellow walker, if I could borrow his. He did not have one, assuming that I would be navigating. He was suddenly very worried; he had lost confidence in the leader and the weather was getting worse. It was not the first time I had set off minus map. But I am never without a compass in my top anorak pocket. At least we would not walk in circles. I closed my eyes and tried to remember the map, guessing that I would have to aim a little west of south to get to Dungeon Ghyll and off the fell as quickly as possible. I set the compass accordingly and off we went, John close at my heels.

Visibility was still very close to nil, and the blizzard was so fierce that it was sometimes not possible to tell where the ground and upper space met. John had hold of my rucksack strap, the depth of snow was accumulating very fast, and I found myself stumbling down holes. After enduring this for long enough I put John in front – his legs were longer than mine! I steered him and progress was slow. Sometimes we had to detour around snags and I had to concentrate hard to make the adjustment; luckily the bogs were frozen. I thought the only real danger was that we might end up on top of Pavey Ark cliff, though I hoped I'd feel the rocky ground around it. Then, after an hour's struggle – miraculously – we reached our destination. An increasing wind tore away the veil of snow long enough for me to recognise the familiar dip between the Pikes, and the head of the gill. Grateful for our axes we made our way down to The New Hotel. 'Brilliant!' said John admiringly as we trudged through the valley's new snow. 'Lucky,' I said, but he did not believe me. Ironically, at this point, the violent snowstorm stopped as suddenly as it started and the sun came out.

High Raise is – just a high raise, with a triangulation column, at 2,500 feet (763m). But its views are very extensive. Virtually every fell range can be seen, and we can see way out to the Irish Sea, the Solway Firth, and Morecambe Bay. Over to the east are the Pennines.

We can also see the round boss of Pike o' Stickle. This is our next objective, and the way to it is over wetland, some of it unusually rich in lime, offering grass favoured by sheep; but there are areas of rushes, bog, mat grass (*Nardus*), and deep beds of peat, some of it containing nodules of iron ore. Drier areas are covered in bilberry, and the air is deliriously loud with skylarks. In an hour we should be scrambling up the side of Stickle Pike to share the confines of the rocky summit with others who are helping to increase the profits of Kodak. Here are airy views again; but the attraction is way below, into the depths of Langdale's valley head.

Descending off the Pike by the route of ascent, we can go around the crag and look down the deep ravine of Pike o' Stickle screes. There, just below us, is the site where the Neolithic stone axe craftsmen worked. The National Trust are urging people not to explore here. So many have been turning over the rock debris in search of axe fragments that they are damaging an important archaeological site. At one time this was a 'scree run', a good way down to the valley floor. I once enjoyed exhilaration in its acceleration! Descending the scree was like walking down a fast-moving escalator. No more. So many were using the scree that it disappeared off areas of bedrock. This was extremely dangerous, for reaching the smooth rock at speed meant a certain fall. There were many accidents here, including some serious ones. There are virtually no safe scree runs left in the Lake District.

We will avoid climbing Loft Crag, the next Pike to the south-east. But a look around its south side shows Gimmer Crag, one of the most famous climbing crags in Britain. There will almost certainly be someone on its walls. We must go back to join the path to Harrison Stickle, crossing a wet area which is often nasty – rather like melting chocolate – and some heavy path erosion. Harrison has the distinction of having two cairns, which once identified it for friends and I when we were in very thick fog: 'Sit there on that cairn and if I find another one to the north we're in business!' Again the drama is below, with Elterwater and stretches of Windermere, and Esthwaite Water.

The way down to Stickle Tarn is by a series of rocky steps with paths deviating on both sides caused by walkers attempting to avoid the excruciating bits. This is not for people in a hurry. It is a trial. A companion with me here was once tried and found wanting – he stumbled, did an acrobatic recovery and used some horrible exple-tives. He happened to be a highly respected minister of religion. In atonement he bought me a cider at The Dungeon Ghyll New Hotel. I promised not to leak the incident to his congregation if he bought me another.

We will need to rest at the tarn to adjust aching downhill muscles for the final trial of the descent to that famous hostelry.

· Great and Little Langdale ·

A Lake District National Park survey in 1987 showed that car touring was the third most popular recreational activity; over half the motorists never went far from their cars. Unfortunately there are places which are quite unsuitable for car touring. They are enclaves without easy exit. Great Langdale is an example. Great Langdale has little to offer the car tourist. The driver will be too preoccupied with avoiding other traffic on the narrow valley road to admire any view. He might squeeze into the car parks by The Dungeon Ghyll New Hotel, but what then if he does not care to walk? He can drive on by Blea Tarn to Little Langdale, but that road is even narrower, and when he inevitably meets car tourists coming the other way, there will be call for a lot of reversing, manœuvring and squeezing; and opportunity to show good manners – or bad temper.

Yet, at holiday times, the Langdales are frequently jammed with traffic, and I find it hard to understand why. If it were possible to restrict road usage to vehicles owned by walkers, climbers, the physically disabled, and local people, would the traffic problem here be solved? I believe that many of the drivers who find themselves in the Langdale jams have no idea beforehand of what the road conditions will be like.

The National Park is not the ideal place for serious car touring, and many car tourists know this. The guesthouse and hotel owners will tell you that they stay one or two days touring the A roads; then they are off to the Scottish Borders. I believe that national parks, using kindly persuasion, should do more to try to break the umbilical cord which binds the able-bodied tourist to his car. Some might cry a little when they are first brought out into the clear air of the real world, but they can surely soon begin to appreciate what true life experience is all about!

What does the car tourist seek? If he wants to enjoy the countryside he is missing the opportunity. The car-bound have only the very vaguest perception of countryside: the pretty green bits between the tourist centres, seen through the windows of a moving box. The motorist needs to be gently persuaded to leave his steel womb now and then, put on some decent footwear, and go for a walk. The National parks' guided walk programmes should be trying very hard to provide an easy introduction, to release the captive into the freedom of unspoilt countryside so that he can learn to re-create himself.

I remember my grandfather, who had a reputation for being careful with his money, saying very firmly to us on a dismal wet day when we were on holiday at Blackpool, 'Put your macs on and get outside and enjoy yourself! This holiday cost good money!' Holidays are precious interludes in the months of toil and trouble. It makes sense to extract the maximum benefit from them. If the value of recreation is in proportion to the degree of contrast to normal urban life, then the car, its great modern symbol, must be abandoned.

The problem with the able-bodied car tourist on the B roads in places like Langdale is that he is diluting the experience of others. He is delaying the walker from reaching his fell, or the climber from his crag – or sometimes preventing their activities entirely. He is also adding to the already great difficulties of local residents in going about their business, particularly the farmers.

From time to time the National Park Authority, and various conservationists, have put forward schemes for dealing with traffic problems on the congested Lakeland roads, but little has been done. One success was the banning of heavy goods vehicles from the main central road through the National Park – the A591 over Dunmail Raise. Other ambitious schemes got nowhere. One of them was a one-way system at weekends on the narrow road on the east side of Coniston Water. Another was a traffic prohibition on the extremely narrow Watendlath road from Borrowdale, with access only by a regular minibus service from the large car park hidden in Great Wood. Planners are very good at devising, not so good at promoting. Good public relations work could, I feel, have brought off both schemes. In the first the local people were hostile because they heard about the scheme before they were consulted, and those I spoke to were not even aware that the proposed system would only operate at weekends. In the second case the owners of refreshment businesses at Watendlath complained that they would lose customers. They could have been convinced that, on the contrary, more people would get to them.

No doubt other schemes will be considered. The Lake District's major conservation group, the Friends of the Lake District, have done much to encourage the National Park Authority to consider the various options. They have suggested traffic regulation orders to restrict traffic on some roads, including the head of Great Langdale, and on Little Langdale. They have also supported the Authority in opposing road 'improvement' schemes, including the daft proposal from the Highway Authority (County Council) to build an Ambleside bypass on the side of Loughrigg Fell. Since heavy through-traffic has been restricted, who needs a bypass? The tourist? Why?

But here we are in the Great Langdale Valley, which I believe, with Borrowdale, boasts the best walking that the Lake District, or anywhere else in England, can offer. Its high upper circuit is superb, from Langdale Pikes by Rossett Pike to Bow Fell at 2,960 feet (903m), which looks like a great church roof with a small spire; then the sweeping crenellations of Crinkle Crags, ending with the Pike o' Blisco. All this amply fulfils the fell-walker's needs; with the added possibility of the great route by Angle Tarn – another of those classic glacial features, backed by the crags of Bow Fell and Esk Pike – to the Scafells.

Look into Great Langdale from any of the heights around, and it is easy to see that this glaciated valley once held a lake fed by the waters of what are now Mickleden Beck and Oxendale Beck, converging into the valley floor's Great Langdale Beck. At some stage the lake waters broke through the natural barrier. The lush green lower valley fields are on the richer alluvial soil and there are a surprising number of farms. I remember an agricultural college student taking in this scene and saying with amazement, 'Look at it. In agricultural terms it isn't worth getting out of bed for: yet generations after generations have made a living from it.'

I wonder what the farmers of, say two centuries ago, would think of the productivity of this land now? There were at least ten working farms in the valley then. Each one would have been just about self-sufficient, though some farmers, or members of their families, would have had to get an added income from work at the slate quarries or from coppicing in local woods. Each farm had its little field of oats, a flock of sheep, some hardy cattle, a pig or two, and some farmyard poultry. They grew a few vegetables, made their own cheese, baked their own oat bread, and most brewed their own ale. They also spun, wove, and made their own clothes; though there would be some local bartering to take advantage of the specialists in one home industry or other.

The cattle, left out on the surrounding hillsides in summer, would have kept down the useless bracken which has now spread over wide areas and is still spreading. The question which probably cannot be answered is how much of the sheep pasture then was infested with the inedible mat grass (*Nardus*) which often results from overgrazing. How much overstocking of the land, if any, was there? And if there was, was it of necessity? In the more recent past, overstocking of sheep has been prompted by the desire for more profit. But more stock causes more problems, and more stock with less manpower causes many problems. In landscape terms it means neglected walls, hedges and drains, a loss of meadow flowers due to applications of agrochemicals, more access tracks to accommodate machinery, more bracken, and more mat grass.

Farming activity in Great Langdale is now much reduced. No small farm can support a family at the living standards expected today without additional income. But there has been no reduction in the number of sheep. And added to the equation is the heavy use of the area by tourists. Off the footpaths, their trampling feet add to the destruction of good grass pasture, and their occasional loose dogs can cause havoc and interruption in the natural movement of the sheep from pasture to pasture. The difficulties of moving about the roads, caused by heavy tourist traffic, add to the frustrations. Yet, against the odds, farming still survives and the farmers are amazingly tolerant.

'What are you thinking then?' I asked one farmer on the fell who was looking, with no sign of emotion, at a struggling line of tourists climbing a footpath.

'Well, it's gey thrang [very busy]! 'There's mare and mare ivry year.' I asked him what he thought about the work party's paving of the footpaths. 'Well then for't most pairt it's good. But I've been watchin' 'em waste time. There was this gert big boulder. It's been there thousands o' years – but it had to come out. Why? God knows! Aye it had to come out! It took 'em all day to shift it.'

Typically, the Lakeland farmer has grown to accept the strange ways of tourists; but he tends to be critical of all workers, usually the much-maligned County Council men, who seem to him – a very practical hard-working man – to be ineffectual. He naturally feels a bit cynical when tweedy men from the Ministry, or land agents with plums in their mouths, who, he thinks, have never done a hard day's work in their lives, tell him he is doing it all wrong.

Farmers like a good grumble. Sometimes National Park staff are the butt. I remember at a farmers' meeting being told that the Park's Upland Management Officer, who at that time was employed to supply practical help to farmers suffering from damage caused by tourism, never seemed to appear in the valley.

'Does the Ranger Service work with him?' I was asked.

'Of course. It's part of our job to keep him informed,' I answered.

'How often do you see him then?'

'Very regularly. In fact I had a meeting with him today.'

'Oh, so that's where he was. Why wasn't he 'ere?'

Sometimes it seems difficult to win, but generally the farmers appreciate what is being done even if they do not always show it.

In the boom days of Victorian tourism the big attraction in Great Langdale was the lower waterfall in Dungeon Ghyll (*gill* or *ghyll* meaning 'ravine'). From the literature of the period it seems that the parties would arrive at Millbeck Farm, order ham and eggs, then go up the gill while the meal was being prepared. At that time the way to view the larger fall was to walk beside the gill and descend a ladder. The ladies in their long skirts must have had problems; but they were made of stern stuff in those days. Now we have to scramble into the recess which receives the impressive fall, and a huge block bridges the chasm. In his poem, 'The Idle Shepherd Boys', Wordsworth wrote:

It was a spot which you may see
If ever you to Langdale go;
Into a chasm a mighty block
Hath fallen, and made a bridge of rock:
The gulf is deep below;
And, in a basin black and small,
Receives a lofty waterfall.

Not Wordsworth at his deepest. The poem records his rescuing a lamb from the gill, and handing it over to two 'shepherd boys' whom he reprimanded for not noticing the emergency.

Nowadays a lot of Outdoor Pursuits Centre expeditioners ascend the gill. All is well if they take care to keep to the rock. The gill is a Site of Special Scientific Interest. The wet soil-covered sides contain some interesting relic flora, some of which has been damaged by scramblers climbing out of the gill on meeting impassable obstructions. This is a matter of long-standing concern; surveys show that this gill has sustained some very serious damage. Having climbed the gill with a group of botanists, I can understand the worry, but I can also understand the attraction for scramblers. Every section of the route is delightful, as the ravine winds around rock walls and into watery chambers, with spectacular views down to the valley. One does, of course, get wet. I failed my first attempt at one pitch. As water poured over me I could not find a firm enough foothold and I descended, sliding slowly and ignominiously, waist-deep into an ice-cold pool, to the great amusement of a companion. But I got my own back. He asked me if I thought the water would be safe to drink. 'Of course!' I said. 'Thoroughly oxygenated!' He drank greedily. When we reached the next pitch above, trapped by rocks in the water, was a very green-fleshed, rotting sheep . . .

The head of Langdale divides into two very different valleys. Mickleden, on the north side is flat and green, and paths leave it for Stake Pass over to Borrowdale, and on upwards by Rossett Gill for Angle Tarn and Sty Head. Coming off the high fells and reaching Mickleden, one is tempted into thinking that the walk is over. But, to the weary, it can seem a long way to the road at Dungeon Ghyll Old Hotel.

Oxendale, on the south side, could not be more different. Below the formidable walls of Crinkle Crags, it is a place of tumbled rocks and waterfalls and nooks and recesses, with the fine ravines of Hell Gill and Crinkle Gill. This is perhaps the area of Langdale which impressed John Ruskin so much when he wrote: '. . . the loveliest rock scenery, chased with silver waterfalls that I ever set foot or heart upon. . . . What a place for a hot afternoon after five, with no wind, and absolute solitude . . .' Yes, oh yes! I once spent an idle hour or two here on a hot day, just exploring, and reading a book with my back to a warm rock.

The original road down the Langdale Valley to Chapel Stile was for the most part too close to Great Langdale Beck; this was often flooded and the present road takes a less natural, higher line. Chapel Stile at the valley foot, is the capital of Langdale. Its 'chapel' is Victorian, built to replace the barn-like building which once served both Great and Little Langdale and was reported to be dilapidated. I like the story related by Harriet Martineau in her *Description of the English Lakes* (published in 1858). Before the chapel was rebuilt, the clergyman of the time, a Mr Frazer, was preaching from his rickety pulpit. He used the text 'Behold, I come quickly', and immediately the pulpit collapsed, catapulting the man into the lap of an elderly lady. He expressed satisfaction that she was not hurt. 'Well,' she said, 'if I'd been kilt, I'd been reet sarrat [rightly served], for you threatened ye'd be comin' doon sune.'

I never pass the church without admiring the well-built retaining wall with the huge stones which must have been tricky to place. The old cottages in Chapel Stile housed the quarry workers. The quarries are still active but, being mechanised, employ fewer men.

Elterwater village is a short step away. Here, from 1824 to 1931, was a gunpowder works. The location was chosen for its access to running water for the waterwheels and supplies of charcoal from the nearby coppice woods. It used to produce 4,000 to 6,000 pounds of powder weekly. Making 'black powder' was apparently a hazardous business, despite the taking of complex safety measures, which included the horses being shod with soft copper shoes which would not spark on stony tracks. Even so, eighteen explosions were recorded during the mill's lifetime, and other mishaps may well have gone unrecorded. The site, now occupied by a timeshare holiday village, is said to be haunted by the victim of one of the blasts. He must wonder what on earth has happened to the place. The scattered stone buildings have gone and the site is now occupied by modern luxury lodges. The result is not an eyesore; there is good screening by established trees, but luxury has been taken to extremes. It includes a sub-tropical swimming pool complete with palm trees, and a gymnasium. A gymnasium in the finest natural gymnasium imaginable! Some people come to the countryside to get away from it all. Some cannot do without it. Here, in Langdale's pure and simple world of fells and crags and byways, are all the trappings of modern suburbia. Why here?

Elterwater (meaning 'lake of the swans') is surrounded by

wetland and is the least accessible of all the lakes. Here, come winter, I watch hopefully for the arrival of the whooper swans from their Sub-Arctic home. One of Langdale's finest photographic views can be seen from the public footpath at the lake's reeded outlet. Following this footpath southwards, we come to the famous waterfall, Skelwith Force. The drop is not great, but the volume of water, pressed into a narrow neck, is often very substantial; it is a busy gathering, taking the flow from Elterwater and fed by Great Langdale Beck, as well as the flow from Little Langdale via Colwith.

Colwith Force in Little Langdale has a longer fall than Skelwith, but it is somewhat difficult to view, particularly when the trees are in summer leaf, as it is in a wooded ravine. The National Trust-owned wood, though, is a splendid place. We can reach it by a footpath from Skelwith Bridge; then by Stang End and the riverside we come to Slater Bridge, an old bridge made of local slate. A path brings us into Little Langdale where the road west goes over Wrynose Pass at nearly 1,300 feet (397m). This narrow, very steep road – in most places too narrow for two cars to pass – is much used by two kinds of motorists: those who want to test their driving skills; and the majority who find themselves there more or less by chance and have little idea of what they are in for. The route more or less follows the old Roman road, the Tenth Iter, from Galava Fort at Ambleside, by Hardknott Fort to Ravenglass; traces of which have been lost between Ambleside and Little Langdale.

There is evidence to show that this Roman road, which was built for wheeled traffic, generally followed a slightly higher line than the existing modern road. The route can be seen more clearly after the crossing of Wrynose Bridge. After the pass summit we can trace it to the left of the modern road but, as we descend steeply into Wrynose Bottom, it is fairly clear as a straight line on the far side of the river.

The Three Shire Stone on Wrynose summit marks the spot where the three counties met before they were merged in 1974. Lancashire lay to the south, Cumberland to the west, Westmorland to the north. I remember being on a mountain search here when a Lancashire policeman asked me with some slight embarrassment whether he was still in Lancashire. I assured him that the road was in Lancashire but not to go beyond the Three Shire Stone without official clearance. The Lancashire Police Authority covered a huge area, but they always seemed to be there when needed; and often very surprised indeed to find themselves in a mountainous area.

Widdy Gill, which has a delightful little hidden waterfall, rises at Wrynose summit and descends into Little Langdale. It was the old boundary.

Sometimes, when I have been bemused by the weekend traffic jams scarring the wild landscape of Wrynose, I have wished Wordsworth's advice in his *Guidebook to the Lakes* was still true: '... this road can only be taken on foot, or on horseback, or in a cart.'

CHAPTER SEVEN

From Hardknott to Dunnerdale

.

We shall have to go into what was Lancashire shortly, but first we must travel with the Roman road to Mediobogdum, the Roman fort on Hardknott Pass. At Cockley Beck, the modern road lies at the bottom of the pass before climbing up to Hardknott. It crosses the River Duddon into what was Cumberland. But the Roman road here went in a straight line south-west and passed Black Hall before turning west and north on a zig-zag course around the line of the present public footpath, eventually to Hardknott's summit, near 1,300 feet (397m).

If the motorist thought Wrynose was tough, Hardknott is far worse; on a busy day the air often reeks of burning clutches and brake linings.

· Hardknott Fort ·

The descent down from Hardknott to Eskdale is very steep indeed. The Tenth Iter went to the right of the present road to the Roman fort, which occupied a dramatic viewpoint. The ruins can be clearly seen and we must dally here, for this is another of my favourite places. Sometimes you come to a place and it feels exactly right. Mediobogdum is one such. Tons of the Roman stones have in years past been carted away for use in Eskdale's buildings. But enough remain to seize the imagination.

Strangely, Hardknott Fort is one of the few places which appeals to me in wet weather. The rain should have the sea wind behind it. Then I can appreciate what the Romans had to put up with. True, those great views will be obscured: down into green Eskdale to the sea; the Scafells to the north; and Harter Fell crowding to the south. But walking through the rainswept ruins one can get the proper feel of the place.

The walls, around 5 feet thick, are backed by an embankment. They form a square about 375 feet across. There was a tower at each corner, and a gateway in the centre of each wall. The main gate is seen in the south-eastern wall. A fragmented large stone of green slate, which must have been carried up all the way from Little Langdale, was found near the main gateway in 1964. The inscription said the stone was erected 'for the Emperor Caesar Trajan Hadrian Augustus, son of the divine Trajan, conqueror of Parthia ... by the Fourth Cohort of Delmatians.' This dates the erection of the stone to between 119 and 139 AD, but it is not known whether the inscription records the building of the fort, or a later repair job. 'Delmatia' was what is now the mountainous area of Yugoslavia. Those who came all the way may have felt not out of place!

We do not really know how long the fort was occupied. It may have been abandoned when the Roman army advanced into Scotland during the reign of Antoninus Pius but, if so, fragments of another inscribed rock suggest a reoccupation between 160 and 163 AD, when the Brigante tribes of northern Britain were growing troublesome. Pottery fragments have been found suggesting that the fort was used until late in the second century. The absence of later pottery implies that Hardknott ceased to be used after that, though the two forts at Ravenglass and Ambleside, linked by the Tenth Iter and defended by Hardknott, were occupied into the late fourth century. One theory is that after the second century Hardknott Fort became merely a staging post.

The 3 acres within the walls would have housed 500 auxiliaries in wooden buildings. Not the smart kilted Roman soldier here, but mercenaries, wearing what most mountaineers wear nowadays – climbing breeches finishing just below the knee. (Also like modern mountaineers, the auxiliaries wore gaiters in winter.) When I visit the site I wonder, how important was it for them to be there? In the second century the Roman defences, in varied forms, stretched from Hadrian's Wall, right around the Cumbrian coast, from Solway to Ravenglass, and probably further south. Roman military strategy was based on a road system. The Tenth Iter between Kendal's fort and Ravenglass, defended by the forts at Ambleside and Hardknott, was built to control the hinterland behind the northern defences. There is evidence to suggest that 'Galava' Fort at Ambleside was burned more than once and men were killed 'by enemy action'. The Brigante tribes in northern Britain were apparently unpredictable, and the northern defences were not only built to keep out the Picts and Scots, but also to prevent their possibly disastrous alliance with the Brigante borderers: a problem which would reveal itself long after the Romans had left.

So who were these backward tribes that the auxiliaries faced? They were clearly strong enough to burn Galava. Did British guerillas also make hazardous the passage of goods and troops on the Tenth Iter? At that time the surrounding hills as high as the fort had a covering of oak woodland – an ideal setting for guerilla raids. Struggling carts going up the steep inclines would have needed a strong escort if they were not to fall prey to Brigante tribesmen.

The tribes were not always troublesome. At times they even enjoyed trading with the invaders; there were villages built outside Ambleside and Ravenglass forts, but not at Hardknott. For the Romans there were probably long periods of idleness. The fort itself would have taken long hard months to construct. Dressing the hard volcanic rock was one problem; then red sandstone had to be carted from the coast; slate from the Langdales; and tiles from a tilery at the foot of Eskdale. Outside the fort there is a parade ground: a large levelled area, the making of which must have been a major physical undertaking. Then there was the road to keep in repair. One section is actually cut through bedrock. Maybe these many hard tasks were set to counter the possibilities of low morale? And for leisure? The parade ground would have been used for games.

Then there was the bath house. We can see the remains below the main gate. It is divided into three compartments: *Caldarium*, very hot; *Tepidarium*, less hot; and *Frigidarium*, frigid, with a cold plunge bath. There are also the remains of a separate round building. This was the *Laconicum*, the hot dry room. Useful maybe for a sentry to rush to, after a cold winter's night duty.

Inside the fort itself the arrangement followed the design laid down in standing orders. The most important building was the *Horrea*, the grain store, as always built very solidly, with walls $3\frac{1}{2}$ feet thick, and large enough to sustain the troops for many months. The grain was probably not only for food; maybe they also used it for brewing beer? In the central position, next to the granary, were the headquarters: the *Principia*. A doorway leads into an open courtyard enclosed between two L-shaped compartments. The next compartment was the *Basilica*, a cross-hall, with the small *Tribunal* on the right. Behind are two small compartments – the chapel stood between them. The fort's centurions would go through the courtyard into the *Basilica* to receive the day's orders from the commander standing on the *Tribunal*. The chapel would contain a statue of the Emperor and the unit's standards. In the two rooms on either side worked the pen-pushers: one the paymaster; the other the general clerk.

The remains of the commander's house can be seen to the left again. There were the obligatory two cross streets. From east to west, across the front of the administrative buildings, was the *Via Principalis,* and from the main gate to the headquarters building was the *Via Praetoria.* Placed around these were maybe six wooden buildings housing the men, and there would also have been a bakery, a blacksmith's, and a cobbler's workshop.

I feel that it is easier to visualise the fort's activity in wild misty weather. The walls then seem to grow to their original height. Probably aided by memories of my own service life, I can almost hear in the wind the orders being shouted, the tramping of feet, the cries from the distant parade ground, the creak of an approaching cart, the challenge of the sentry. Standing outside the north gate, which overlooks a precipice and could have served little purpose, I imagine what the sentries there may have felt: perched on the end of the world, thinking sadly of home, and cursing the waste, and the slow pace, of time.

It is unlikely that the fort was attacked. Why should it have been, when there was more to gain from robbing the supply columns or laying ambush? A Roman fort, in any event, was not merely a defensive position; it was primarily a base for patrols. If the fort was threatened the troops would run out to meet the enemy.

The Lakeland fells are full of places where men have come, left their spoor, and passed away. The axe-makers, Britons, Norsemen, and Normans; and here – some men from Yugoslavia? When Roman activity was at its height, was there some local hillman giving the road-building work a critical look, and wondering why the passes were suddenly 'gey thrang'?

· *Dunnerdale* ·

We will make one sortie from the Roman fort: from the pass and down the Roman road into Dunnerdale, for the dale of the River Duddon is very special. Not that this is the obligatory route into the valley. The easiest way is from the valley's foot, at Broughton. When I first enjoyed Dunnerdale's bounty I did not know that Wordsworth admired it so much that he wrote 'A Series of Sonnets' on the River Duddon. Regrettably, many of the lines are not his best; but I recently recognised with new enjoyment a piece which I had previously read many times in my much-travelled and tattered pocket anthology:

> ... Still glides the Stream, and shall for ever glide;
> The Form remains, the Function never dies;
> While we, the brave, the mighty, and the wise,
> We men, who in our morn of youth defied
> The elements, must vanish; – be it so!
> Enough, if something from our hands hath power
> To live, and act, and serve the future hour ...

The River Duddon is a delight along its whole length: fed from oozing mosses high along the southern slopes of Crinkle Crags; gathering in the hollows of Mosedale, Gaitscale, and Wrynose Breast, it flows then with urgency down to and along Wrynose Bottom;

then proceeds with less haste on the flatter valley below Cockley Beck Bridge. There is drama and beauty all the way as it flows and falls, on through hidden ravines and beautifully wooded banks, for 11 miles into the sea sands.

Dunnerdale is one of the less visited valleys; probably because it needs more effort to reach it, and it has no lake. However on one visit I was appalled to find myself in the middle of what was apparently a day's competition to determine who could thrash out the greatest number of miles. There were several hundred competitors and throughout my walk I met these strange people hurrying by me in a lather; some, it seemed, looking scornfully at my slow progress. It appears that so many nowadays, as far as countryside is concerned, want quantity rather than quality. To me the idea is as outrageous as those occasional public house competitions to see who can eat the most sausages. Fell races are traditional at local sports meetings. I will accept those. I have thrilled to see a score of fit men or women race to the top of the nearest fell, and hurl themselves down it to get back to the sports field first. I have acted as marshal at longer-distance races in the past, but no more – not with the present pressure of popularity. There should be a limit to the numbers taking part in these mass events on our fells, the main purpose of which is usually to promote some sponsor's supposedly indispensable item of outdoor gear. Not only is the competition an assault on the sensibilities of those who are trying to get away from the crowds, it also adds very much to the rapid rate of footpath erosion.

Some of these large-scale events have become a regular feature. And added to them are the company competitions: executives in some large industrial conglomerate decide that it would be a great idea to test the organising capabilities and moral fibre of their staff by sending them on a tough outward bound-type competition, with generous prizes. Where? Somewhere challenging – like the Lake District. The great machine rolls forward: a score of coaches, squadrons of company cars; campsites for the rank and file, hotels for the management; the fells alive with the sound of mobile telephones and the gasps and shouts of the competitors. It is probably raining. Only the fittest complete the course. Others are tumbling off the fells, and climbing over walls in all directions, to be picked up by the company's patrols.

But back to Dunnerdale. Following the bridleway from Cockley

Beck by the river, we are soon on the site of an old battle between conservationists and the gentlemen of the Forestry Commission. Date: January 1935. It is revealed in the press that the Commission have purchased 7,000 acres in Dunnerdale and Eskdale, intending to plant trees there. February: alarm raised by Lakeland enthusiasts who have already reluctantly accepted afforestation in Ennerdale and Thornthwaite. Commission turn down an offer to buy them out to preserve the land. Herdwick Sheep Breeders Association resolve to protest at the intrusion into the central fells. Statement in the Commons by Forestry Commission's spokesman: '... there are always a certain number of people who prefer that land should produce nothing rather than trees'. Sheep are nothing.

No less than 13,000 people sign a petition during the summer holidays against the planting in Eskdale and Dunnerdale, or anywhere else in the central fells of the Lake District. The petitioners include many eminent people – eight bishops, several high sheriffs and lord-lieutenants, landowners and residents, academics and MPs of both houses, as well as holidaymakers – and they are led by the Archbishop of York. There follows a series of meetings with the Forestry Commission, the Council for the Protection of Rural England (CPRE) and the Friends of the Lake District. The petition is delivered in October. The Commission make a long rejoinder in *The Times*. Nothing is conceded.

In 1936 the Commission reach agreement with the CPRE, ending any plans for afforestation of some 300 square miles of the central fells. Planting begins in Dunnerdale and Eskdale, but there is consultation with conservation bodies as planting proceeds in subsequent years.

What we see now is a forest thrust upon us despite much opposition. But, because of that opposition, it is a scene far less horrific than Ennerdale: a mixture of trees and a mixture of ages; but of course mainly alien conifers. These cover the greater portion of the eastern and southern slopes of Harter Fell. Pyramidal Harter Fell is a gem but the popular route from Dunnerdale, by Grassguards Gill to its 2,140-foot (653m) summit, is spoiled by the planting.

Still the climb must be made, for Harter's rocky height has a special character. The actual summit is on an outcrop which is attainable by a scramble. A walkabout offers some stirring views. In the northern half are most of the high fells. Mediobogdum, down below, looks especially impressive. To the south-east we have a near view of the great bulk of the Coniston Old Man Range, still in the Borrowdale Volcanics; while down south the Volcanics tumble away, to be superseded by the waves of softer Silurian landscape, heap upon heap, falling fold upon fold, to the sea.

With luck we will have Harter Fell to ourselves, for it is the perfect place to indulge in solitude. (I am assuming that two compatible people – hardly three – can indulge in solitude together.) Harter Fell is one of those places where, even if the summit is occupied, you can move around or, if you prefer, find a comfortable seat with back to a rock, and enjoy the views and the congenial atmosphere. Your mood then will depend upon how your attitude of mind is affected by this splendid environment.

After Coleridge had made the very hazardous descent from Scafell into Upper Eskdale he sheltered from a storm in a sheepfold and, in a mood of mad euphoria, shouted out the names of his friends and his children, listening happily to the echoes. He wished, he said, that he could have stayed there for ever! Surely every adventurer feels so, when the main business of the expedition is over, and the whole world takes on a special beauty. A similar exhilaration is felt by those who have been seriously ill, when after a time in successful convalescence, it is as if life gushes deliriously back with an overpowering surge, and the world seems to burst into song.

I remember, as a boy from a smoky Lancashire industrial town, first standing on a hill, more modest than Harter's, but looking out over the rolling moorland of the Peak District, and feeling awed at the measureless immensity of opportunity. I felt as if I had been a prisoner, and I almost wept with a sort of happy fearfulness at the prospect of release. The feeling returns when I am in quiet countryside, time and time again, even to this day. Sometimes I want to shout, like Coleridge, and delight in the echoes. (But of course I still have inhibitions. One cannot destroy the quietness which others around you, out of sight, may wish to enjoy.) I must admit, though, that I have occasionally burst into song, and sometimes then been embarrassed at an unexpected encounter with fellow walkers.

It is as if you are so full of extreme happiness that it must burst out. Young children feel it; young animals feel it, particularly dogs. Wild animals too: otters sliding down a muddy bank; young hares tossing heads and skipping in a field; roe deer fawns running in a mad circle. I remember an ornithologist friend telling me that birds have no emotions, that their song has a purely biological function. I am as keen an observer as my friend, not a sentimentalist, and no one can convince me, that they are not sometimes – very often – pouring out a song of joy at being alive!

Sometimes I admit to feeling strangely guilty about enjoying the bliss of solitude, on a hill such as this or in the woods. It is rather like over-indulging at a great feast, then thinking about the millions who must go hungry. The bliss of solitude is a regrettable self-indulgence. I want the whole world to enjoy the experience!

Sometimes there is a very different feeling and it is difficult to explain. In Cumbrian it would be called a 'dowly' mood: a sad wistful feeling that I am only very nearly a part of the perfect equilibrium that is wrapped around me. That glory of the sky, the peaks, the green woods, and the sea; the flowers, the grass, the birds, and animals, seen and unseen; all in harmony. It is as if I am poised, standing at the threshold of heaven, knowing that the door is locked and I cannot go in.

Now and then, after spending several hours on the hills alone, my perception has become so strangely detached from the normal that my sense of time has become unreal, or even lost. I am half afraid that when I get down to civilisation time will have fallen away from my grasp, and I shall be an object of curiosity in a strange twenty-first-century world!

But back downhill to Dunnerdale. We have, of course, to see Birks Bridge, a stone arch which spans a gorge near Hinning Close. Here the river narrows to pour through a gap in the hard rock. The gravel picked up by the river in its dash to this place has been swirled around for centuries, grinding and honing the base rock into curves, cups, cavities, and hollows as smooth as glass, and it is bleached white. The water is deep and green; for light too is bent and moulded in the swirls and whirls; and we can see down to its deepest depths. It overwhelms attention. I daresay the same effect could probably be had by looking at a large pure emerald placed on white satin.

If we go over the bridge and on for a short distance beyond Birks (once a farmhouse), we can pick up a path through the forest which goes southwards for a mile to another old farm, Grassguards.

In the eighteenth century there were five buildings here, for it was the centre for a rural industry – weaving cloth, rugs and carpets. From here there is a bridleway, still going southwards, presently between walls. And here is something else that always seizes my imagination: walls! Walls? Are there not walls enough? Ah yes – but look at this. It is craftsmanship in absolute perfection; it should be protected by a preservation order. This is the Mona Lisa of the waller's art! I have not seen anything better anywhere. I suppose I am especially excited about it because I have sweated and laboured at wall-building and know how difficult it is to get it just right, so that every stone fits and locks itself close to its neighbour and follows a straight line. This wall is almost miraculous. Some of the stones are quite large and the task of turning them until they fitted exactly and absolutely correctly must have required strength as well as skill. Walk on to where a stile crosses the wall on the right, stand on the stile top, and see more of this amazing craftsmanship. Each time I come here I approach the place fearfully in case some calamity has despoiled this masterpiece. I pay its maker humble homage. No doubt he is laid to rest in some dale churchyard, to fortune and to fame unknown. But this is his superb memorial!

Following the bridleway further on, we pass by Wallowbarrow Crag, ugly and vicious-looking to some, beautiful to a rock-climber. At High Wallowbarrow farm we turn left to go under the crag; then along a grassy terrace, into a birch wood, and we come to a lovely arched bridge. This is another place to linger and enjoy the river. The path continues, meandering around rocks and trees and over four small bridges, to bring us to the hamlet of Seathwaite-in-Dunnerdale.

Here, according to *Sylvan's Pictorial Handbook of the English Lakes* (published in 1847), was a little chapel, 'a low oblong building, with a plain porch, similar, in outside appearance, to a labourer's cottage, only at one end a bell hangs, with a bell rope outside'. The Victorians got rid of all this. A product of that confident age, H. W. Schneider, who had made a fortune in the Furness area's iron industry, had the chapel replaced by a new church in 1874, in spite of protests. Dedicated hard worker that he was, Mr Schneider was no doubt attracted to Seathwaite by the story of its earlier incumbent who had died seventy-two years earlier.

We must pay our respects to that cleric. The Robert 'Wonderful'

Walker legend was repeated many times in popular Victorian literature, as an example of what everyone, particularly the young, should aspire to. Wordsworth himself refers to this remarkably saintly and industrious man. We are told that Walker was born in 1709 in Seathwaite, the youngest of twelve children. Being too sickly for 'real' work, he was encouraged to be a scholar instead. He was a schoolmaster at Loweswater before entering the curacy at Seathwaite in his twenty-sixth year, for a rich salary of 5 pounds per year and a cottage. Shortly afterwards he married into money – his new wife brought him a fortune of 40 pounds!

At that time families were raised in dozens, and the Walkers were no exception; though, also typically for the times, four died. We are told that the clergyman taught school in the chapel, spinning wool while the children studied. He took fees only from those who could afford to pay them. The cloth was then woven at home and his wife made all their clothing. The family were fed frugally on oatmeal every day, with meat only on Sunday. (Oatmeal was the staple food in eighteenth-century Lakeland.) Walker hired himself out to the local farms and, with the help of his sons, kept a few animals himself on 2 acres of land. As there was no inn then, he brewed ale and sold it. He cut his own peat for his fire, and made his own rushlights, candles being an occasional luxury. He supplied parishioners who had travelled far to his Sunday service with broth; and he was, it is said, generous to the needy, and a regular visitor to the sick. He also acted as scribe and lawyer to the illiterate. All this, yet at his death he had been so thrifty that he left a fortune of £2,000. He and his wife lived to the age of 93, and are buried in the· churchyard.

Come now, the man must have had some faults? Maybe his sermons were boring, and he sang the hymns off-key?

Sylvan's Pictorial Handbook says that tourists visiting Seathwaite 'will be much interested in the primitive simplicity of the inhabitants'. The 'primitive simplty' probably meant poverty. In fact there was a great deal of poverty in the Lake District then. A bad yield of oats at harvest-time could be disastrous. Harriet Martineau, writing at about the same time in her *Description of the English Lakes*, states:

> ... The unhealthiness of many settlements is no less a shame

than a curse, for the fault is in Man, not in Nature. Nature has fully done her part in providing rock for foundations, the purest air, and amplest supplies of running water: yet the people live – as we are apt to pity the poor of the metropolis for living – in stench, huddled together in cabins, and almost without water. The wilfulness of this makes the fact almost incredible; but the fact is so ... there are fever-nests, as in the dampest levels of low-lying cities.

Harriet Martineau places the main blame upon the Lakeland land-lords. But there was always the problem of lean land supporting too high a population. Many were forced to go to the industrial towns to become factory fodder. There was also the lack of decent roads, and the absence of good agricultural know-how. Hard times produced a grim but typically Lakeland humour. By the time the rough cheeses made on the isolated farms came to market, it was said by the *Lonsdale Magazine* of the period, they were rock hard. The cheese, it was claimed, was used as shoe leather and as a substitute for iron soles on clogs. Some cheese, it was reported, could be used instead of flint to light a fire, and a soldier had once used a paring of cheese for a flint in his rifle. A blacksmith swore that he struck sparks when he tried to cut a cheese with an axe. And when some heather moorland caught fire it was said to have started when a couple of cheeses fell from a cart and struck sparks on the cobbled road!

Just north of Seathwaite there is an old packhorse-and-cart link with Coniston over Walna Scar. This is a great scenic route, now only a bridleway, which crosses the heights at just under 2,000 feet (610m), below Brown Pike on Coniston Old Man. South of Seathwaite, at Hall Dunnerdale, a narrow branch road goes south and crosses the craggy hills to Broughton Mills. This road gives access to the Dunnerdale Fells, some of the quietest. It is very easy to get lost, but sometimes one needs to lose oneself – to shun Ariadne's thread and dare the labyrinth – though it is hardly possible to get lost for long. Here there is a choppy landscape of scattered knots, elbows and pikes, up to 1,000 feet high, and a cluster of little tarns.

But we are not very far up the narrow road, about to start the climb up Kiln Bank, when we see a wall on the left – yes another wall – which boggles the mind! Here it is not the precision, but the enormous size of the stones. Remember that each stone has to be manhandled, placed and manœuvred. When I showed this one to an elderly farmer friend, a great waller himself, he pushed back his cap and exclaimed, 'What gurt wallakin mak o' man [what big make of man] built this wall!' There may be something to be said for a diet of oatmeal.

If we go down the valley towards Broughton we reach the edge of the Borrowdale Volcanics. Sometimes the beauty of a valley is all in its head. Duddon is one of the exceptions. It is a place of tempting hills and lovely woodland. The road divides at Ulpha. A very narrow branch to the right goes past Duddon's Old Hall. There was probably once a pele tower here. These towers were mainly constructed in the fourteenth and fifteenth centuries as a defence against border raiders. At the sight of advancing marauders, valued cattle were put into the base of the tower and secured with a heavy door. Carrying their possessions, the villagers would climb an outside ladder to the upper storeys, and pull the ladder up behind them. There they would wait until the 'Scots' (who could well be English borderers pretending to be Scots) went away.

If we take the other, more direct road, following the river, we might see another interesting ruin on the skyline to the west. This is Frith Hall, the stuff of legends. Until the seventeenth century it was a hunting lodge owned by the Huddlestons, lords of Millom, and what we see around us was a deer park. Later it became a hostelry, being beside the old packhorse route from Dunnerdale to Millom. And there the legends start. Apparently it had a reputation as a wild lawless place. In the eighteenth century it was the place for runaway marriages – another Gretna Green. Seventeen marriages were recorded here in 1730. In October 1736 a man died – either, it is said, the victim of a drunken brawl, or a murder. He was buried here and, of course, is reputed to haunt the place.

Broughton in Furness is only a short distance now and we must pay a visit to this unspoiled village which is a special and friendly place. It was built largely in the eighteenth century when the vernacular architecture was untainted by foreign influences, though a plaque on the market hall facing the square announces that the square was designed 'by a London architect' (no less!) in 1766. John Gilpin, who donated the land, has his memorial in the shape of an obelisk.

Stone slabs, for the market stalls, are still in place.

Sylvan's 1847 *Pictorial Handbook* contains a remark about the mild air contributing to the longevity of the local inhabitants, pointing out that a tombstone in the churchyard records the death of Mrs Anne Walton at the age of 104 (died 1791) and of Mr T. Walton, at 101 (died 1748).

Yes, there is a lot to be said for an oatmeal diet.

CHAPTER EIGHT

From Coniston to Grizedale Forest

•

The Coniston Old Man Range spreads over about 28 square miles of the Borrowdale Volcanics, with several peaks just over 2,000 feet (610m): Brown Pike, and Dow Crag with its great east-facing cliffs over Goat's Water, famous for its rock climbs; the Old Man, highest point 2,635 feet (804m); Grey Friar and Swirl How with an arm reaching down to Wrynose Pass; Black Sails; and the long north-eastern hulk of Wetherlam, 2,503 feet (763m), a magnificent corpulence, which seems to thrust itself into most viewpoints of the central fells, like a formidable aunt in a family photograph.

The range holds several tarns: Blind Tarn in the south, so-called because it seems to have no exit flow; Goat's Water, one of the scenic best; Low Water, which is always strangely bright blue, probably because of its copper content; and two which have been dammed to provide water supplies: Levers Water above Coppermines Valley; and Seathwaite Tarn in a wild area on the Dunnerdale side of the mountain.

· Coniston Old Man ·

Climbing the Old Man is no problem to the reasonably able-bodied. (Why 'Old Man'? A 'man' is a cairn, a heap of stones. There is a cairn on Coniston's mountain, as on most other peaks. But the question is confused by the fact that a miner was once also called an 'old man', and the mountain is riddled with mines.) The most popular route is from the fell gate on the Walna Scar road and up the quarry road, picking up the well-worn path via Low Water and struggling up the loose way to the summit. I hate it. Its only good feature is the proximity of lovely Low Water. Our choice of ascent must be by Walna Scar, past the fell gate, and by Goat's Water, once known as 'Gates Water', a name which makes more sense if the 'gate' is the Walna Scar Pass (Old Norse *gat*, meaning 'opening or passage').

The way takes us under one of Lakeland's largest quarries, but we are too near, and too far below it, to see its massive scar. Coniston slate, a tuff, almost metallic in its hardness, has long been in great demand. Nowadays it is favoured for the facings of modern buildings, because it can be highly polished to shine like glass. Much of it is exported. The slate is formed from volcanic ash deposited in water; deep layers became solidified by their own weight. If it had remained at this stage the resulting slate would be easy to split horizontally along its bedding plane. But the strength of the Borrowdale Volcanic slate here – and in the other major quarries on Honister Pass, above Borrowdale, at Kirkstone Pass and at Elterwater – is due to the fact that the original deposits were subject to the violent lateral pressures of subsequent earth movements, which realigned the natural grain of the rock so that it tends to split *across* the original bedding plane. When polished, it can show some especially beautiful features. Ripple marking is one, and some pieces show 'raindrop' markings, caused by showers of other volcanic material which dropped into the ash mud.

The ugly scars left by quarrying are a frequent cause for complaint. The quarry owners argue that the work is traditional and gives local employment. But the working methods are certainly not traditional. Nowadays quarrying is highly mechanised, involving rapid extension of the quarry face; and great masses of waste are pushed down the mountainside, which in earlier times would have been worked and used. Mechanisation also means less local manpower. The eight quarries within the National Park only employ 200 people between them.

We are here on the edge of the rugged Borrowdale Volcanics. To the south of the track there is a softer heathy landscape where the geology gets complicated: that hardly seen, narrow band of Coniston limestone; then the Silurians, stripped down by glaciation to the lower layers, the Wenlockian, in another band; then, below this, to the shores of Coniston Water and beyond, the Ludlovian, a higher layer of Silurian. Suffice to say that the walking is pleasant, in season loud with skylarks. We pass by Boo Tarn, which is only a small tarn in very wet weather; then we begin to come to grips with hard rock as we go through a narrow cutting. Dow Crag comes into view and we take a path north-westwards towards it, marked in places by cairns white with quartz. Now we reach Goat's Water, and a memorable scene.

Dow Crag is opposite, and demands attention. It is a 500-foot (153m) high wall, nearly half a mile wide, with five heavy frowning buttresses separated by cavernous gullies. The whole is gnarled and furrowed, creased and crinkled, notched and folded, grooved and knuckled, warped and buckled; like a huge mass of clinker from a giant's furnace. This is another of those great crags on which the first rock-climbers ventured a century ago. It seems made for the sport. From the tarn, one can imagine the many thousand hand- and footholds, though a closer look at the beetling face makes one less confident. There are many climbing routes here, from what a rock-climber would call 'moderate' to 'extremely severe'. Some are exhilaratingly exposed.

Goat's Water is a model glaciated feature: a mountain tarn cupped in rock, devoid of much vegetation. Though sheltered from the prevailing south-westerlies, I have never seen it calm. Maybe I have yet to see it in early morning, but whenever I am there the clean, cold, clear water is lapping on the rocks. It is a scene which might haunt the dreams of a wanderer in a desert.

Our route then climbs to Goat's Hawse. I remember once reaching this exposed point, to be met by a westerly gale which helped lift me to the summit ridge. Great! Except that once I reached the ridge I practically had to crawl on my hands and knees to avoid being blown off the other side. A good lick of a wondrous westerly wind enhances the enjoyment of a walk. There is a delightful effervescence; even a slight intoxication; maybe there is an increase in oxygen intake. All my dogs seem to have had moments of rejuvenation with a wind in their tail, going mad, like puppies, with glee; and it is an entertainment to watch the effect on loose horses.

The strong wind is less welcome if it hurls rain like bullets. On the Lakeland fells, wind with rain is a far more serious hazard than snow because of the high wind-chill factor. It can be a killer. There is not only the problem of the rain beating through ineffectual waterproof clothing, but the rapid rate of cooling through evaporation. In fact it is a summer danger. Mountain accident records show that it is possible to have fell-walkers suffering from heat exhaustion on a day in July, followed two or three days later by casualties from hypothermia. Two unfortunates once attempted to break the record for the ascent of the top three mountains in Britain: Ben Nevis, Scafell Pike and Snowdon. They had already done Ben Nevis and had left their car at Seathwaite. They were wearing only thin running gear when they were faced with gales and rain on the fell. They both died.

The dangers have been well publicised. It is necessary for fell-walkers to carry good waterproofs – including over-trousers – even if the day looks set fair. There should also be some 'iron rations' – food to stoke the boiler and to maintain the energy which bad weather will test. Then the danger signals have to be recognised. Bad weather wind-chill works fast. There have been occasions in the distant past when my protective clothing was not as good as it should have been, and I have experienced creeping demoralisation in violent weather. There is a gradual feeling of coldness and then a reluctance to battle with a flapping map, or a compass, or a torch, with numb hands; a reluctance to stop, get out the warm sweater, take off the anorak, and put the sweater on. Will *must* triumph over chill.

When the body's inner core becomes cold the brain can cease to receive its vital supply of warm blood and begin to malfunction. Then the normal person starts to act irrationally. Rescue teams have found victims dead of hypothermia who had untouched warm gear and food in their rucksacks. Mountain leaders who have received the necessary warnings recognise the common symptoms of hypo-thermia: the person slows down to the tail end of the party, as their energy is consumed by efforts to keep warm; there may be complaints of feeling cold; pale face; impaired vision; irrational behaviour, including bad temper, perhaps violent resistance to attempts to help. Brain malfunction indicates that the person has reached a very critical phase. Inducing rapid movement, to help the person generate heat, actually has the opposite effect; it involves the burning up of more vital energy. The casualty is a stretcher case. The only thing to be done is to wrap him up, place him in shelter, offer him hot drinks (not alcohol) if possible, and call out the Mountain Rescue – fast!

Here, though, there is sometimes a problem. A youth leader familiar with the symptoms of hypothermia, had, foolishly, taken his party on to the fells in the rain. One of the boys was hanging back, looking pale, complaining about feeling cold, acting irrationally. The leader noted this with concern and called out the rescue team. We were given an approximate idea of the party's position but when we arrived, in the wet mist, there was no sign of them. A descending walker informed us that he had glimpsed a party, apparently helping someone, descending off the path to the east. We radioed the infor-mation down to base and continued the search. No sign. We searched, opened out our party, widened the search area, continued to inform base, and met another walker who thought he had seen someone helping someone. After a considerable time there was still no sign and we reported our exasperation to base.

At last our leader radioed down in frustration, 'Where is this [unrepeatable] casualty?'

'We don't know,' replied base, 'but if you get a glimpse of him shoot him in the legs!'

Here the problem was that the party leader had remembered the vital symptoms of hypothermia, but had completely forgotten that young Nigel, his supposed casualty, was quite normally slow, always complaining, usually uncooperative, and seldom acted in a rational manner!

We caught up with the party eventually. Though the leader had reacted wrongly in attempting to walk the boy off the fell, if the boy *had* been a hypothermia case, we were reluctant to criticise him too strongly, having pointed out his errors. A rescuer has to be philosophical.

One thing I continually fail to understand. Why on earth do parties, time after time, go on the fells at all – particularly with young and often reluctant people – when the weather forecast is completely hostile? Are there not low-level paths enough?

The Old Man summit is soon reached from Goat's Hawse, as our feet rattle over rock which is split up into plates. There is a splendid view over the cliff to blue Low Water. Towards the north-east and east we can see three of the lakes: two parts of Windermere, Esthwaite Water and, of course, Coniston Water.

Southwards there is the distant view over Morecambe Bay, and westwards, on a clear day, we should see the Isle of Man. There is a good view of most of the Scafells, and the mountain panorama includes the Skiddaws, Helvellyn, and High Street. But the Old Man is very popular. Best to move off northwards, away from other walkers, to the next summit, on Brim Fell then to Levers Hawse, from whence we shall carefully descend to Levers Water.

Levers Water is another natural tarn, but dammed to raise its level for a reservoir. It does not look too artificial. In fact it has a long history as a reservoir, as it supplied a head of water for the operation of the extensive copper mines. Sir Daniel Fleming of Coniston Hall and Rydal Hall, who wrote his memoirs in the 1680s, records of the 'Coningston' area:

> In this Lordship are very high Fells or Mountains, wherein are Mines of lead, and where (besides Limestones and excellent Blew Slate) is great Store of Copper Oar. In these Hills heretofore was much Copper Oar got & carried on Horseback into Keswick in Cumberland where it was smelted.

He also records that the 'Coningston' lordship came into the hands of the Le Flemings by marriage in the reign of King Henry III, in about 1240. We can be fairly certain that there has been some winning of metal ores here since ancient times. However, true mining did not seriously begin until the founding of the Company of the Mines Royal in 1564 by Queen Elizabeth I, with agreement with the Master of Savoy, and a large business house of Augsburg. German miners were then brought to the Keswick area, and to Coniston. It is fascinating to learn that the copper ore was carried on horseback to be smelted at Keswick, and not only ore. Sir Daniel

Fleming noted a record in family papers which showed that in 1570 'William Fleming Esq. did for £280 sell 2000 Seme of charcoals into the Governors, Assistants & Cominalty of the Mines-Royal'.

A seam was one packhorse load. Imagine long trains of pack-horses, loaded with ore and charcoal, winding over Dunmail Raise into the industrial smoke of what must have been a busy, noisy, and sooty Keswick! After that time the mine workings on Coniston Old Man became very extensive indeed. In their most productive period in the mid-nineteenth century these mines employed around 600 men, women and children. The very extensive workings descended to 600 feet below sea level.

As we reach Levers Water, mine levels and holes are evident. Walking round the front of the tarn to the dam a fearsome hole, known as Simon's Nick, is passed. We should resist the temptation to throw a stone down this, or any shaft. There could, just possibly, be a mine historian exploring down below! The whole of this fell is riddled with holes and levels. One shaft, from the crags to the south-east of Levers Water, goes down 1,700 feet. So extensive are the excavations beneath our feet that when the economics of mining here proved unfavourable, and the pumps stopped pumping water out from the lower levels, it is reported that it took five years for the workings to fill until water flowed out of the lowest surface tunnel.

There have been a number of accidents involving walkers in this area. It used to be my duty to see to the fencing-off of dangerous shafts near paths into which people might fall by accident. Incredibly, I have often seen people climb the fences to peer down the shafts. I once even saw a family having a picnic *inside* the Simon's Nick fencing. Asked why they were there, father replied that it was nicely secluded and sheltered from the wind! Other accidents have been caused by walkers entering access tunnels without torches. Groping along the tunnel in the dark they have not realised that partway along there is a great hole in the floor. When a number of such accidents happened in one tunnel I accepted the offer of a mines expert to put a warning chain across it just in front of the hole.

Mine workings once caused me some anxiety when I had a mountain search dog. We had to train our dogs to help us search the workings for missing walkers. With better eyesight in the dark, and a better sense of smell, the dogs soon overcame their initial fear, occasionally disappearing from our sight and having to be called back. My German shepherd dog, Claife, was so anxious to please me that even on an ordinary fell-walk if she caught sight of a hole she would be into it! She once squeezed down a hole into a drain and disappeared. I called her back and, to my horror, she could not climb out. If I thrust my arms into the hole to get hold of her the space became even more restricted. The ground around the hole was completely solid and I was afraid I might need to get a pneumatic drill. How long would that take? Maybe I would have to leave her and return with food and water. After many efforts, however, and almost in complete despair, I managed to get one arm down and pull her out by the scruff of the neck. This was no easy task – a German shepherd dog is no lightweight. Having extricated her, the wretched beast bounced around with glee, and I had to restrain her – she was about to go down again!

I have occasionally explored some workings with mine experts. At such times, my amazement at the extraordinary skills of man has been tempered with fear, as we have come across rotten timbers and collapsing roofs. Walking a plank across a deep hole, or walking below a stope (vertical working) or air shaft criss-crossed with poised and broken timbers is not an enjoyable experience.

'Is it really safe?' I asked my guide as we looked up at a soaring stope apparently filled with tons of rotten timber supporting more tons of rock.

'Yes,' he replied, 'but for gawd's sake don't sneeze!'

No. Let us leave mine exploration to the experts. I like daylight and fresh air.

If we cross to the far side of the tarn we join a path descending through the devastation of Coppermines Valley, past the youth hostel and the waterfalls in Church Beck, to Coniston village. We have seen only a small part, and a popular part at that, of the Coniston Old Man Range. But there is material here for a lifetime's exploration. The southern and western part is remote and hardly visited. The complicated landscape of crags, valleys, and footholds in the northern portion receives attention and deservedly so. No one can leave without thoughts of return.

As we reach the village of Coniston we turn our backs on the turbulent landscape of the Borrowdale Volcanics and find ourselves among the softer Silurian rocks. This side of Coniston Water was once called 'Fleming-Coningstone', to distinguish it from 'Monck-Coningston' situated on the other side of the lake, on land owned by the monks of Furness Abbey. (The name 'Monk Coniston' is still used in that area.) Coniston village is not handsome. This was a miners' and quarrymen's settlement, with the addition of some Victorian buildings inspired by tourism. The oldest building is three-quarters of a mile south, by the lake shore. This is the sixteenth-century Coniston Hall, distinguished at a distance by the massive round chimneys of the period. It once stood in a park. To quote its one-time master, Sir Daniel Fleming, again:

> In this Demesne is a large Park, call'd Coningston Park, which was charter'd in the Reign of K. Edw. I & is well wooded and replenished with Fallow-Deer. This Park is bounder'd on the West by Coningston Fells & upon the East by Water; in which Park near the bank of the said Water is plac'd the Manor-House, a fair Building, Call'd Coningston Hall; which was much beautifi'd, if not Rebuilded by Will. Fleming Esq. about A.D. 1570 (Glased A.D. 1572. Wainscotted 1575).

The hall is now in the care of the National Trust. And what was the park is occupied by farmland, a campsite and a caravan site.

Coniston Water (once called 'Thurstain' or 'Thurston Water') is 5 miles long and has always held a firm place in my affections. It is wholly within the softer landscape of the Silurian rocks, which were formed by sediments accumulating in layers in the seas for forty million years at the end of the Ordovician layer of Coniston Limestone. If the successive layers were of uniform hardness or softness we would not see the lovely convoluted, folded and knotty landscape that is so typical of southern Lakeland. Glaciation and the major earth movements had very varied effects. Although the rock is generally much softer than the older rocks, it can be quite hard in places. Hard Silurian slate has been quarried south of the district for centuries. Indeed at Kirkby in Furness, a mile or two south of the park boundary, is the largest slate quarry in England. Generally, though, the more friable acidic material has supported extensive woodland since time immemorial. The roe deer, and the red deer that are still here, first occupied the area long before its human settlement.

Since by-laws prohibiting boat speeds of over 10 miles per hour were approved in 1974, Coniston Water has been relatively quiet; indeed, out of season it is a haven of peace. The lake was long a highway for the transport of ore, slate, and charcoal. And pleasure boating began in earnest when the Furness Railway reached Coniston in 1859. Here again, this beautiful track from Foxfield on the coastal line was built for industrial use but the owners immediately saw its tourism potential and introduced their own pleasure 'steamer' on the lake in June 1860. Alas, the railway line has gone. But the Furness Railway's eccentrically appealing *Gondola* was resurrected by the National Trust in 1980 and plies the lake for pleasure once again, thanks largely to the support of the apprentice training scheme at Vickers Dockyard in Barrow in Furness. A trip on the *Gondola* is a step back in time; the quiet steam engine a model of supreme engineering.

There is a delightful walk along the lake shore from Coniston Hall to Sunny Bank. Part of the path by Torver Back Common, in the Park Authority's ownership, I had to clear and engineer with the help of volunteers. We were working on this path on the day in January 1967 when Donald Campbell made his fatal bid for the water speed record. We had heard the boat run down the lake and later make its upward run, when the roar of the engine was suddenly cut. We could see nothing from where we were, assumed that the engine had failed, and thought little of the incident as we had heard practices before. It was only when we finished our work, and became aware of a sudden increase in traffic on the far side of the lake, that we realised there might be trouble. I was of course horrified at the news. However I must come clean and admit that I have always thought it wrong that this lake in a national park should be used for a world water speed bid. It was, I was told, the only possible one. But then, to me, water speed records in this age seem an irrelevance.

In several places along this west shore there are the remains of 'bloomeries', where iron ore was brought by boat along the lake to a suitable woodland site and a simple smelting hearth was built. (It was more practical to bring the ore to the fuel than vice-versa.) The sites can be identified by lake-shore clinker. Bloomeries may have existed here since Furness Abbey's commercial heyday. The ore would have been carted from deposits in Low Furness, and the Abbey had permission from the Baron of Kendal to ply one boat to carry 'what might be necessary' on Thurstain Water. However, in 1565 private enterprise bloomeries all over Lakeland were made illegal. Charcoal consumption was such that soon there would be no woods left! Green politics from Elizabeth I? Well, it was really the fact that the Crown needed a plentiful supply of charcoal for the Mines Royal. Politics was ever a devious business...

· *Grizedale Forest* ·

The ability of the Silurian soils to support woodland is nowhere more obvious than on the east side of Coniston Water, for here, from a scattering of woodlands, has grown the Forestry Commission's Grizedale Forest, covering 8,715 acres over Monk Coniston Moor, southwards to Bethecar Moor, and the whole of Hawkshead Moor over the horizon. There are a number of good things to be said of Grizedale Forest, and one is that it still retains some native deciduous trees: 10 per cent of the whole. It was also the first forest to welcome the general public on to its land, and then actually promoted public access. Today Grizedale produces leaflets and maps inviting walkers on to planned routes, and there is a cycleway.

Grizedale has an excellent visitor centre and shop; and the Theatre in the Forest attracts some of the best national and international musical talent. What better atmosphere could one have for Bach, Mozart, Chopin, Schubert, folk and jazz concerts, plays, and even Gilbert and Sullivan operas?

A few years ago I realised one of my ambitions in Grizedale Forest: to fell a tree with a Neolithic axe which could have been 4,000 years old. A TV film about the Lake District with Melvyn Bragg gave me the opportunity through the kindness of the historian Dr Bill Rollinson. An axe was produced; the ash shaft of course was new. At once I did not like the way the axehead was mounted on the shaft. I felt that the wedge shape of the head would split the ash as I delivered the blows. However it was said to be as near as it was possible to get with the rare examples which had been recovered from archaeological sites. We chose our birch tree, the camera whirled, and I began the cut some way up the trunk, for the cutting profile of the axe demanded that there had to be an upwards as well as a downwards blow. Partway through the tree, the shaft split, as I had predicted. A spare one was produced and the head mounted. The second shaft also began to split but luckily the tree was felled on camera. We had not, I said, got the shaft right. It was pointed out again that the mounting was based on the one example with a preserved shaft remnant in the British Museum. I have seen that axe and that shaft seems to have split too. Maybe the Neolithic axeman split the shaft and hurled it away in a temper, eventually to be discovered by the archaeologist!

The whole of the Silurian landscape in southern Lakeland was once densely covered in natural forest, and in spite of the many centuries of human depredation, most of Lakeland's deciduous woodland is still found in this area. If this region were left to itself for long enough, it would return to native forest. I was recently reminded of this when I saw with surprise that a paddock, previously occupied by stock for years but lately abandoned for four, had a covering of birch scrub. Birch is the coloniser. If stock is kept away from the scrub, dominant trees will develop at the expense of the weaker ones, and there will be birch woodland. If there is no further interference from then on, other tree species will appear among the birches. As there are oak trees by the river beyond the paddock, their acorns would certainly germinate in the birch's leaf litter.

Generation after generation has benefited from the harvest of the Furness woodlands – that is, the south-western area – most of which was once in Lancashire. I have lived here for most of my life and the woods are my natural habitat (they gave me my first work experience in the Lake District), so it is hardly surprising if I enthuse about what woodland means to me.

If we walk through one of these splendid woodland areas we will be seeing both relatively new trees and older ones. There is no natural woodland left. Most of what we see has been planted, or has been allowed to regenerate from previous planting. I say most, for it is not possible to say how much. It is very likely that some of the woodlands have always been woodlands, so their stock will have a long ancestry. Certainly, given some restriction of access to too many grazing and browsing animals, the quick growers, such as birch, hazel, and alder, will have always been there.

A large area of woodland, particularly between Windermere and Coniston, provided profit for the monks of Furness Abbey for many years, and it is interesting to read the species listed by the King's Commissioners in 1537 at the dissolution of the Abbey. The dissolution followed a period of heavy exploitation, but there was still 'Byrke' (birch); 'Holey' (holly); 'Asshe' (ash); 'Ellers' (I am sure alders rather than elders); 'Lynge' (a puzzle, did the Commissioners think that the ever-present 'savins' (juniper) was a tree version of Ling or heather?); 'Hasells' (hazel); 'Crabtree'; 'thorn' (hawthorn); 'lytell short Okes'; and 'other undrewood'. The same species are seen today in those woods which have not been converted to spruce, though not all the oaks are 'lytell'. But there are some surprising omissions. There must have been yew trees, 'gean' (wild cherry), and Scots pine (Scots fir). The absence of the last-named might be due to the fact that the species does not readily recover, if at all, from heavy cutting.

In addition to the local native trees we will see some non-natives introduced in later years: notably sycamore and beech, both of which romp away, sometimes to the exclusion of other species; and sweet chestnut. There is also rowan (mountain ash), but this is a tree of the open, not completely at home in woodland.

We must look for signs of local woodland animals, such as the ever-present roe deer, the lightest and handsomest of our native deer. In some woodlands we can hardly fail to see them. Indeed, their numbers sometimes present a problem. Since we have done away with their natural predator, the wolf, the deer can increase to the extent that their browsing prevents woodland regeneration. Given a naturally regulated deer population, and minimal human interference, a woodland should be self-generating in perpetuity. As trees die and fall the light allowed in through the gap in the canopy allows dormant seedlings to take over.

Roe are often seen in small family groups. One sign of a buck's presence is the fraying of the bark of young saplings. When the buck is growing new antlers in the spring he rubs them clean on the young trees, at the same time leaving his scent to mark his territory. The red deer, our largest wild animal, is also present in the southern woodlands. It is larger and heavier than the red deer which have adapted themselves to the different environment of the eastern fells, being better fed on woodland fare. The sound of a roaring stag in the quiet of the evening at October's rutting time is strangely exciting – even sometimes disturbing – raising the scalp hair. Maybe it stirs up some deep-down hunting instinct.

Then there are the signs of the day-shy badger to look for. Their populations fluctuate and from time to time they are dreadfully persecuted for no real reason. The worst villains are the diggers and netters, usually from the towns and cities, sometimes many miles away, who take the animals for badger-baiting – a hideously cruel activity which has nothing at all to do with sport. All who deplore this criminal activity should support the efforts of the Cumbria Wildlife Trust which has a badger set protection policy.

We must also watch out for red squirrels (no grey squirrels here), best seen when they are collecting the autumn harvest of hazelnuts and acorns and getting themselves into a terrible twist trying to cope with them all, scattering as many as they pick up. On occasions a squirrel will have the audacity to confront us and swear at us most disgracefully for encroaching on its patch.

But I also look for signs of old human presence. It is strangely moving to come across a fern-covered hearth, well built of dry-stone, but with the chimney gone. They can be stumbled upon in many places in the woods. The hearth is all that remains of a woodland hut occupied by workers long ago. The huts were roughly oval. From low walls a roof structure of wood was raised and the whole covered with sods. The door was of wattle.

The huts here were probably occupied by barkers. (Oak bark was in great demand for use in the tanning industry until imports depressed the home market in the mid-nineteenth century.) The barker would strip the bark from the lower part of a standing tree in early spring when the sap was rising, then take off the rest of the bark when the tree was felled, lifting it with the leaf-shaped head of his barking iron. I have done such work myself when I needed stripped oak poles to build outdoor furniture. The bark peels off easily with a satisfying tearing sound, though some skill is needed to strip off the tighter bark around the branches. The barker would then stack the curves of bark to dry. Hides soaked in oak bark tannin liquor for several months made the best leather, particularly shoe leather, and shoe-making is still a major industry in Kendal. In spite of cheap imports, I can still remember oak bark being stripped and sold, and the occupation has even been revived in recent years.

Charcoal burners also lived in these woods, and there are signs of their activity everywhere. Charcoal is produced by heating wood to an extreme, while denying it sufficient air to allow its complete combustion. It was in huge demand for centuries for smelting ore and heating metal, and for making gunpowder. Sometimes, wandering off the path, we come across a level platform on the slope, now perhaps overgrown by trees. In some woods we can stumble across them everywhere, but charcoal burners preferred sheltered places near water. These platforms (called 'pitsteads') were made by building a low wall on the lower end and cutting and filling from above. The collier built his stack on the platform around a central stake about 6 feet high. Short lengths of coppice wood were built up in layers around the stake into a beehive shape; then the whole was covered with bracken, sods and earth. The central stake was withdrawn and hot coals dropped down the hole, which was then capped. From then on, the slow burn had to be tended night and day. It could not be allowed to break through the sides to let air in, so soil, sods and buckets of water were on hand to seal any gaps. If a strong wind blew up, problems increased! Depending on its size, a burn could take from two days to a week or more, and the man had to look after several burns while preparing others. His hut therefore had to be a temporary home close to his work, so it was cruder than the barker's – a pyramid of sods.

Later the task was simplified by the use of iron kilns. It is very pleasing to see that the craft has recently been revived, as charcoal is now being produced for cooking, particularly on outdoor barbecues. A Furness man working in the woods near my home has made his own iron kiln.

Charcoal burners, swill makers (*swill* or *spelk*, meaning 'basket') who made their boat-shaped baskets from strips of oak, and coopers and bobbin turners all used coppice wood from the Furness woodlands. Coppice wood is produced by felling a tree in winter and allowing the new shoots produced from the root stump ('stool') to grow up into stems, racing upwards for the light, for around twelve to sixteen years. These shoots can then be cropped, the stool produces more stems, and the rotation continues.

Coppicing was once quite profitable, but it declined early in this century, largely because of the iron industry's conversion to coke ovens. Everywhere in the deciduous woodlands (conifers will not coppice), we can see signs of the old coppicing, for many tree trunks – in some areas most of them – spring severally from one stool. To allow some regeneration of these old coppice woods, attempts have been made to revive the work. I must say, though, that I am very disappointed at some of these attempts. Firstly, it is necessary to cut the trees close to the ground, otherwise *branches* are grown from a *stump*, instead of new stems from the root. Secondly, skill is required to produce a sloping cut so that rainwater runs off and rotting is avoided. It is also debatable whether one can do the job successfully using a modern chainsaw. The saw cut leaves ragged edges which tend to trap water – far better to make a clean cut with an axe.

It is, I know, very difficult to coppice with a felling axe. This was one of my earliest jobs, and I learned the hard way: in those first pitiful weeks my hands blistered and bled, and my back cried for mercy! After that I found it the most satisfying job I have ever done. I had to learn to use the axe left-handed as well as right-handed, and it had to be kept sharp. At one time I even lived in a hut of my own making. So I feel an affinity with those men of old who earned their living among the trees.

We can see the past work of man writ large in the great ruined castles and forts, the fine houses, the churches and cathedrals. But the marks left here in the woods are mere scratches. The trees, and the silence, have closed about them and claimed them. By one pitstead a collier has left the bowl of his clay pipe. It is as if he has spoken to me.

· *To Hawkshead* ·

Below Grizedale Forest, close to Coniston Water shore, is the large white house, Brantwood (*brant*, meaning 'steep'), which was the home of John Ruskin from 1871, the year after his election as first Slade Professor of Art at Oxford. Ruskin was a rare genius. At the height of his fame he was art critic and 'interpreter', artist, author, lecturer, philosopher, naturalist, geologist and prophet. His strong views (considered too extreme in his day) on war, social inequality, work and the dearth of craftsmanship, and the hypocrisy and self-interest of the Industrial Revolution, offended many, and his move to Brantwood was perhaps partly a retreat from growing isolation. However he had his faithful disciples, including his remarkably talented secretary, W. G. Collingwood, who was a fine artist and historian in his own right. Ruskin was an ardent conservationist and, like Rawnsley, a defender of public footpaths. 'Of all the small, mean and wicked things a landlord can do,' he wrote, 'shutting up his footpath is the nastiest.'

Towards the end of his life he suffered from bouts of mental illness, but became and remained a well-loved figure in the community, remembered long after his death in 1890 for his kindness and generosity. Brantwood is open to the public, but a visit must also be made to the little Ruskin Museum in the village. The memorial cross in Coniston churchyard was designed by Collingwood.

From Monk Coniston the road to Hawkshead crosses a steep hill on the northern end of Grizedale Forest. Hawkshead is a much-photographed small village of timber-framed houses built around narrow streets. Although the old buildings remain, and the village centre is virtually unspoilt, I have seen some regrettable changes here over the years. The car park built by the National Park Authority in the 1960s is too large, and proves that no matter how large you make a car park, vehicles will still overflow the available space. Did the Park Authority really need to make a car park there in the first place? It should not be in the business of making car parks for village users; that is the job of the Local Authority. It *is* the National Park's job to provide facilities for those who wish to enjoy the countryside. Hawkshead, fine though it is, is not countryside.

The size of the car park means that the village is hopelessly overcrowded at times. And an entrepreneur saw the opportunity to open a large clothing store which in itself attracts even more visitors. A visit must be made to Hawkshead, but preferably not at peak holiday times and weekends. There is one great improvement: through-traffic used to snarl up the narrow village street, and one particular house with an overhang used to have bits knocked off it quite regularly. A simple bypass has relieved the situation.

The oldest building in Hawkshead is the Old Courthouse, a fifteenth-century outpost of Furness Abbey. One of the more curious events in the history of Hawkshead took place here in 1548. The Vicar of Urswick and his chaplain stayed at the Old Courthouse, where they were besieged for two days by a 'tumult of insurrection', an assembly of men armed 'with swords, bucklers, staves, bills, clubs, daggers and other weapons'. They broke through an outer door but could get no further. Being unable to reach the Vicar, they demanded that he should come out 'for they would have one of his arms or legs before going away'. They were eventually dispersed by neighbours. What on earth was going on?

We must visit the old Hawkshead Grammar School which was endowed in 1575 by Archbishop Sandys, who was born in the area. Wordsworth received his early education here, from 1779 at the age of nine to 1787, before he went to Cambridge. If it had not been for his first teacher there we would probably not have had one of our greatest poets. The Reverend William Taylor was himself keenly interested in poetry and doubtless encouraged William's efforts. William acknowledged this debt, and was much affected by his teacher's death at the age of 32. Much later, in 'The Prelude', he wrote:

> He loved the Poets, and if now alive,
> Would have loved me, as one not destitute
> Of promise, nor belying the kind hope
> Which he had form'd, when I, sat at his command,
> Began to spin, at first, my toilsome Songs.

Wordsworth always thought fondly of Hawkshead and nearby Esthwaite Water, 'That sweet valley where I had been rear'd'. He lodged here with kindly Anne Tyson: first in a cottage in the village (now owned by the National Trust), and later at a cottage called Green End at nearby Colthouse. He wrote movingly of his gratitude to Anne, 'So motherly and good', in 'The Prelude': 'While my heart/Can beat I never will forget thy name.'

Wordsworth recalls that he would walk around Esthwaite Water, a distance of 5 miles, before school. As classes started at 6 a.m. in summer and 7 a.m. in winter, he must have been up betimes. Nowadays the tracks he walked on are narrow tarmac roads, and one is in constant danger from traffic, though if we were to walk it at 5 a.m., as Wordsworth must have done, I daresay we might be safe.

Apart from the famous Hawkshead Grammar School, there was a school for Quaker children, a girls' school, and Mr Mingay's 'Hawkshead School and Military Accademy', which taught, amongst other subjects, 'writing in all hands ... geography and the use of globes, fencing and music'. The Wordsworth accounts show that Mr Mingay was paid £2.18.6 in 1785 for teaching the Wordsworth brothers to dance. In fact William was an enthusiastic pupil. Some years later, while on summer vacation from Cambridge, he spent a night of 'dancing, gaiety and mirth' some 2 miles away from Hawkshead. On walking back to the village over a hill from which he viewed mountains and the distant sea, in a dawn 'more glorious than I ever had beheld', he made the decision to devote his life to writing poetry. He describes this moment in 'Summer Vacation', *The Prelude* Book IV:

> My heart was full, I made no vows, but vows
> Were then made for me; bond unknown to me
> Was given, that I should be, else sinning greatly,
> A dedicated Spirit...

Where was the viewpoint on which he made the momentous decision? I can only accept the suggestion that it was Latterbarrow, now crowned with a tall cairn, to the north-east of Hawkshead. A visit on a clear day, if not a glorious dawn, could inspire the poet that hides in all of us.

CHAPTER NINE

Ambleside and Troutbeck

•

Ambleside has its back to the Borrowdale Volcanics. If we were to climb on to its nearest fell, Loughrigg, and take a south-facing viewpoint, we would be standing among the somewhat stark Volcanics and looking down the length of Windermere into the quite different, rather lush landscape of the Silurians. Ambleside's position, close to the lake at the front, and to the central fells around, has made it one of the top three Lakeland holiday bases.

I once worked for a week with a man born and bred in Ambleside. I should have followed it up by writing a paper on, or making recordings of, his particular Cumbrian dialect. For a start, Ambleside was most definitely 'Amalsit'. Much later I learned with great surprise that an ancient spelling of Ambleside was 'Amalset' (from the Old Norse/Irish *Amalseatr*, meaning 'The shieling of Amal or Hamal'). Coincidence? He would greet me as his 'marra' which is Cumbrian and Northumbrian for 'workmate'. I think the days have probably gone when such local dialects can be studied; TV, modern transport and tourism are killing them.

I think the days have gone too when Ambleside had a distinct character of its own. Young people move out to find careers, and homes they can afford. In come retired people who can afford to buy houses at inflated prices; and the entrepreneurs hoping to make a pound or two out of tourist enterprises. Hotels, guesthouses, restaurants, and giftshops change hands more quickly than they once did. The old familiar names in the telephone book gradually disappear. I am not saying that the place is worse than it was. My love/hate relationship with it continues. It is just different.

· Ambleside, Past and Present ·

Ambleside's changes in the past were even more extreme. It was once a place of many mills. Waterwheels powered corn mills, fulling mills, bark mills, cotton mills and a paper mill. They could change their function according to varying economic demands. With the rapid growth of textile industries in Lancashire and Yorkshire, mills changed over to making bobbins, and there were scores of bobbin mills throughout this area. Southern Lakeland was particularly suitable, because of its bountiful supplies of coppice wood. One very busy mill (now converted into holiday flats) was in Stock Ghyll. As well as supplying Britain's demands, bobbins also went for export. The business declined due to foreign competition in the 1870s, but in other parts of Lakeland bobbin mills were still working in the 1970s.

Early tourism brought the next series of rapid changes. Wordsworth, for one, regarded Ambleside's transformation with utter distaste:

> Many of the ancient buildings with their porches, projections, round chimneys and galleries have been displaced to make way for the docked, featureless, and memberless edifices of modern architecture, which look as if fresh brought upon wheels from the foundry where they had been cast.

Much of the new building was taking place in 'Ambleside Below Stock' (Stock Ghyll), for Ambleside had previously been two villages. The distinction was greater before 1676. Until then, there being no consecrated ground in Ambleside, the dead of 'Ambleside

Below Stock' had to be carried to Bowness to be interred, while those of 'Ambleside Above Stock' had to be carried to Grasmere. The old right of way through Rydal to Grasmere is still referred to as 'the corpse road'. Ambleside Above Stock was the older part. The early chapel of St Anne was built there, possibly on an early pagan site (a 'henge' or stone circle). It was replaced by a Victorian building in 1812 and later abandoned in favour of the new church of St Mary (1850), with its quite alien steeple, in Below Stock.

Wordsworth was right. There is now nothing of great architectural interest in Ambleside, except a tiny eccentricity, the Bridge House (owned by the National Trust), which belongs neither to Above or Below Stock, for it spans the river. A seventeenth-century folly or summerhouse, it once belonged to Ambleside Hall which no longer exists. Early tourists were told that it had been built by a Scotsman who wanted to avoid land tax. It has been both residence and shop. Incredibly, in the 1840s it was occupied by a Mr and Mrs Rigg who, despite the diminutive proportions of the house, raised a family of six children in it. It has attracted painters, including J. M. W. Turner, and nowadays on occasions queues of photographers.

Painters, both amateur and professional, were amongst the early tourists who came here, and there are many pictures of the area in galleries all over Britain. The best-known local artist of great merit was William Green, a Manchester man who settled here in 1800 and was accepted by the Wordsworth circle. His prints became very popular (they are now collector's items), and he did much to promote Ambleside as a tourist centre.

Some aspiring artists were less skilful. It was said that the 'lion' on the signboard for The White Lion Inn was based loosely on the likeness of a lamb, probably painted by a local shepherd. A lamb with teeth and claws? It was reproduced by the artist Allom who had been engaged to illustrate a guidebook by Thomas Rose. The book was commissioned by Cumbrian Henry Fisher, a printer in London. Allom assumed that the animal on the signboard was a faithful reproduction of a Lakeland lion which inhabited the fells, or so he was told. There was a lot of such leg-pulling of tourists in the old days. I suppose it still goes on. A charming foreign lady on one of my guided walks asked me in all seriousness if it was true what a farmer had told her – that the fell sheep were bred with two longer legs on one side so that they could graze easier on the steep slopes!

There was another inn sign which raised a laugh. One of the earlier inns was called The Cock. The Bishop of Llandaff, Richard Watson, was resident at Calgarth, between Ambleside and Windermere. He acquired some property, including The Cock Inn. Out of deference to the new owner, the innkeeper had a sign painted which was supposed to depict the bewigged bishop, and he renamed the hostelry The Bishop Inn. Competition for customers was very keen in those days and another innkeeper instantly called his establishment The Cock. The innkeeper at The Bishop was furious and had a sign painted under the picture of the Bishop which read 'This is the old Cock'.

The railway reached Windermere in 1847 and Ambleside's popularity grew. Roads were improved and the volume of traffic increased. Below Stock was extended to Waterhead at the head of the lake; the steamer pier was built in 1850 by the Windermere Steam Yacht Company; and the first traffic queues occurred in the 1880s. Four-in-hand coaches, carrying up to twenty passengers, were in keen competition then. (Remembering as a young lad how I used to scrape a penny or two for pocket money with my small barrow, I reckon some local person must have been making a killing, collecting and selling horse manure. Gardens were developing about new property everywhere.)

From the earliest days of tourism one of Ambleside's big attractions was Stockghyll Force, the splendid waterfall situated in a woody ravine behind the village. Seeing its commercial value, a Mr Mackareth purchased the site in the latter part of the nineteenth century. He then fenced it off and charged people an entrance fee. Canon Rawnsley expressed his outrage in verse, there was an instant claim of a long-standing right of way, and on one occasion the iron gates were torn down. In the end a town committee was formed to acquire funds to buy out the landowner. The plan succeeded. However, to pay off the money they'd had to borrow, the new owners still had to make a charge – but only a nominal one of three pence. Though entry is now free, the old iron turnstile should be retained as a historical monument. Strangely, nowadays, not many visitors to Ambleside are aware of the waterfall's existence only a matter of yards from the town centre. Its interesting wooded setting adds much to its special attraction.

The Furness Railway Company opened a line to Lakeside, at the foot of Windermere, in 1869. At this time two rival steamer companies were competing with each other on the lake with cut-price fares and on-boat entertainments. The Furness Railway Company bought them out and in 1900 decided that a bigger pier was needed at Waterhead across the mouth of the bay. Those who hired out rowing boats saw their livelihood being threatened and supported an action by Bowness Council who were faced with a similar threat to their bay. An injunction was sought to prevent the Furness company from obstructing the highway of the lake. Eventually they proved their point and the pier at Waterhead was extended outwards rather than across.

The Furness Railway Company became the London Midland and Scottish, then British Rail, and each continued to operate the 'steamer' service (in BR's case, even after the line to Lakeside was closed and taken over by a private company). The three steamers, *Swan*, *Teal*, and *Tern*, are now once more the property of a Windermere Iron Steamboat Company.

At some time when Ambleside was being developed, the stones from Galava, the Roman fort at Borrans field (*borrans*, meaning 'a heap of stones'), west of Waterhead, became a free quarry for the builders. There is now little left of the fort apart from its foundations. In 1913 the field was bought for the National Trust by public subscription for £4,110. As prices went in those days I reckon it was a rip-off. Currently (1990), the fort remains are in the guardianship of English Heritage which has organised a dig. Eventually, probably by 1993, the National Trust hopes to display the foundations in an acceptable form with an interpretative display.

The fort had a jetty so that supplies could reach it by the lake; some of its stone was sandstone and must have come by lake from Furness. Galava was built to defend the Tenth Iter – the road over Wrynose and Hardknott, by Hardknott Fort to the sea port at Ravenglass. (Its routes with the fort at Kendal, and the route to High Street for Brougham, are as yet unknown.) Archaeological evidence shows that there was an earlier fort on the site, built of turf, clay, and wood, around the end of the first century. In the next century it was replaced by a more solid stone structure, with towers and principal buildings built on an artificial platform of earth and gravel to raise them above flood level. At that time the River Rothay was closer to the site than at present and acted as a moat on the west side, with Windermere itself as a defence on the south side. To the north was a civil settlement, Ambleside's first town (Below Stock). Up to 500 auxiliaries occupied the fort over a period of about 250 years and times were not always peaceful; there is evidence that the fort was damaged by fire on perhaps three occasions. In 1963 a tombstone near the site was excavated. Part of it read:

TO THE GOOD GODS OF THE UNDERWORLD
FLAVIUS ROMANUS RECORD CLERK
LIVED FOR 35 YEARS
KILLED IN THE FORT BY THE ENEMY.

I wonder how Flavius the clerk died. Was this man, who worked so humbly for a cause, also prepared to die nobly for it?

· *Troutbeck* ·

It is my belief that the Roman link from Galava to the High Street Roman road to Brougham climbed into what is now Skelghyll Wood. It then followed the present bridleway all the way by High and Low Skelghyll and by the contouring route along Robin Lane into Troutbeck. From then on, to reach High Street, it would have crossed the river and gone straight up north by Troutbeck Park along the line of another bridleway. It follows a very good easy line and it makes a pleasant walk.

Skelghyll Wood (Old Norse *skalar*, meaning 'summer hut') is an important mixed woodland, thankfully in the care of the National Trust. Easily reached from a lane at the south end of Ambleside, it is of interest to geologists because that narrow band of Coniston Limestone can be found running through the wood in an easterly direction. It is not easy to detect, for overlaying much of it is a layer of calcareous shale and mudstone, and the limestone itself is dark-coloured. Fossils are not easy to find in this particular limestone, but there are shells, graptolites (a branched plankton) and trilobites (that shelled animal that looks rather like a woodlouse), and corals.

Of interest to everybody is a superb viewpoint on a crag. Jenkin Crag overlooks the northern end of Windermere as far south as Belle Isle and Bowness. On the opposite shore we can make out Wray Castle, the Victorian folly; Blelham Tarn is behind. Then southwards along the lakeside slopes is the lovely woodland of Claife Heights which makes a very generous contribution to the Windermere scene, again in the ownership of the National Trust. In the background is Wetherlam on the Coniston Old Man Range, then right of it Wrynose Pass, Crinkle Crags, Bow Fell, and the Langdale Pikes. The view is one of the classics and, as it is so near Ambleside, we could expect to see it thronged. In fact I have even visited the crag on bank holidays and had it to myself.

As the bridleway leaves the wood there is a limestone outcrop on the left, noticeable because of the distinctive way in which limestone weathers. As rain is slightly acid (it has always been so, since long before we became concerned about 'acid rain'), it reacts with the lime, and forms fissures and holes. The result reminds me of boiled dumpling!

At a bridge past High Skelghyll Farm, the bridleway climbs to a higher contour, then turns south-east on a very intelligently engineered walled track. Surely this is the Roman road? In less than half a mile there is a stile on the left over a wall. The early tourists were directed by Father West's guidebook to fixed viewpoints or 'stations'. There is a station just above this stile marked with a small pillar. This is not West's and I assume that this is 'Station 4', marked by local ex-deep-sea sailor and Excise man, Mr Peter Crosthwaite, self-styled 'Admiral at Keswick Regatta, Keeper of the Museum at Keswick, Guide, Pilot, Geographer, and Hydrographer to Tourists'. He was an extraordinarily talented and energetic character who in 1783 surveyed and made fairly accurate maps of the lakes (including Windermere), with his own stations, and Father West's marked. We are higher here than Jenkin Crag so there are more extensive views to the high fells. It is a pleasant place to sit and refresh ourselves before we continue the walk. And perhaps I should quote Peter Crosthwaite's verse, appended to his Windermere map:

> Here lies Great Windermere in Princely State,
>   With Mountain basis [sic] for its Royal Bed.
> Their variegated sides form curtains great;
>   And splendid sky's the canopy o'er head
>
> Grand furniture beyond the art of man!
>   'Tis Nature's self, the workmanship Divine!
> The Living Landscapes, numberless and Grand,
>   Peep out (as you advance) on every hand.

Not Greece, nor Rome, those northern lakes outvie,
  For mountain Prospects, we them both defie.
And now invite the noble Tourist down,
  To take this splendid Walk and Feast thereon.

I think I would have liked Peter Crosthwaite. He was a true, and
very clever, Lakeland eccentric. (His popular museum's exhibits
included the straw hat of a sailor who was with Bligh on the *Bounty*,
two barnacles from the bottom of Captain Cook's ship, and a stuffed
'lamb with claws instead of hooves and wool of three colours' –
could this be the Lakeland mountain lion?)

The bridleway after the station becomes Robin Lane, and curves
gently down into Troutbeck village, a series of dwellings grouped
around common wells. Three of the main wells are preserved – St
James's, St John's and St Margaret's – and the groupings are Town
End, Crag, Longmire Yeat, High Green and Town Head. It is a
fascinating place, and I became captivated by its uniquely Cumbrian
qualities when I was responsible for the population census of this
area in 1972.

Although, inevitably, there have been changes in the village, a
walk through its streets reveals some vernacular architectural features
of the seventeenth and eighteenth centuries. Many of the solid-
looking stone houses have round corbelled chimneys, mullions and
crow-stepped gables. We must visit one of the houses owned by the
National Trust, which is open to the public. This is Town End,
home of the Brownes, a notable local family. The present house was
built around 1623 by George Browne (1596–1689), and the Trust
acquired the contents with the house in 1947. What we see inside is
not a collection of museum items from other areas. Everything
belongs where it is, and if you like carved oak, as I do, you will find
plenty to admire in the fixtures and furniture, all made and carved
by the Brownes.

Until the nineteenth century, villages such as Troutbeck wre
largely self-sufficient. In 1851 Troutbeck had its shoemakers, joiners
and blacksmith, miller and stonemason, parson, schoolmaster and
schoolmistress, and innkeepers, as well as its yeomen and tenant
farmers. An old saying has it that Troutbeck had 'three hundred
bulls, three hundred constables, and three hundred bridges', which
was true in a sense, because the township was divided into three

sections called 'hundreds'. Each hundred had six cattle 'gates' (grazings) of 2 acres on the common, a common bull, a constable and a bridge.

One peculiarity is that the church is not in the village itself. A series of lanes and paths lead down to where it lies, at the bridge by the river; for this church had to serve a larger parish, of which Troutbeck was only a part. I like the story told of the Reverend William Sewell, the very down-to-earth incumbent at Troutbeck during the first half of the last century. There had been a long drought and one Sunday his clerk said that the farmers wanted him to pray hard for rain.

'Where's wind?' asked the clergyman.

'In Blue Gill Heead [north-east].'

'Why then,' said the clergyman, who knew all about the area's weather, 'it's nay use praying for rain.'

The Reverend Sewell was another man I would have liked to meet. He was at Troutbeck for forty years, and headmaster at Ambleside Grammar School for over fifty. In 1839 he rescued a woman who was almost dead from exhaustion; she had been caught in a storm north of Troutbeck on Kirkstone Pass. The Reverend decided a shelter for travellers was needed there and caused the building of the inn in 1840. This inn used to have a claim as the highest inhabited building in England – Kirkstone is Lakeland's highest road pass at 1,500 feet (457.5m).

One memory I have of the inn was of a media gathering there to launch a record, to which I had contributed. It was a very good disc and deserves remaking; but it did not sound very good that day. The organisers did not know that there was no mains power to the inn. The power was from a generator and was definitely not at the right voltage. To the horror of the organisers, when the record was played, it groaned and wailed out at a tortuously slow speed. One or two of us had to rush outside, unable to suffer the pain of suppressed convulsions of laughter.

One cannot leave Troutbeck without mentioning at least two of its notable characters. One is legendary. Hugh Hird was the local strongman, the 'Troutbeck giant', who apparently lived there in the fifteenth century. He is said to have held off the marauding Scots single-handed. Another of his feats was to lift a main beam during the building of Kentmere Hall which ten men had failed to move.

It is said that he had an audience with the King who was much impressed by the giant's strength. Asked what he lived on, Hird replied: 'Thick poddage [porridge] and milk that a mouse might walk upon dry-shod, for breakfast, and the sunny side of a wedder to his dinner when I can get it [a whole sheep].' I am surprised that the poddage had to be only thick enough to support a mouse. Some of the poddage I ate in my youth, I swear a farmer could have walked over in his wellies!

Another character who lived in Troutbeck for a short time, after a spell at Ambleside early last century, was a very talented painter who rejoiced in the name of Julius Caesar Ibbetson. He was a man with a sense of humour. He it was who painted the original inn sign at Troutbeck's Mortal Man when Sally Birkett was the proprietor. The present reproduction, showing a red-faced and a pale-faced man, still reads:

> Thou Mortal Man, that lives on bread,
> What is't that makes thy nose so red?
> Thou silly ass, that looks so pale,
> It is by drinking Sally Birkett's ale.

Sadly, the modern substitute for Sally Birkett's ale is not as effective, and people are not as colourful as they used to be.

CHAPTER TEN
Bowness and Windermere
•

The hamlet of Birthwaite is in the township of Applethwaite, and was renamed Windermere after 1847. This was because the new railway line got that far, and the railway company had to make it known that their station was the station for Lake Windermere. This has caused confusion ever since, as tourists still alight at the station expecting to find the lake practically lapping at their feet, and are surprised to find that there is a walk or a bus ride of over a mile. The confusion increased when the Furness Railway opened a line to Lakeside, at the foot of the lake, in 1869; then there was another Windermere station, this time as near to the water's edge as one could get. When both lines became the property of the London Midland and Scottish, one had to be very careful when booking a ticket to make sure that the clerk was told the correct station, Windermere or Windermere Lakeside. Even then luggage sent in advance might go to the wrong one.

Once the railway came to Birthwaite, the hamlet vanished under the frantic building of holiday accommodation, workers' houses, shops, business establishments, workshops and gentlemen's homes, which eventually reached down and affected the true lakeside village of Bowness-on-Windermere. Soon the whole area was transformed. Wordsworth viewed the changes with sadness:

> It has always appeared to me that a person of feeling mind, beginning the excursion with Windermere and descending directly upon Bowness would not only be disappointed but perhaps in no small degree disgusted, with the bustle, the parade and drest-out appearance of so many of the objects immediately around ... The appearance of the neighbourhood of Bowness, within the last five and thirty years, has undergone many changes, and most of these for the worse, for want of due attention to those principles of taste ...

The changes were not confined to Birthwaite and Bowness. The surrounding roads also had to be improved to take the increasing traffic. In the season of 1855, as many as 21,480 carriages passed and repassed from Windermere to and from Ambleside; and 15,240 paid the toll on the toll road between Grasmere and Thirlmere. Traffic congestion is by no means a new phenomenon.

In 1887 the railway company proposed pushing the line on from Birthwaite to Ambleside, and there followed a storm of protest. By this time all the hillsides overlooking the lake, over which the line would have to pass, were taken up by the residences of eminent and influential people who could claim to have 'principles of taste'. They petitioned. They had determination and influence. The railway bill had no chance.

A number of Manchester and Liverpool businessmen with residences in Windermere were using the railway line constantly, and a special luxurious 'club car' was eventually provided by the company for their use at scheduled times. Many a deal must have been struck over a glass and a cigar or two between Preston and Windermere. What a contrast to rail travel today! Travellers must now change from the main line at Oxenholme to a rail bus which decants them at a shelter behind Windermere's supermarket.

Up above the supermarket, from the far side of the A591, a track winds through attractive woodland to one of Lakeland's classic viewpoints. Orrest Head is a delightful surprise. Within a half-hour's walk we have a breathtaking view of much of the lake; in the background a great deal of the central mountain mass including the Scafells; and to the east the Yorkshire Pennines. When I had an office in Windermere a stroll to Orrest Head was a wonderful lunch-hour escape from paperwork, to remind myself of what a national park was all about. Quite a lot of it is there in full view.

· Bowness ·

Before the tourist boom in the eighteenth and nineteenth centuries, Bowness was a tiny village, with a nearby ferry serving the route between Kendal and Hawkshead. There was a parish church for the scattered farm communities, and a few people earned a little from fishing. Even in 1850, by which time tourism was becoming a major local industry, there were only two rival hotels and about a dozen boarding houses. But the bigger changes were still to come. The railway was bringing a wider clientele and the need for more tourist accommodation was being met. Local businessmen got together in the 1870s and formed the English Lake District Association to promote the area for tourism. They also provided some amenities: iron seats at viewpoints (a few of which still exist!); stiles and gates; paths, footbridges and signposts.

In the 1860s and 1870s Bowness promenade, by all accounts, became a real tourist honeypot; it has been ever since. People who are critical of the Bowness crowds now should remember that Bowness always *was* crowded at holiday times, though maybe we would have found the nineteenth-century scene more colourful. Boatmen touted for trade; the steamboat companies vied noisily for custom, one offering the attraction of a brass band; stalls sold their wares; buskers and an organ-grinder provided a tuneful accompaniment.

Against this background appeared another of those slightly batty characters which the Lake District has always attracted. Each season John Close, son of a butcher in Kirkby Stephen, hiked the 35 miles over to Bowness and set up stall to sell his appalling 'poems' to the hapless promenaders. His aggressive style of self-promotion and salesmanship would probably place him top of the class at any modern business school. He buttonholed and bullied, flattered those who bought, and abused those who refused. Styling himself 'Poet Close' and 'The Bard of Westmorland', he sent his compositions to royal and titled people, and made the most of their polite acknowledgements, boasting that he 'corresponded' with 'crowned heads, the late Majesty of France, and England's glorious Queen, and also her future King'! Who then would dare not to buy one of his books!

The extraordinary fact is that Close got his 'poetry' recognised and even got himself on the pension list. It happened that the then Lord Lonsdale was about to get married. This called for a suitable Close poem, a sample verse of which is quoted here:

> The Honourable William Lowther,
>   Our Secretary of Berlin, he,
> Respected much at Prussia's court,
>   Kept up our dignity.
> His nephew, now Lord Lonsdale,
>   Upon his wedding day,
> We wish all health and happiness,
>   All heartily we pray.

At least it almost scans, for this was one of his best! The composition was sent to the Honourable William Lowther with an appeal for help. Did the honourable gentleman read the verses? Or could he really have believed that this was the work of genius? Whatever, he influenced Lord Palmerston to place John Close on the pension list. Did Palmerston read the verses? Some MPs did eventually, and insisted that the pension be withdrawn. And so it was, after Poet Close had received the first payments and £100. Do any of his books still exist? Maybe his execrable verse was no worse, in its way, to some stuff which pretends to be poetry today.

The changes to Bowness continued. Even St Martin's, the fifteenth-century parish church, did not escape the blight of Victorian restoration. At least the fifteenth-century stained glass, said to have been acquired from Cartmel Priory, was preserved. More and more guesthouses and hotels filled the space between Bowness and old Birthwaite. More and more gentlemen bought land and built their country seats. Storrs Park, a lakeside estate of impressive houses running south of the ferry, was still known as 'millionaire's row' when I was a lad. Maybe it still is.

Having known Bowness for more years than I care to tell, I must add my regrets to Wordsworth's for the changes that I too have seen. It is partly, of course, nostalgia for the old days; maybe something of the past seen in rose-tints. And there is also that instinctive dislike of change, which subconsciously threatens security. In my teens, Saturday shopping in Bowness renewed many regular local acquaintances. I remember going to Martin's, the family grocer's, which smelled so deliciously of cheese and freshly ground coffee; meeting friends at Atkinson's cosy little café for tea and scones; exchanging greetings in the street; being ticked off at the cinema for making too much noise with my hobnailed boots; getting all the news from the barber shop and technical advice from the bike shop; rowing on the lake past the jetties and the huge corrugated-iron boat sheds; watching the steam-driven ferry; hearing the bus conductor's banter.

Tourism then benefited old established businesses run by local folk. Now it has all altered, thanks to a tourist boom on an unprecedented scale. Giftshops, cafés, and take-aways change hands at a remarkable rate. The boat sheds have been replaced by a modern edifice which looks as if it was designed by the same architect as the Sydney Opera House (predictably, it won an award). Green fields have been covered with cars. Dear old Bowness, what have they done to you? To me, a visit is slightly shocking, like coming across someone you knew as a decent and guileless young girl, now painted and dressed up like a tart.

Speculators are moving into the countryside 'leisure market' all over Britain. As they see it, the principal purpose of a picturesque scene is to provide an attractive backdrop for modern leisure activities, like shopping, squash courts, trim-gyms, fun pools, and the rest. Bowness is a prime target. The crowds are already there, and there is apparently not enough for them to do (or, rather, spend their money on). There is talk of exciting new commercial developments and many more car parks. You cannot, I am told, stop progress. There is property to pull down. Get rid of the old cinema, the ugly Victorian buildings. Exciting prospects of modern development, bringing more wealth to local businesses. Those green fields by the lake – dead land – worth a fortune to a developer. Somewhere to enjoy leisure activities in bad weather? It would provide many jobs. And it could all be so *tasteful*! The best landscape architects money can buy – designer landscape. There is a lot of capital sloshing around and waiting to be spent – if only those nasty National Park planners would give some leeway...

Bowness receives many knocks. It has always been criticised for its crowds, particularly back in the late twenties and early thirties. Its bustle is not infrequently compared to that of Blackpool. That is grossly unfair. As yet, Bowness has no golden mile, no amusement arcades, no pleasure beach or candy floss. And one must give full marks to the council gardeners who somehow manage to keep the flower beds on the promenade looking so superb. But there are traffic jams; and hordes of people, tramping round the shops, eating chips and ice-cream, gazing at the lake, watching the 'steamers', queuing for cruises, watching other people. Gregarious souls are in their element here. (Among those I must count my father who thinks the colourful pageant is all marvellous.) I do not dislike people. But I, and others like me, must escape them in the mass, and Bowness in the season must be given a wide berth.

In Snowdonia National Park a boundary line was drawn around Blaenau Ffestiniog, excluding it, even though it was in a central area, because the devastated landscape of the quarries was at variance with the concept of a national park. When depressed by the sight of rampant commercialism, I have sometimes thought that if things were to get too far out of hand the same policy could be adopted in the Lake District National Park, excluding Bowness and Windermere. Crowds and greedy money-making have nothing to do with national parks.

But Bowness out of high season is fine. Bowness then is a different place, and still has much to offer. There are great viewpoints from easy strolls around the village. The prospect across the lake in November, with the autumn colours in the woods climbing to Claife Heights: that is very special. I have not yet, like some Lakelanders, quite given Bowness up for lost. The National Park Authority, the Friends of the Lake District, and many concerned residents, are together holding a line which the would-be developers and investors constantly try to cross. Bowness does very well as it is. Enough is enough.

We will go down to the shore not very far from Bowness in the still cool air of early morning, when the only sound is the song of an awakened blackbird. On the distant shore there is a brief protest from a green woodpecker. The lake is flat calm, and still sleeping under its thin night-time bed-sheet of mist. Then it picks up the lemon yellow from the dawn sun. Beyond and above the mist, the trees on Claife Heights very gradually begin to blush their spring green. The yellow turns brighter, and then the mist begins to lift, vanishing into air, its remnants on the lake surface curling like strands of silk, drifting lazily, then rising. The lake flat calm, the reflection of the Claife woodland a perfect reversal of its reality. Then – as we enjoy the luxury of silence – for no apparent reason, the water begins lapping gently on the shore. The lake is rising and falling almost imperceptibly as if it is taking breath. That is the signal. The lake will accept us. Now, and only now, will we dare to push out our boat and sink our oars. Off around Belle Isle, to the islands of the Lilies of the Valley. A spring morning on Windermere. Not a dream. It happens. But the opportunities are rarer than they once were.

England's largest lake has not changed over the centuries. (You cannot build on water.) It is the most beautiful. I know that many will argue the case for Ullswater, or Derwent Water or Coniston; but among the princesses Windermere is the queen. Sometimes, contemplating the scene in July and August, or on bank holidays, people might say that Windermere is a write-off; that it is now far too crowded and noisy. But for sheer physical beauty I say that Windermere is in a class of its own. The steamer trip from Lakeside, outside the main holiday period, along the lake's 10-mile length, reveals most of its scenic charms. To know the subtlety of its shore lines, with its nooks and 'nebs' (promontories), we would need to row around for years in all seasons.

The steamer starts from the jetty at Lakeside railway station. Alas, the railway closed in 1965, but a private company now runs the short 3-mile stretch from Haverthwaite with steam trains. As a lad, that station, right on the water's edge, was to me an idyllic place. To have steam engines and boats together was something – but in such a place! I remember enjoying a cup of tea with the station master in his house, looking out on a grand view of the lake and the waiting steamers. It was magic! The camping coaches in the siding were always in great demand – it was a perfect place for a holiday. The 'steamers' on the lake are diesel nowadays, but one of them might be one day re-converted to steam.

The scenic interest begins as soon as we leave the pier, through wooded banks. Straight ahead the Fairfield Range is in view, with Helvellyn's summit behind. Silver Holme is the first island on the left, so-called, because a 'kist' (chest) of silver is said to have been hidden here. The Esthwaite Valley lies behind the woods. Here, during the glacial periods, a sheet of ice met the main sheet ploughing down from the north, and the combined weight deepened the trough which is now around 150 feet deep. Grass Holme, the next island, covered in reeds, was always a nesting site for mute swans. Beyond and behind it, before the promontory of Rawlinson Nab, at Hammer Hole, was once a jetty to which iron ore was brought to be smelted at Cunsey Furnace. There was a forge in the woods behind; its waterwheel-driven hammers could be heard pounding as far as Hawkshead in Wordsworth's day. He mentions 'The distant forge's swinging thump profound' in his poem, 'An Evening Walk'.

Opposite then, on the east shore, is Storrs Hall. Now a hotel, in the days of the Lake poets it was owned by Colonel John Bolton, the man who introduced the iron plough into the Lake District. In 1825 the house became a centre of fashionable culture, when Sir Walter Scott paid the Colonel a visit. William Wordsworth was also present at jollifications which included moonlight boatings and culminated in a grand regatta when 'not fewer than fifty barges' decorated with flags and streamers, accompanied by music, processed around the lake. The shores were thronged with spectators. The odd little octagonal building on the promontory is the 'Temple', owned by the National Trust, and built in 1804 to honour Admirals Nelson, Duncan, St Vincent, and Howe.

The ferry run between Bowness and Sawrey, which links the old market towns of Kendal and Hawkshead, has a long history, although the present craft only came into use in 1990, replacing an old friend that had been converted from steam to diesel. It pulls itself across on cables. I recall one occasion when the cables were being renewed and I boarded the temporary boat on the Bowness side. It was a foggy evening and we got lost. One of the regular passengers remarked that we seemed to be a long time reaching the far shore.

And when we arrived, there was no sign of the Ferry House landing! Gingerly approaching land at last, we found we had drifted into Ling Holme, over a mile down the lake.

When gales blow up, as they often do, the ferry is suspended. The ferry skipper must make the sometimes controversial decision.

'When does he decide to suspend?' I asked a frustrated Sawrey resident as we stood forlornly in the squally rain at the Bowness end, looking at the immovable craft, and the so-near-yet-so-far opposite shore, beyond which was shelter, warm home fires and food.

'When the wind is strong enough to blow the ash off his cigarette,' was his gloomy reply.

The only accident I have heard of, though, was the terrible one on a night in October 1635, when a boat sank – probably overloaded, with a wedding party from Hawkshead – with the loss of forty-seven passengers and eleven horses.

Before reaching Bowness Bay the boat passes Belle Isle with that round house which some called 'the pepper pot' or 'tea caddy'. It was built for a Mr English in 1774 and was surrounded then by formal gardens. He felled an old tower (the seat of the Philipsons) which had endured a siege in the Civil War, to build it. Before that the island had the local manorhouse, and there are signs that it may previously have held a Roman villa. Mr English thought the unique building would embellish the beauty of the lake. However there were 'people of taste', including Wordsworth, who thought it a nasty intrusion. The embarrassed owner sold the house before it was completed. It was bought by a Mrs Curwen, of a family who had made a fortune from coal-mining in West Cumbria. She and her husband considerably planted a screen of trees around the house. Thanks are also due to the Curwens for the extensive planting of woodland on the hillsides of the western shore, now in the care of the National Trust, which make a major contribution to the beauty of the lake.

On the far side of Belle Isle are three islands: Thompson 'Tommy' Holme and the two well-named 'Lilies of the Valley' islands. In 'The Prelude' Wordsworth says:

> ... an Island musical with birds
> That sang for ever; now a Sister Isle
> Beneath the oaks' umbrageous covert, sown
> With lillies of the valley, like a field ...

One must have a special regard for beautiful places which have demanded one's hard labour. I spent many happy hours of two cold winters thinning out the trees on the islands, letting light on to the woodland floor to encourage regeneration, and letting ice-cold water into my waders. There is nothing more pleasurable than getting dirty hands and aching muscles, maybe even enduring a little discomfort, in the practical work of conservation. It is important to contribute with a cheque book or the ballot box; but to bend the back to some task, no matter how simple, opens up portals of perception. It intensifies a love of the countryside. It brings that satisfying, enjoyable feeling of husbandry that is largely lost to us with our comfortable modern lifestyle. It is true recreation.

Beyond Bowness, the next island is Lady Holme, which once held a chantry devoted to the Virgin Mary. Nothing remains of it, which is scandalous. On the shore here is the Steamboat Museum, which holds some of the lake's oldest boats, beautifully restored and maintained. Then, beyond the next bay, is Rayrigg Hall, once the summer residence of William Wilberforce, famous for leading the fight to abolish the slave trade. He wrote: '... in the early morning I used to row out alone and find an oratory in one of the woody islands in the middle of the Lake [meaning Lady Holme].'

Up above, on the east bank, is the excellent viewpoint, Adelaide Hill, owned by the National Trust and named after Queen Adelaide, widow of King William IV, who enjoyed a visit here in 1840. Millerground Landing is just below and beyond. Here another ferry, said to belong to the Monks of Furness Abbey, linked this shore with Belle Grange on the other, from whence there was an ancient paved track to Hawkshead, now a bridleway. This seems to have been a more civilised arrangement than the Bowness ferry. At the latter place you had to shout for the ferryman, whereas at Millerground you rang a bell. As the lake curves slightly to north-west we approach the deepest water; in fact the bed is below sea level.

Brockhole, the National Park Visitor Centre, is now on the right. Opened in 1969, it was once the residence of Mr Henry Gaddum, a Manchester tycoon, and the garden has been magnificently restored to its original plan. When the Park Authority acquired the property it was a lapsed Merseyside women's convalescent home. It was not popular with the ladies – far too quiet and not near the shops! Now the place seeks to bend the public's mind to conservation and a better appreciation of what the National Park has to offer. There are walk-through displays, demonstrations, lectures and courses, and a café. A visit here is an enjoyable necessity.

On the opposite shore is Wray castle (owned by the National Trust). Built by a Dr James Dawson, a Liverpool surgeon, in the middle of last century, the castle is entirely Victorian bogus, even including specially constructed 'ruins' in the grounds. In the 1970s when the Trust had drainage problems, with subsequent damp and dry rot, under the strange rooflines of the building, they discussed the option of gutting it and just leaving a shell. The terrible wrath of the Victorian Society was about to descend, but luckily such extreme treatment did not become necessary. The building is now let to a school for Merchant Navy radio officers.

The views of the Langdales and Wetherlam are excellent at this point, and the water here is around 200 feet deep. To our right is The Low Wood Hotel, once a famous coaching inn frequented by many famous folk, now a bit up-market. In the last mile, views of Fairfield dominate the scene over Ambleside.

Now and then we have a winter which starts early and continues without respite. At such times Windermere can freeze over. The last time was from January to March in 1963, and the ice was so thick that some foolhardy people even drove cars over it. I was able to walk to Ambleside from Bowness in record time. Crowds enjoyed the novelty of walking to the islands, and visiting friends on opposite shores, and there was skating for weeks on end. But the real surprise was the noise the ice made. In the quiet of the night I listened to it groaning and howling and booming like some huge monster. This sound changed key and increased in volume when the thaw eventually came. Ironically, the ferry, which had been kept going beyond its usual time limits to keep its lane open, was finally defeated and bound to the shore by the moving ice flows. Another surprise was the amount of flotsam I collected after the thaw. Piers and jetties had been wrenched out of the lake bed by the ice, and their timber, including some huge balks, ended up in the shoreline alders and willows.

At times I have thought despairingly that Windermere Lake

should be excluded from the National Park. This is when I have observed with disgust the chaotic amount of traffic on the lake in the high season, and endured its noise. For those who are besotted with mechanical toys, who like a bit of noisy fun, or who need to boost their egos with a sense of power, Windermere is ideal. Anyone else – those who like a quiet form of water recreation, or who just want to stroll or sit quietly on the shores may well feel frustrated.

Here we have a recreation area overrun by motorboats. Some years ago the National Park Authority introduced a by-law compelling all owners of motor-powered vessels to register their craft. This enabled them to be identified in the event of an offence being committed. The Home Office allowed the introduction of the by-law on the condition that it would not be used to limit the number of boats on the lake, or to make a profit on licence sales. In 1990 the number of current licences had grown to something like 14,000. Of course the likelihood of all, or a majority of, the licensed craft running on the lake at the same time can be discounted; even so the position is ludicrous. Authority to put a limit on the total number of certain vessels is being sought by the National Park as part of a Lake District Protection Bill, which it is hoped, will be presented to Parliament in the near future.

In high season the lake scene can only be described as chaotic. There have been accidents, including some fatalities, but it is little short of a miracle that there have not been more. Here we have fast boats, cabin cruisers, water-skiers, yachts, canoeists, rowing boats, wind-surfers, jet-skiers, anglers, swimmers, sub-aqua groups, all competing for the available water. There is some regulation: for instance there are speed limit areas, and other by-laws compelling boat owners towing water-skiers to have two operators (one to navigate, the other to observe the skier).

As a ranger I always had to try to be unbiased in my approach to the public. I must confess, however, that I found this very hard in relation to water-skiers. Some of them proved to be the most difficult people to deal with, a view shared by my colleagues in the National Park and the National Trust. To begin with, the sport needs a large amount of water; and yachtsmen, rowers, and anglers complain that skiing activity interferes seriously with their enjoyment. But that is not all. There are very frequently too many skiers for the available space. Not only do they demand water, but after launching they need an area of shore on which to deposit equipment and from which to operate. The pressure is such that they appropriate private land (in spite of warning notices), obstruct rights of way, and occupy National Trust land provided by benefactors for the quiet enjoyment of the public. To add insult to injury, some light fires, leave litter and use the lakeside woods as lavatories.

When, at the request of landowners, I have very politely asked skiers to leave private land I have been subjected to unprecedented abuse. Why that should be I do not know; I merely record it as fact. The Water-Ski Club, based at The Low Wood Hotel, say that the trouble is caused by 'cowboys' and not by members of their club, who must observe the club's rules. I am prepared to accept that, but we still have this trouble. If walkers are seen to trespass habitually they rightly bring down the wrath of farmers and landowners. Yet habitually offending water-skiers seem to get away with it; they know that no one is likely to take action against them, and they persist.

Other 'cowboys' I would like to see the back of, are jet-skiers, motorboat speedsters, and clowns pulled along on large inflatable doughnuts. People who tear around other lake users on jet-skis, the water equivalent of motorbikes, are the subject of many complaints. In their defence it is pointed out that they make little noise. Noise, though, should not only be measured in decibels; there is also the irritation caused by high pitch. Motorboat speedsters cause other problems. It is almost impossible to prove their excessive speed in restricted areas, and there are the odd occasions when they harass other craft for fun (very dangerously in the case of rowing boats). I have even seen them chasing ducks and swans. To try to deal with these – at times almost intractable – problems, we have the lake's traffic wardens and a park ranger. Occasionally a police launch will appear.

Any reasonable person who uses the lake, lives around its shores, or walks around it, must see the need for regulation. In a discussion document to test reaction to the proposed Protection Bill the Park Authority has suggested the following measures: compulsory third party insurance for owners of power-driven vessels; revision and extension of speed limit areas; a 6 mile per hour speed limit between sunset and 7 a.m.; prohibition of jet-skis; prohibition of towed passenger-carrying inflatables; no water-skiing among moorings;

limits on numbers of powerboats; a licensing system for launching sites; parts of the lake to be closed either seasonally or permanently to protect wildlife, and a ban on activity when the lake is partially frozen, which makes wildlife vulnerable; more specific noise restriction, with powers to test individual boats.

All this might seem reasonable, but the commercial interests on the lake have banded together. This, they say, is 'the thin end of the wedge'. The Park Authority has already placed severe restrictions on other lakes; is Windermere to be the next? In the consultation procedure which any democracy must observe, they will have their say, and they are a powerful lobby backed by money. They will kill the bill if they can, in every detail. For instance, to go for the bare-foot skiing record, calm water is apparently needed – best before 7 a.m. One commercial user even argued that wildlife *likes* the human recreation activity! The yacht clubs can speak for themselves, the Cumbria Wildlife Trust must surely speak, but who is to speak for the thousands of other individuals, not in any grouping, who simply wish to enjoy the lake environs? I can only think of the Friends of the Lake District. (And it is refreshing to be told that the Friends do not need money – just a large membership.)

The main, distorted, argument against the introduction of what are sometimes called 'draconian' regulations is that they are a threat to the ancient rights of navigation. Do traffic regulations on our roads interfere with ancient rights of usage? It can no doubt be argued that navigation rights have existed on the lake from time immemorial. But there is no ancient right to use the lake as a funfair. Rights imply journeys, for this is the purpose of public highways. I would like to see someone try to argue the right of a car-owner to tow someone behind on roller skates.

If we think of national parks as offering what they were meant to offer – quiet enjoyment of unspoilt countryside – Windermere in July and August and on bank holidays is a nonsense. The noise is often intolerable. A motor boat is said to be no noisier than a car – between 75 and 85 decibels normally – but when too many of them operate together on the sounding board of open water the total noise becomes unbearable. Even without the Protection Bill, the Park Authority has the power to increase the speed limit areas. In theory it could place a 10 mile per hour limit on the whole lake, but that would be tantamount to a declaration of war. The alternative of sensible regulation should get general support.

The value of quiet countryside cannot be measured in monetary terms. It is becoming increasingly precious. Commercial pressure must never tempt us to rethink the basic reasoning behind national parks. That commercial pressure is powerful. Tacitus, in the first century, remarked that 'In seasons of tumult and discord bad men have most power. Mental and moral excellence require peace and quietness.' Some order needs to be brought to this noisy chaos.

Windermere is an example of a recreational area in the grip of lucrative business interests. It is happening everywhere in the world, among the mountains as well as on the lakes. But the businessmen must accept reasonable control when their dividends are produced from a capital stock that belongs to us all.

CHAPTER ELEVEN

Eskdale and Wasdale

•

In looking at the central fell areas I have omitted two of the most important dales, Eskdale and Wasdale, because a great part of their landscape is not of the rock type known as Borrowdale Volcanic. When volcanic activity takes place as a result of earth movements, not all the molten magma reaches the land surface. A great mass of it boils up into a blister-like dome beneath the surface, and subsequently cools more slowly to form granite, a rough-textured and usually coarsely crystalline rock containing shiny specks of mica. Generally the slower the rate at which the magma cooled, the larger the crystals. Granites vary in colour, depending upon their particular composition. In Eskdale, Miterdale and Lower Wasdale, and north towards Ennerdale, the basic rock type is a coarse-grained granite, mainly pink-coloured because of its iron content, and generally called Eskdale Granite. Although this was formed beneath the earth's surface it has become exposed as a result of Ice Age erosion. There are other, smaller, granite exposures elsewhere: in the Skiddaw Slates; and particularly at Shap, where the rock has been profitably quarried for many years and has been used in some of London's notable buildings, including St Pancras Station and the Albert Memorial.

The granite can be examined in the dry-stone walls. It is cobbly, nobbly stuff, and I think most difficult to work with. Not only is it very rough to handle, but it is hard to make a good jigsaw match, and 'throughs' (slabs to bind both sides of the wall together) are absent. Often walls built from this type of rock are of wide, tapering construction, to make up for the lack of throughs. Otherwise a few acrobatic sheep can start an upper breach that might result in a 'rush' (an avalanche), and another maintenance job for the hard-pressed farmer.

· Eskdale ·

I reckon the best view of Eskdale, given a clear day, is the famous one from the terrace walk at Muncaster Castle. It covers a vast stretch of Eskdale, with the high fells in the background. It is very grand, indeed sensational, lacking only a fanfare of silver trumpets and clouds of angels! Not all the viewpoints are high ones and the preserve of the agile. This is an easy stroll. Yes, we must visit Muncaster Castle, particularly when its gardens are adazzle with rhododendrons and azaleas in early spring.

The castle is near Ravenglass, a village which has been a port at least since Roman times. Here was the Roman fort of Glannoventa (meaning 'the town on the bank'). Unfortunately only dim traces remain, for the stone has long since been stolen, and the mainline railway was driven through it in 1850. However there is one remarkable remnant in woodland to the south, to which we must pay our respects: the bath house, long called Walls Castle, for some strange reason. Its walls actually stand to the original height. Glannoventa was linked to the fort at Hardknott by the Tenth Iter, but the road's route is largely a matter of speculation. This fort was also linked with a defensive system along the seaboard all around the Cumbrian coastline to Hadrian's Wall.

Ravenglass has long since silted up and ceased to be a bustling port. Now it is just a very attractive one-street hamlet, its water the resort of pleasure craft.

The popular way to start an exploration of Lower Eskdale is on

'Laal Ratty' (the Ravenglass and Eskdale Railway), the narrow-gauge line which runs the 6 lovely miles from Ravenglass to Dale-garth near the village of Boot. The line was built in 1875 to carry iron ore from Eskdale mines, and also granite, to the mainline railway and port at Ravenglass. The train is often pulled by scale models of steam locomotives but it would be a mistake to think of it as a toy railway. It is genuine public transport which serves the valley well, and rewards the traveller with a wonderfully scenic ride through woods and fields.

At Boot there is a working corn mill restored by the County Council. Eskdale had a number of mills and one or two iron mines; one that the railway served is on the fellside above Boot. But of course the main occupation here was farming. When the Romans built their road through Eskdale, the valley would have been more populated than it is now. To the south there were extensive farm settlements on Birker Fell, and on the northern slopes of Eskdale Moor. When the Roman columns marched along the Tenth Iter, farmers were producing rye (a crop said to have been introduced by the Romans), barley, and possibly wheat, as well as grazing animals. This has been borne out by excavations, pollen counts and radio-carbon dating of material in old field systems above the Esk at Brantrake Moss.

Almost opposite Dalegarth Station, a very minor road leads to Stanley Force, a waterfall in a narrow ravine (National Park). Actu-ally the ravine is so narrow at the main falls that the best views require a scramble which is not for the less agile, the nervous, or both. But there is a delectable walk along the beckside paths, through the mixed woodland, to the base of the fall. It is very pleasant to listen to the conversation of a beck – a chatter here, a murmur there, a calm whisper, an amusing titter from a feeder, a deep grumble, and then as we approach the fall, an angry roar. The mossy wood-land – with its tall trunks, rich green banks and curtains of growth everywhere, generated and sustained by the moist air – is the nearest thing we have to rainforest. There are male ferns, lady ferns, and carpets of beech fern; polypody ferns, which grow up the trunks of trees, and everywhere sheaths of moss and liverworts. On the forest floor, among the grasses and rushes, we find wood sorrel, the fragile flowers of cow wheat, the white foam of heath bedstraw, and mauve towers of foxglove.

The bird residents are best heard in the evening or early morning: the dipper with its flute-like song snatches; the blackbird with the most plaintive song of all; the laugh of a green woodpecker; and the wren, with that miraculous sustained trill, such a mighty sound from a mite, here in its element among the secretive little rock caves and undergrowth.

From near the base of the falls a path climbs steeply, a little forbiddingly at first but more easily above, and curves off towards the top of the gill to another of my favourite viewpoints. It is on the edge of the ravine so children and dogs need to be tethered! It gives a superb view of the Scafells framed in trees; if we need to peer over the ravine at the falls below, it might be as well to do it on all fours!

The River Esk rivals the Duddon for sheer beauty and variety, slow at its meandering foot, higher when hurrying through farms and woodland; and higher still, tumbling and churning down some of the remotest areas in Lakeland, under the highest land in England, whose savage slopes feed the river's source. Away from a public road this is a remote and quiet place and has the best routes to Scafell and Scafell Pike; but it is a full day's hike. Here, around the Upper Esk, the monks of Furness Abbey had several thousand acres of sheep pasture, and their enclosure walls, or dykes, can still be seen. When the then Lord of the Manor, John de Hudleston, granted a licence for the enclosure it was stipulated that the dyke should not be so high that it would exclude deer and fawns.

· *Show Time* ·

There is one time of year when the quiet dale below Hardknott takes on new and colourful life, with tents and trailers, pens and cars, and lots of people. Show time! Observed from the fell road high above, the scene is a novel one; but what is strange is the way the sound reaches us in waves on the wind: the distorted and modulated chatter and laughter; like hearing a distant colony of sea birds.

Many of the dales shows in Cumbria and other country areas are less localised and traditional than they once were, thanks to ease of personal transport, and increasing commercialism. But the shows in all the western dales are truer to the old type. 'Eshd'l Show', or Eskdale Show, is an example. Here all the local hill-farming clans, including the toddlers and grandparents, gather for 'a bit of a crack' (an exchange of news); and some of them for 'a bit of a stir' (a bit of fun). If we mingle with the throng we can enjoy the true country flavour.

There is no canned music from the loudspeakers, but there is so much conversation that greetings, to reach above the noise level, have to be loud. A typical exchange between two farmers might go like this:

'Why Willie, hoo ista, y'owd boogar!' (Hello Willie, how are you, old friend!)

'Noo then Tommy! Aaz grand as owt! 'Ow's tha?' (I'm fine! How are you?)

The loudspeakers announce that the next event will take place at three o'clock. Everyone looks at their watches. It is already half-past three. 'Nay use lookin' at yoor watches,' bawl the speakers. 'The'll be on foreign London time – 'ere it's Eshd'l time!'

Dominating the livestock show are the traditional Herdwick sheep, handsome little creatures. Here their white faces are powdered like Edwardian ladies' and, for reasons lost in time, their fleeces are dyed red with iron oxide. The judge looks at them very carefully. Good Herdwicks need to have 'daylight between their legs' if they are to withstand winter snows, and they should have a good covering of that wiry fleece. There are several classes: 'yow hoggs' (the year's grown ewe lambs); the one-year older 'gimmers' (yet to bear lambs) and 'shearlings' (once sheared). Hounds, terriers, and sheep-dogs are also judged, and the children have brought their family pets.

There are the usual product tents, and the stalls sell everything a countryman might need. There is a competition for shepherds' crooks. They are always amazing. The curved crook of sheep's horn can be carved and coloured by the local craftsmen: one may be in the likeness of a leaping salmon; or it could even be a fox with the hounds in full cry behind; the hazel or ash sticks are straight as billiard cues.

Then there are the races for young and old. The most exciting is the fell-race (traditional at all the dales shows) which is strictly for the very strong and fit! The route is all within sight of the valley, up a line so steep we almost have to lean backwards to view it. It goes up to well above 2,000 feet, and if the rate of ascent seems astonishing, the descent speed is unbelievable. The runners come down in great leaps. The first one in has completed the course in less than half an hour; covered in perspiration, he flops on the grass, gasping and only able to nod acknowledgement of the congratulations. 'Good lad Charlie!' 'Cummon Tommy!' The followers sprint in, to applause and shouts of encouragement, trying to outdo each other in a last burst of speed, doubling up after passing the line, hands on knees, chests heaving.

The other great excitement is the 'hound trail', a fell-race for hounds. The bookies start it by shouting the odds, and there is much discussion and advice, some good, some optimistic, from gathering punters. Meanwhile a runner has left the field unseen, dragging a rag soaked in aniseed and paraffin. At the halfway point on the fell, his 'drag' is picked up by another runner who must complete the mountainous course of around 10 miles, back to the field. The hounds, dressed in colourful jackets, are brought to the starting line and the noise of excited baying and howling is deafening. The whole valley echoes to it. There is something quite basic about the sound which stirs the adrenalin!

The clamouring hounds are dancing about like kites at the end of their leashes. Jackets are removed, the hounds held close; the flag is raised, then dropped. Immediately the hounds are loosed the baying stops. It is as if a switch has been thrown, and all that can be heard is the padding of their feet as the pack takes off across the field to leap the walls. Everyone wanders off then to other attractions.

Forty minutes later the hound owners are behind the finishing line. They and the reassembling crowd watch the fellside anxiously and with gathering anticipation. A shout is raised as the first hounds appear over a wall, tiny in the distance. Watchers with binoculars try to guess which is in the lead. The hounds scatter down the distant slopes, dropping down crags at an amazing speed, and, as if aware that the finish is near, accelerate through the intervening fields, bouncing like rubber balls over the walls. Then the owners start shouting and blowing whistles, and waving flags. This time it is the humans who are raising the echoes. As the hounds begin to approach, owners wave bowls of tempting food, screaming their dogs' names. The hounds leap the last wall and stream towards the line, clear it one by one and dive into the bowls of food held out by their owners. The human din dies down. Lucky punters run off to find the bookies.

Less lucky owners still stare and shout and wait for the remaining animals. When most have come in and gobbled their food there are always one or two owners still waiting sadly, holding their food bowls, to watch their beasts limping home. It usually brings a lump to my throat!

This hound race goes way back to the days of the Border raids when cattle-rustling was a way of life to some of the Border families. According to Border law, owners of stolen cattle could cross into Scotland to recover them, on condition that the crossing was done in 'hot trod', and not much later. To help in pursuit, 'sleuth dogs' (trained hounds) were used to follow the warm scent. In those bad old days a good hound could command a high price. Indeed, a good hound today is similarly prized. They are cosseted, and each owner has his secret food mixture for his dog, sometimes containing maybe just a dash of brandy?

A less serious canine race, traditional in the western shows, is the terrier race. Terriers, as a breed, are not natural racers. They also have wills of their own and the first difficult and lengthy task, which usually causes a great deal of hilarity, is to get the wriggling excitable beasts into the race traps. The announcer calls: 'Will any spectators wi' dogs please put 'em on a leash. 'T'last time we ran this race there were ten starters and fifteen finishers!'

The 'hare' (a fur bundle) is on a line pulled along with a string on a geared winch. After being waved in front of the dogs' noses to get them excited it is loosed, the traps are opened, and the terriers tumble out. Two immediately start a fight. Three more disappear into the crowd. The rest run after the hare. Two make the winning line together, immediately and noisily dispute ownership of the quarry, and have to be dragged apart by their tails. The barbarous winner is a lovely little Jack Russell, looking very fetching in the winner's blue ribbon, with an expression that says it would not growl at a goose.

There are other races: for young children; for toddlers and mothers; sack races, three-legged, egg and spoon. There is produce to be judged; best pair of hounds; best turned-out huntsman. And meanwhile there is a lot of activity around the beer tent. As the other events come to a close the beer tent becomes the centre of attraction, and the merriment extends well into the evening. Dalesmen with stentorian voices compete for a songster's prize. Some of the traditional hunting songs have many verses and require an unhesitant memory. At a time when normally only owls are heard in the valley there are lights around the beer tent – a novel sight from the fell road above – and again the sound comes in waves: a whisper from the soloist, interposed with some volume as every pair of lungs shouts out the chorus.

· Wasdale ·

There is no direct road over the fell between Eskdale and Wasdale. But there is the old pack-pony route – now a bridleway – from Boot over Burnmoor, a wild stretch of moorland, to Wasdale Head. Just below the highest part of the crossing, at 820 feet (250m), is Burnmoor Tarn. This is larger than most tarns, and is not in the usual setting below some towering crag, but in a bleak open area. It is a remnant of post-glacial meltwater, trapped in a bed of clay. Burnmoor Tarn is as large as Rydal Water and I am sometimes asked: 'What is the difference between a tarn and a lake?' Scenically it should be obvious. The tarn is of the austere mountain landscape; the lake is of the lush valley. If a scientific definition is needed, it has been suggested by Dr T. T. Macan, of the Freshwater Biological Association: the typical lakeside plant is the common reed; whereas in the case of tarns it is the bottle sedge (*Carex rostrata*).

It seems hard to believe now, looking at this open moorland, that in prehistoric times the land here was settled by farmers. There are Bronze Age burial circles hereabouts, particularly to the south-west, and pollen count evidence shows that there were agricultural fields in woodland clearings. Greater tree clearances took place later, probably around 1,000 BC, and the soil, deprived of leaf mould and the natural cycle of nutrients, rapidly deteriorated. When the climate changed, around 500 BC, heavy rainfall did further damage in the area, and the inhabitants left the place they had done most to destroy. It is an old story, ending when the remaining tree cover was cleared in the second and third centuries AD.

There is no denying that the walk over the moor is enjoyable. It is good when the heather is in bloom, but I have also found it exciting in the early summer when that large moth, the Northern Eggar, was in flight. Hard to get interested in an insect? This one has a wingspan of up to $3\frac{1}{2}$ inches! I have also enjoyed struggling my way over the moor on a keen winter's evening, leading a bunch of students and knowing that at the end of the walk there would be warmth and a hot meal waiting.

The track descends easily out of the granites to the small settlement at Wasdale Head. It is a place patterned with massive stone walls, some parts of them bulging out into great swelling platforms. They were not built to withstand sieges – they represent many centuries of field clearance, for the ground here grows stones better than anything else. To grow grass or oats has been a back-straining exercise for many generations. Wasdale Head used to have a much bigger population. It once supported over a dozen farms and was a self-contained community. Although it declined in the eighteenth century there were still enough people to man a bobbin mill, a corn mill, and a small woollen industry a century later. The little school was in use into this century.

The tiny chapel, loved by many, probably dates from the sixteenth century. It is popularly claimed that the roof is constructed from a ship's timbers, one suggestion being that they came from a wrecked Spanish Armada vessel. Cumbrians are thrifty folk and it is possible that the timbers were rescued from a breaker's yard. On the other hand the story may have been invented because in later years, when Wasdale Head had been denuded of its old woodland, it was hard to believe that there were once oak trees in the valley capable of providing structural timbers.

In the churchyard there are memorials to those climbers who have died hereabouts. Wasdale Head has been a climbers' centre for over a century, and the early mountaineering pioneers often lodged at The Wasdale Head Hotel. This is the nearest England has to an Alpine centre, for the high mountains stand shoulder to shoulder around it and there is immediate access to all – the Scafells, Gable and Pillar. Yet the settlement itself sits cosily among them. It is a mere 260 feet (79m) above sea level. I have enjoyed warm spring weather here when the summits have been gripped by ice and snow, but therein lies a danger to the uninitiated. Tempted by the valley's mildness, unsuspecting fell-walkers can find themselves ill prepared for the arctic conditions above.

Down valley is the famous Wastwater, England's deepest lake. From the west side road in its lower reaches, we see behind it the steep chaotic slopes of Wastwater Screes falling from about 2,000 feet (610m); a great spilling of broken rock, largely volcanic, but also with shoots of Eskdale Granite. Here the glacier carved its way into the mountainside, leaving a steep unstable wall which has been crumbling away into the lake ever since – for 9,000 years. The steep slopes continue downwards into the lake's clear depths, for 250 feet (76m). Some say they find the awesome scene rather sinister and depressing. Perhaps they are influenced by the old guidebooks which suggested it was so.

In the eighteenth century it was customary to stand with one's back to a countryside view and hold up the 'Claude-glass' (a pocket mirror). The prospect was thus suitably framed into a usefully sized picture. But we all carry mental Claude-glasses; our views are modified by our attitude of mind. Wasdale Screes are sinister, we think, before we see them. We see them and we agree. It is not necessarily so. Actually if we walk out to the shore, at the point where the lakeside road joins the road from Gosforth, we see some memorable views: not only the length of the Screes but up into the remarkable mountain backdrop at Wasdale Head. This is the essence of the Lake District – deep water and high summits – which was adopted as the emblem for the Lake District National Park logo (although I do not like its cartoon form). Actually I think the best view is further down the lake: from the National Trust's footpath on the shore at Low Wood, near the lake's outlet. This takes in the whole length of the lake as well as the mountains, and the Screes take on a less dominant role.

The lake is so pure that it supports very few aquatic animals and plants, though it does contain some trout. I was once driving along the lakeside after an unusually exhausting day on the fells. There was a bronze evening light reflected on the calm water and I saw a ripple start off from the shore. I assumed that a person standing out of sight had let a dog go for a swim. But I could see no one and, although I was tired and hungry, curiosity made me stop. There were in fact two ripples which came and went at intervals. I took out my field glasses and swept the lake. And there, close to shore, a head was raised for a second, then disappeared. Was it – could it be? Then, unmistakably, the head was again raised, and this time raised high. The animal appeared to be standing upright with half its length out of the water – an otter! Its head turned and then I saw what it was looking for – there was another head cruising towards it. Two otters! I watched them as they played together, 'porpoising', swimming over on their backs, diving and coming up locked together in mock fight. I was transfixed with enjoyment for half an hour until the fading light made viewing difficult.

I knew that otters could not stand disturbance and I assumed, alas, that they were no longer resident in the Lake District. Sightings are very rare and one can never meet anyone who has seen them at first hand. People know other people who thought they saw... I also knew beforehand that Wastwater was so pure and unproductive that it could not possibly support otters. I knew that before I looked at the lake. But I saw what I saw. It was magic. One must be ready to open the mind as well as the eyes.

West of Wasdale we reach the rim of the sandstone country. Between 350 million and 270 million years ago, the land was engulfed by sea. It was a sea rich in life – mainly corals, molluscs, and crinoids – and then the first vertebrates made their appearance. From the accumulated debris and the mud on the sea floor came the Carboniferous Limestone. At the end of this period there were violent earth movements, followed by arid conditions which lasted for 90 million years. At this time the equator was only 250 miles south of what is now Britain. There were vast deserts of drifting sand which were to consolidate and become the New Red Sandstone (to distinguish it from the Old Red Sandstone of an earlier period).

The best of this sandstone provides splendidly adaptable building material. Cumbria's sandstone was used in the walls of its castles and abbeys. The stone was also relatively easy to carve, and if we stop before reaching Gosforth, at the churchyard, we will see something unique and exciting.

I have said that the Vikings had settled here in great numbers; according to the thirteenth-century historian Snorri Sturluson, they came as refugees from Harald Finehair, King of Norway, in the tenth century. There is evidence that many came from Ireland where they had been influenced by Celtic Christian faith. Here in the churchyard is a very tangible sign of their presence – we can touch the carved cross made by a Viking craftsman 1,000 years ago.

This incredible slender cross stands about 15 feet high. But St Patrick would hardly have approved, for on this Christian symbol are also carved pagan myths. We can recognise, on the east face,

Christ on the cross, with a Roman soldier about to pierce his side. But what on earth (or heaven, or hell?) is happening elsewhere? First of all the pattern on the base part is a stylised representation of the bark of an ash tree, or *the* ash tree. For this cross also represents Yggdrasill, the sacred world ash tree whose branches cover all the regions of the world and whose roots are in the realm of the gods, the realm of the giants, and the realm of the dead.

We need to know something of Norse mythology to recognise the various characters which appear elsewhere. But here, above the crucifixion (the Christian symbol of the ultimate victory over evil of the Son of God), it would appear that Vidar, son of the great god Odin, is triumphing over the two-headed wolf (or dragon?) Fenrir, the symbol of evil. Surely the carver was making a point?

On the base of the west face, Loki, the wicked one, lies bound with the sinews of his slaughtered son, Narvi. Meanwhile his wife, Sigyn, holds a bowl over him, attempting to catch the venom from a snake which has been suspended over him. According to the legend, each time she empties the bowl Loki squirms under a missed drip of the poison and this causes the world's earthquakes. On the same side is Heimdal, with his horn in his left hand, the watchman at the rainbow gateway into Asgard, the world of the gods. His eyes were so keen he could see vast distances, and his hearing so sensitive that he could hear the grass grow.

Inside the church there is the 'fishing stone' which represents the Norse legend of Thor in the giant Hymer's boat, attempting to catch the Midgard serpent using an ox head as bait. There are also two hogback tombstones. The carving on one represents two armies facing each other in battle order.

Not very far from the Viking cross – just over 2 miles as the crow flies – is another remarkable one. In the churchyard at Irton is a cross made a century or so earlier. But in contrast to the slender Viking cross, this is a stolid, stout 10-foot-high *Anglian* cross. It is rich in decoration and again remarkably well preserved.

The Angles had already settled the area when the Vikings came. The two races may not have been competing for the same land. The Angles would want the level land which could be turned with their ox ploughs; the Norsemen might have been content to find a place up in the fells with their flocks and herds. The distribution of placenames certainly suggests that this was so. Placenames of Anglian origin are found around the coastal plains, while Scandinavian names are more generally clustered around the central hills. Christians, even when they were Angles and Norsemen with warlike traditions, could live together peacefully. Surely the proximity of the two crosses is tangible proof.

Finale

•

So we must go north out of the rim of sandstone, through the limestone, and over the River Crake, into the Silurian and into the National Park, and soon we meet the traffic of visitors. Some come casually, some eagerly seeking the elusive butterfly of recreation. 'Recreation' can simply mean a change from the routine of daily life. But it can also mean much more – a re-creation, a coming back to life, a return to reality.

There is a lot to be said for solitude in a place where the air is clear and the earth is green and the prospects wide; where there is rest; and a return to the simplicity of countryside, unspoiled and unsoiled by human activities. At its best, such an experience stirs the dull embers of the spirit, breathes into it a rekindled fire. Many of us know of that need. Where to fulfil it, if not in a national park?

It is hard, though, for any concerned conservationist not to be depressed at times. It seems to me, when I see the damage done to some parts of our countryside by unsightly development, or when

I help the teams of volunteers who clean up the mess left by visitors in the National Park at the end of the season, that we have lost our way. In spite of all the political hot air, we seem to regard our countryside, even our special places like national parks, with complete indifference. We have done more damage to our land in the last half-century than our forefathers did in the previous four. We quite rightly show concern for what is happening to the tropical rainforests while letting half our indigenous woodland be destroyed. We are rightly concerned about the loss of some of the world's wildlife, while letting our own vital habitats, such as a thousand miles of our hedgerows, and nearly all of our flower-rich meadows, disappear.

If our countryside were threatened with a foreign invasion we would defend it to the last. Yet we treat it so badly. We even abuse it. We are too often like parents who ill-treat their children, but do not care to listen to those who suggest a need for care. No one has the right to ill-treat a child, even if it is his own. Neither should anyone have the right to ill-treat our land. It is a heritage that belongs to us all.

If everyone really cared for the countryside aright, there would be no need for national parks or for conservationists. As it is, the countryside must be protected from those who would change it either unknowingly, or deliberately, or for greed. It must be protected, not just for ourselves but for the generations which are to follow. That does not mean preserving the landscape as a museum. People are part of it, and the way of life of many is wedded to it. A balance has to be struck for the landscape to live.

So far, we have relied on feeble stop-go and utterly inadequate legislation to try to provide the balance. There are confusing systems of grant aid; committees and councils, statutory and voluntary; conservation groups; and a comparatively small number of dedicated professional people. And all these usually uncoordinated systems, which are supposed to be concerned with the protection of the countryside, are bedevilled by petty differences, national and local politics, and pathetic under-funding. But worst of all is the general national apathy. The feeling that 'they' ought to do something, when so much depends on the efforts of us all.

What then must be done? Much of what can be done in the Lake District National Park depends upon what can be done nationally.

And there will be no political will for action unless we all convince our politicians, who need our votes, directly or through our support of conservation societies, that our national parks are very special places needing very special care.

Hill farming obviously has a vital part to play. It gave us the colour and character of the landscape we all enjoy. Yet its survival is threatened. Any farm financial support system which only matches grants to productivity cannot benefit the hill farmer working on marginal, lean and exposed land. It works against him. It also tempts him to increase the size of his flock to levels above those his fell grazing area can sustain. The European Common Agricultural Policy must move much more rapidly away from the system which produces food mountains and benefits the rich farmers on fatter land. Help must be readily and more generously available for farmers in the Less Favoured Areas of our national parks, to enable them to farm in traditional ways based on small family units, with sensible stocking levels, and with the higher grants scaled to favour the most environmentally handicapped. Hill farming can then play its part in the overall agricultural scheme by preserving the purity of stock breeds.

It is nonsense to offer to pay farmers for doing nothing. As well as farming their land, they should be adequately rewarded for conservation schemes which should include tree planting and woodland management, restoring flower-rich meadows, and the maintenance of walls and fences. They should also be given help in providing recreational facilities, such as modest tourist accommodation and campsites for back-packers. Most importantly, they should be paid to maintain our public rights of way, with no confusion from conflicting agencies, no red tape, and with the maximum of sensible advice and support. This has to happen. There has to be a commitment. Farming families should no longer have to look pessimistically into an uncertain future.

There are already very promising experimental schemes working in some national parks where farmers are being given some payment to reduce stocking levels and to look after the landscape. Parks have been given the powers to launch such initiatives, but must find the funding as best they can. With the pitiful financial support national parks currently receive, that is not good enough.

There are urgent social, as well as environmental, issues here.

The young rural population need local employment. Traditional skills should be revived and encouraged. There should be support for small-scale rural industry. Houses should be available to local people way below the sky-high prices prompted by the demand for holiday and retirement homes. The National Park Authority should have clear powers to link planning permission for new housing for local people only, with legal agreements ensuring that they remain in local hands.

The proof of the effectiveness of good planning by the Park Authority is in what you do *not* see. Unsightly development anywhere in the National Park is rare. However the Park Authority must continue to be firm on planning, even at the expense of some local popularity. I believe it is too kind, too often. Part of the trouble has been that if the Authority is too hard on a planning applicant, he might well win on appeal to the Minister for the Environment who can be far too lenient. In the late eighties, 47 per cent of Lake District appeals were scandalously allowed by the Ministry.

New legislation is also needed to place forestry under planning control. The present consultation procedure between the Forestry Commission and the National Park Authority has not prevented the replacement of native broadleaf trees by alien conifers to the extent that the latter now outnumber the former. It is heart-breaking to see the old woodlands go. Grant schemes which do not support the management of broadleaf woodlands, but favour their felling to make way for faster-growing conifers, are out of order. Many of the Lake District's present 50,000 acres of broadleaf woodlands (75 per cent of them ancient) are crying out for proper management. It is heartening to hear of a recent coming together of a range of local statutory and voluntary organisations into the Cumbria Broadleaves Group which has the object of trying to save the Lake District's native woodlands.

The military should be brought to account. Many people believe that it is only in non-democratic countries that the armed forces are a law unto themselves. Not so. It is costly nonsense to produce an official report on low flying which recommends restrictions on very low flying but is then over-ruled by the Ministry of Defence. There has to be somewhere to escape from the strident noise of modern civilisation. National parks should be sacrosanct.

The Park Authority should have control over highway 'improvements' and transport policy. We have already seen a lovely part of the Lake District degraded by the ploughing-through of the A66; and the stealing of grass verges in road-widening schemes has put pedestrians at risk. An Ambleside bypass alongside the Rothay and Loughrigg, proposed by the County Highway Authority, should not go ahead. Another link-road scheme there should also be opposed. Some traffic control measures, such as 'park and ride' schemes, should be tried.

There should be more adequate government funding. It is ludicrous that support for all ten national parks amounts to less than the cost of a mile of new motorway. The Lake District National Park should be better able to acquire important areas for conservation or public access when they become available. The Authority should be able to employ more staff, particularly workers in the field. The Park should not have to rely on sales of tourist bric-a-brac at information centres, in competition with all-too-common giftshops, to top up their budget. Information staff should be skilled in informing rather than selling.

The objective of all information activities, in centres or on guided walks, should be to win us over to a fuller appreciation of our countryside, and its importance as a national park. The public should not be told too much about what they should *not* do, but what they *can* do to get the most enjoyment.

Locally, the National Park Authority must take a much higher profile. Why do we have to wait so long for park entrance signs? How can the public be expected to support their National Park if they do not know where it is? The Park staff should not be bashful either; they should show themselves. The Authority's vehicles are recognisable in their standard admirably muted colours, yet the staff usually remain incognito. There is a British aversion to anything approaching a uniform, but there should surely be some simple, standard, easily recognisable working gear for all field and information staff. They must be required to wear it at all times, particularly the rangers and voluntary wardens who work among the visitors. How can the public respect and listen to National Park staff when they do not know where or who they are?

The Park and the National Trust, with the help of the British Trust for Conservation Volunteers, and other volunteers, should continue their splendid work on footpath improvements. But I believe that there should be more concentration on the lower-level paths, used by the majority, which are crying out for attention, rather than on the fells. The latter work is high-profile and no doubt attracts public notice and popularity, but I believe that valuable resources are sometimes thrown away on the restoration of fell footpaths, which cannot be afterwards maintained. I also share the reservations of other mountain enthusiasts about any obvious man-made intrusions on the high fells. There is nothing, I believe, to complain about now, but we must take very great care. Mountains are the last refuge, our most valuable recreation resource, and a great source of spiritual inspiration. If walkers complain about loose rock on fell footpaths they should not be there in the first place. A mountain is a hostile environment. That is its challenge. The path erosion, which causes so much concern to some, is the mountain's response to the human invasion. The presumption, also by some, that all the hundreds of miles of boot-ploughed paths can be restored, is absurd.

If the footpaths within the National Park's boundaries are unob-structed, I am afraid that the same cannot be said yet for those in the county outside. It is part of the strategy of the Cumbria Tourist Board to attract holidaymakers away from the too popular areas within the Park. They should ensure that the rest of the county does its part in opening and maintaining footpaths. There will, of course, be complaints of lack of resources. In the rest of the country things are even worse, despite the efforts of members of the Ramblers Association. Country walking is the most popular recreation, enjoyed by millions. Yet Local Authorities prefer to spend huge sums on prestigious sports centres, rather than providing the modest funds needed to put their countryside paths in order.

The Park Authority should be given the power to sort out the chaos on Windermere. There has to be a restriction on numbers of lake users; and the types of activity by a few, which spoil the experience of the many, should be banned.

There should also be much more closer cooperation between the National Park, the National Trust, the Forestry Commission, the Water Authority, the Tourist Board, and the County and Local Authorities, on the best use of resources to deal with environmental and access problems of mutual concern – not a talk shop but a workshop. Of course there is some cooperation; but occasionally there have been unresolved clashes of opinion, a jealous guarding of individual interests, a wasteful duplication of services.

The National Park and the National Trust need to take care not to overmanage their properties. Subtlety in management can ensure that woodlands look to be in a bit of a tangle to give the impression of wilderness. No part of a national park should look like a neatly managed municipal park. Too many obviously engineered paths, and an over-profusion of interpretative information boards, detract from the natural beauty we are supposed to enjoy.

Sadly, the high standards normally set by the National Park and the National Trust sometimes slip. It may be lack of vigilance, or lack of staff, or mistaken priorities. But after nearly forty years of experience it is really time that the Park's problems were solved. It should have outgrown the experimental stages and got down to some serious management work.

Lastly there is a fundamental point that must be made. It is grievous to see how the purity of the countryside is defiled by rubbish. Litter dropping seems to be a way of life in the centres and suburbs of our cities and towns. Concern and care begin in the place where we live. The fact is that many towns and cities are a disgrace. If the local urban authorities did more to clean up and make their environments more attractive, the public might learn to respect their surroundings. But the argument again is that funds are not available. I believe that there is also too often a lack of will. Regretfully, I have to say that one could criticise some of the towns and villages in and around the Lake District on this score: long-lying litter and dirty public lavatories are not unknown. The discerning public remember these things. They spoil their experience.

I do not wish to be overly critical, or to paint too gloomy a picture of what has not been done and what still needs to be done. I am optimistic for the future because more and more people are beginning to care. As I write (in 1990), the national parks system is under review to consider 'the means by which national park purposes are pursued'. I hope that they can be more actively pursued, and quickly overtaken!

And we can, in our Lake District National Park, look back with some satisfaction at what has been accomplished in spite of all the odds. Thanks to the parallel efforts of the National Trust, and the support – sometimes usefully fanatical – of the conservation groups, concerned local people, and the hundreds of willing volunteers, we have managed to hold off most of the threats to our precious and unique countryside. Nobbut just!

And so, we are soon in one of the woodlands of the High Furness. A track meanders through the woods which, thankfully, have not yet suffered the attention of tidy-minded foresters. The landmarks are still here: the fallen oak propped on its side branches as if trying to claw itself upright; the woodpecker tree; the bent larch, its fingers stretching to leeward; the bilberry-covered slabs of outcrop.

The resident jay complains of our coming, but we are here, on this familiar tower of rock. The rich woodland falls below us to the restful levels of the long lake, and on the opposite shore another climbs to the curve of the hill. Behind are the heads and shoulders of the everlasting fells, brushed by drifting clouds.

I always reach this place with some nervous anticipation; for it was here that I came so long ago, and had the first dawning of an awareness. I saw a new meaning in the exciting, living world around me: trees, plants, birds, insects, lichens, water; and that panorama – that magnificent shrugging of the earth!

At that first awakening I thought I had begun to hear the heartbeat of the living world. Its appeal to my senses was immediate, but it also spoke of something deeper, which brought me that first strange haunted feeling – half-fear, half excitement – as the horizons of inner thoughts strained to reach out beyond the horizons of sight.

It has seemed to me sometimes since, that the hills sit quietly like very old wise men who have seen everything and who know everything, but who say nothing. Yet they offer *something* – a strength – just by being there.

It seemed to me sometimes that the pleasure of the company of the trees about this place made all the petty questions that troubled my mind irrelevant.

I have come here again many times: at one stage in loneliness; which is not to be despised, for it is a step towards the better appreciation of solitude. I have come here in the happiness of relaxation, and again in the tired satisfaction that follows a hard day of physical work. I have come in the hope of reward. Sometimes, coming here weighed down with worrying thoughts, reward has been meagre. More often, with mind easy and open, I have been refreshed.

I have come here in winter when needle-ice has crackled underfoot, when the rock was like cold iron to the touch, the lake below me lay like lead, and mist smoked from the white-capped hills. Or when the crunching of the snow under my boots has violated the utter silence of the woods, when the trees were crouched under their snow burdens, the rock was disguised by drifts, and the hills were white against the dark blue sky, looking so close that I could touch them. And in the thaw when the frost had fallen like rain from the trees, the lake rippled with westerlies, and the hills were asleep behind grey blankets.

Or when, even if the wind has blown so cold that I was cocooned in wool and windproofs, I knew that the winter had ended, that it had lost its fight, and that spring was the victor. An inexplicable sense of excitement at a time when I could see nothing of promise; but a feeling in my bones that in the depths below the dead leaves, the grey grass and the brittle bracken, there was a stirring, an awakening. The trees suggesting a mere breath of expectancy, a faint whisper; the hills blue with frigidity. But the spring, I knew, was rising and would become a green crescendo soon. Even when I was sure that there were cold snaps to come and that there would be snow in May, I could be certain that the clock had started and the advent was irresistible.

Then I have rejoiced with the birdsong in spring, when the woods were a hundred shades of green, the lake below rippling with laughter, and the hills wearing their white caps jauntily on the sides of their heads. And in the heat of summer when the woods smelled of wealth, the lake was all adazzle, and the hills in a haze of perspiration. And the magnificent autumn when the woods blazed with warm colour so lavish it was even smeared across the levels of the lake. And the hills were brown like baked bread; and bright leaves began to break bonds and spill in the wind like sparks from a bonfire.

The hills and the woods of this supreme landscape have called to us and we have explored, and enjoyed their generosity. I hope that we can think gratefully – if not now, then in time – of the discoveries that they have brought: their hidden valleys and quiet glades; the surprise of summits undreamed of. And we might feel even deeper gratitude knowing that there are exciting possibilities of discoveries yet to come.

This can be our great discovery. This is the true happiness. We look out from our viewpoint into the natural world, and our senses absorb the impressions from the nearest deep-down greenness to the outermost hills. But our feelings, our perceptions, are centred in heart and mind. We enjoy the world aright when we gather the impressions to the centre. We then become a part of what we see. We have come out of the cold. We belong. We accept membership of this glorious land.

Some Useful Addresses

Lake District

The British Trust for Conservation Volunteers
Brockhole, Windermere, Cumbria LA23 1LJ.

The Cumbria Tourist Board
Ashleigh, Holly Road, Windermere, Cumbria LA23 2AQ.

The Cumbria Wildlife Trust
Badger's Paw, Church Street, Ambleside, Cumbria LA22 0BU.

The Friends of the Lake District
Number 3, Yard 77, Highgate, Kendal, Cumbria LA9 4ED.

The Lake District National Park Authority
Brockhole, Windermere, Cumbria LA23 1LJ.

The National Trust
North West Region, The Hollens, Grasmere, Cumbria LA22 9QZ.

The Wordsworth Trust
Dove Cottage, Grasmere, Cumbria LA22 9SH.

National

The British Mountaineering Council
Crawford House, Precinct Centre, Booth Street East,
Manchester M13 9RZ.

The Council for the Protection of Rural England
Warwick House, 25–27 Buckingham Palace Road, London
SW1W 0PP.

The Friends of National Parks
Council for National Parks, 45 Shelton Street, London WC2 9HJ.

Friends of the Earth
26–28 Underwood Street, London N1 7JQ.

The Open Spaces Society
25a Bell Street, Henley-on-Thames, Oxfordshire RG9 2BA.

The Ramblers Association
1–5 Wandsworth Road, London SW8 2XX.

The Woodland Trust
Westgate, Grantham, Lincolnshire NG31 6LL.

Index

·